KT-234-950

2000321761

NEATH PORT TALBOT LIBRARIES

THE BEATLES

A CELEBRATION

THE BEATLES

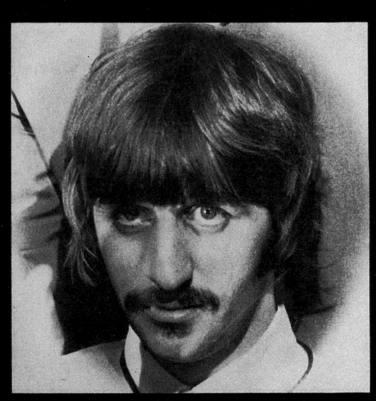

HELLO, GOODBYE

GEOFFREY GIULIANO

THE BEATLES
A CELEBRATION

SIDGWICK & JACKSON
LONDON

WEST GLAMORGAN COUNTY LIBRARY

742385   £14.95

FEBRUARY 1989
CLASS NO 784.500922

LOCATION
CE — BRITON FERRY

Copyright © 1986 by Geoffrey Giuliano/Skyboot
Productions

First published in Great Britain in 1986
by Sidgwick and Jackson Limited

Originally published in Canada by Methuen Publications

All rights reserved. No part of this book may be
reproduced or transmitted in any form or by any means,
electronic or mechanical, including photocopying, recording or by any information storage and retrieval system,
without permission in writing from the Publisher.

ISBN 0-283-99380-4

Every effort has been made to trace the ownership of all
copyrighted material and to secure permission from copyright holders. In the event of any question arising as to
the use of any material, we will be pleased to make the
necessary corrections in future printings.

DESIGN: Brant Cowie/Artplus Ltd.
Printed and bound in Hong Kong
by Scanner Art Services Inc., Toronto

1 2 3 4   86   90 89 88 87

NEATH PORT TALBOT
LIBRARIES

CL ANF 784. 500922

DATE

LOC BRI

NO 2000321761

Contents

Foreword

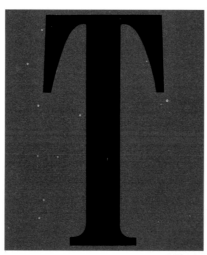

The Beatles brought something new to popular music which I call "the modern art of pop." Before 1955 it was all straight, melodic music. When the white man's rock 'n' roll came out in the fifties, though, and when it started to divert, the Beatles finally came along in '64, they began a new cult. They helped to establish rock as an art form. You just couldn't go out and buy some sheet music and then learn to play their songs. You had to *hear* the music as well, listen to what it was saying to *you*. People like Dean Martin, Frank Sinatra, Tony Bennett, and Bing Crosby never really succeeded after that because they all stayed back. They denied the challenge of that new sound. But the kids who were growing up with it were able to adapt, and *that*, my friends, is what the Beatles gave to a generation.

TINY TIM

New York City

The Beatles in the wood outside London during the filming of their second feature.

Introduction *What's the News Mary Jane*

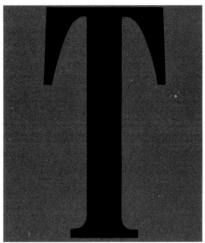

There is good reason to celebrate the Beatles. A lot of it has to do with our own heady associations with them during the turbulent days of our somewhat misspent youth (mine anyway). Or perhaps it's that the ultimate drudgery of so many expectant lives was so successfully anesthetized by the apparent glamor and excitement of theirs. Better yet, maybe it's simply because Beatle music is just so damned extraordinary! This is not to say, however, that loving the Fabs these past twenty years has always been easy. Generally regarded with great suspicion by our parents when first experienced one dreary winter's eve on Ed Sullivan's "Really Big Shoe" way back in 1964, the Boys' own souped-up brand of Anglo-American R & B rapidly became a controversial addiction for the impressionable, teenybopping youth of the world.

Further down the road, the Beatles' brazen escapades into the realm of illicit self-medication weren't all that easy for some folks to swallow, either. For in 1967, when they sang they'd love to turn us on, we had no doubt whatever but that they really meant it! Later, as the mid-sixties love jones paled and a generation of free-living flower children wondered out loud what would happen next, John Lennon suddenly counted himself in on violent revolution. Almost overnight Chairman Mao and Stokely Carmichael

Beatle autographs signed by the mechanized "auto-pen" of the Official Beatles Fan Club. 1966.

became as celebrated as, say, Frankie Avalon and Annette Funicello had been a few hazy lifetimes before.

Unfortunately, the Beatles' near-omnipotent reign over popular culture did not extend much beyond the shadowy perimeters of the swinging, acid-soaked sixties and soon sank under the incredible weight of its own convoluted momentum. John, Paul, George, and Ringo were far from finished, though. During the next decade each member of the group went on to distinguish himself as a highly creative, commercially successful artist in his own right. And while breaking up is definitely hard to do, the Beatles remained close, having shared the unparalleled experience of being the most wildly popular group of our time. All of that changed forever, though, when on December 8, 1980, the world lost John Ono Lennon to the demented dreams of one nameless nowhere man, and all at once an entire generation was forced to face the prospect of its own tenuous mortality.

This collection, an unabashed celebration of the fabulous Beatles, is nothing less than a memoir for that generation. And it holds something more than you might expect to find in a book about the past — shades of the present! It represents a delicate resurrection of our own waning youth, reincarnated for what may be the very last time — this time around.

God bless you, Beatles. Love and thanks to Joe Jelly, Perna, Brenda, Sesa, and Devin Leigh. Aisumasen Yokosan. Now I'd like to introduce to you the act you've known for all these years . . .

Beatle wallpaper.

10

THE BEATLES

A CELEBRATION

1

Like Dreamers Do

Liddypool

"There is a lot to do in Liddypool."
JOHN LENNON

"Liverpool is the pool of life."
C. G. JUNG

"Liverpool life is the best apprenticeship in the world."
MIKE McCARTNEY

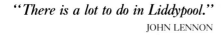
The Silver Beatles hang tough outside the Cavern. Circa 1962.

ack Lennon, John's grandfather, had always looked forward to returning home to Liverpool to retire. Born in Dublin and raised in Liverpool, he spent many years in America as a founding member of the Kentucky Minstrels. After working so long on the stage as a professional singer, dancer, and comedian, he finally returned home, a happy man. Soon after he had settled down in a comfortable, lower-middle-class neighborhood on the outskirts of Liverpool's bustling city center, his third son, Freddie, was born. Five years later, in 1917, Jack Lennon took sick and died suddenly, leaving the care of his three young sons — Charlie, Sidney, and Freddie — to Liverpool's Bluecoat Orphanage.

Freddie Lennon left the orphanage at fifteen and soon secured a respectable job as an office boy. A short time later, while sitting in Sefton Park on one of his numerous "unscheduled" afternoons off, he met Julia Stanley, a chatty, vivacious, good-natured schoolgirl whose father, George, was an officer with the Liverpool Salvage Company. Freddie and Julia went out together on and off for the next ten years, but certainly not with the blessing of the Stanleys, who considered themselves a definite cut above the careless, freewheeling Lennon.

13

At sixteen Freddie signed on as a steward on a passenger ship in the White Star Line. Although the work was grueling and tiresome, he enjoyed life at sea and quickly worked his way up to the responsible position of headwaiter in the posh dining hall of the luxurious ocean liner. On one of his infrequent shore leaves, against the wishes of Julia's family and without so much as a pound note between them, Freddie and Julia were married on December 3, 1938, at the public register office at 64 Mount Pleasant Road. The happy couple spent their honeymoon at the cinema, and the next day Freddie sailed away to the West Indies for a three-month tour of duty.

A little under two years later, during another of her husband's extended stints abroad, a very pregnant Julia Lennon packed her tiny suitcase and checked into the Maternity Hospital in Oxford Street. Just after seven o'clock the next morning, on October 9, 1940, with Liverpool under heavy bombing from the Nazis, John Winston Lennon was born. He was immediately placed under his mother's sturdy iron bed to protect him in case the overcrowded hospital suffered a direct hit. Julia's sister Mimi (who later raised John) remembers, "The minute I saw John I was overjoyed. I went on and on about him, almost forgetting my poor sister."

John quickly grew into a very clever, dreamy little boy. His first recollection is of walking along the Pier Head with his Grandpa Stanley. He must have been wearing new shoes, he thinks, because he remembers his feet hurt so his grandpa slit the heels with a pocketknife, making them fit better. By the time John was three years old, Freddie and Julia had called it quits, and John went to live with his Auntie Mimi and Uncle George in Woolton. "Julia had met another man by the name of John Dykins," says Mimi. "Taking John would have been very difficult for her, so I offered to look after him myself. We had no children, and John was such a lovely, bright little child I couldn't bear to see him hurt. Both Fred and Julia wanted me to adopt him, but I could never get them both down to the office to sign the papers."

John's first school was Dovedale Primary. He was a cheerful boy, full of fun and mischief, who impressed both schoolmates and teachers with his natural leadership and naughty sense of adventure. He was also quite creative. By the age of seven he was even writing his own books. One of them, "Sport, Speed and Illustrated. Edited and Illustrated by J. W. Lennon," contained a witty collection of poems, caricatures, and short stories that hinted at his talent as a writer with a keen sense of the absurd.

When he was twelve, John left Dovedale for Quarry Bank Grammar School just a mile or so away from his aunt's house on Menlove Avenue. Then in June 1953 his beloved Uncle George died unexpectedly from a massive hemorrhage caused by an undiscovered liver ailment. His death was a terrible blow to John. His Aunt Mimi believes it was George's sudden death that strengthened John's early resolve to isolate himself emotionally from things too personal or painful for his sensitive, artistic psyche to handle.

Liddypool, home of the fabulous Beatles.

"Strawberry fields forever."

Freddie Lennon, John's unpredictable dad.

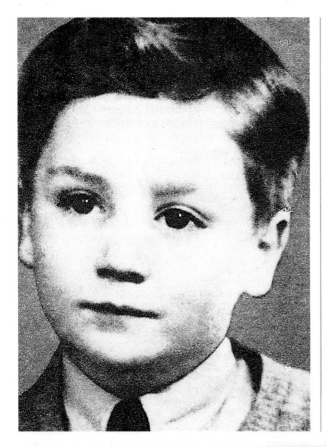

"John was such a lovely, bright little child, I couldn't bear to see him hurt."

Auntie Mimi in the comfortable Liverpool home where John grew up.

John Lennon
251 Menlove Avenue
Woolton

Quarry Bank Grammar School as it looks today.

John's years at Quarry Bank were characterized by the consistent academic failure and random creative achievement of a young man struggling with the seed of genius sown in the soil of middle-class conformity. He recalls his early frustration: "People like me are aware of their so-called genius even as a kid. Didn't they see that I was cleverer than anyone else in the school? And that the teachers were stupid, too? I used to say to me auntie, 'You throw my bloody poetry out and you'll regret it when I'm famous,' and she threw the stuff out! I never forgave her for not treating me like a genius when I was a child. Why didn't they train me? Why did they keep forcing me to be a cowboy like the rest of them? I was different, I was always different. Why didn't anybody notice me?"

At the age of twenty-eight Jim McCartney had attained a level of security in his job as a salesman for A. Hannay and Co., cotton merchants, that few from his working-class background could ever hope to achieve. Even when the Cotton Exchange closed during the war, Jim was secure, working at Napiers, the engineering works. In 1941 he married Mary Patricia Mohin, a former midwife and visiting nurse who shared Jim's love of family and a common Irish ancestry.

A year later, on June 18, 1942, in a private ward of Walton Hospital, James Paul McCartney was born. Jim was allowed to see the baby almost immediately but was shocked to see that his only son and heir looked, in his words, "like a horrible piece of red meat." By the next day, however, Jim had reconsidered and decided that "he was looking better and better all the time. He turned out to be a lovely baby in the end, you know." Eighteen months later their second son, Peter Michael, was born, thus completing the close-knit, clannish McCartney family.

Paul and Mike first attended school at Stockton Wood Road Primary in Speke. They both got on well with their studies but were soon moved to Joseph Williams Primary School at Gateacre when Mary realized that Stockton Wood was becoming overcrowded. It was absolutely imperative that her boys receive a first-class education. Apart from school and other more whimsical boyhood pastimes, young Paul especially enjoyed listening to popular music. He recalls: "I used to like the radio a lot and the music from old films. Fred Astaire I loved. From a very early age I was quite interested in singing tunes. My dad used to play a lot of music and even had his own little group called Jim Mac's Band, so I suppose I was quite influenced by him. He had to give it up eventually, though, because he got false teeth and couldn't play the trumpet properly anymore."

Just after Paul turned fourteen, his mother began to suffer violent pains in her breast. Doctors put it down to the menopause, as she was then forty-five, but Mary had spent too much time with seriously ill patients and knew better. One day Mike came home from school early and found her sobbing quietly in her bedroom. A month later, after undergoing an operation to remove a breast tumor, Mary McCartney was dead from cancer.

"It was very quick," says Mike. "One minute a loving, warm, hugging mother, the next — nothing. Mum's death affected us more than we'll ever know." Mary's passing devastated Paul and Mike, but it was Jim who was left with the problem of caring for his two sons on a weekly salary of less than eight pounds. At fifty-three he had to face the fact that the Liverpool cotton industry was in deep decline and that his prospects of finding a better job were indeed doubtful.

Like Freddie Lennon, Harry Harrison started out as a steward for the White Star Line in 1926. He was at sea for ten years and met his future wife, Louise French, while on shore leave in 1929. A year later, on May 20, 1930, they were quietly married in a civil ceremony at Brownlow Hill and immediately moved into 12 Arnold Grove, Wavertree, Liverpool. They lived there in the simple terraced house with two rooms up and two down for the next eighteen years. In 1931 their first child, Louise, was born, with Harry Jr. following in 1934. Two years later, unable to support his growing family on his meager eight-pound-a-month salary, Harry came ashore, but Liverpool was in a deep recession. He was on the dole for fifteen months, but in 1937 he managed to find a job as a bus conductor and a year later was promoted to driver. In 1940 the Harrisons' third child, Peter, was born; then, on February 25, 1943, along came the family's dark horse, George Harold Harrison.

Paul McCartney
20 Forthlin Road
Allerton

The Harrisons felt it very important to provide their children with a stable, loving environment free from any inherited prejudice or hatred. Mrs. Harrison especially made sure that they developed a firm sense of fair play and compassion. As a result, George grew into a bright, kindly little boy with an independence and candor far beyond his years. Like John Lennon, George's first school was Dovedale Primary, but John was three years ahead of him, so the two never met. Young George insisted on walking unescorted to and from school ever since his second day and invariably shunned the gossiping mothers who waited for their children outside Dovedale. Always impatient with intrusions into his personal life, George Harrison valued his privacy from a very early age.

In 1954 George left Dovedale Primary and started classes at the Liverpool Institute. Paul McCartney was already there, one year ahead of him. As it happened, George and Paul shared the long bus ride back and forth to school and soon became friends. George remembers: "It took us an hour to get home in the evening to the outskirts of the Speke estate. Paul McCartney, being in the same school, wore the same uniform as I did. Anyway, I started hanging out with him; besides, he had a trumpet!"

George was regarded by his teachers at the institute as a capable but generally uninvolved student. The math and geography classes he was forced to attend were tedious and impractical. The problem was, what would he do when it came time to leave school? George couldn't think of anything he really enjoyed doing all that much beyond playing a little

"Penny Lane is in my ears and in my eyes. There beneath the blue suburban skies."

George Harrison
12 Arnold Grove
Wavertree

The Liverpool Institute and School of Art.

Richard Starkey
10 Admiral Grove
The Dingle

skiffle guitar. And everybody knew you could never make a proper living doing that!

Richard Starkey, known to close friends and family as Ritchie and later to the world as Ringo, was born at home just after midnight on July 7, 1940. His mother remembers thinking, because of her baby's alert, wide-eyed expression, that he must have been here many times before. She also recalls lying in bed hearing the screaming air raid sirens for the first time — Hitler's Luftwaffe was in flight over the Mersey.

Nellie Coutts lived only a few doors down from the Starkeys and later became loosely related to the family through the marriage of her nephew to Ritchie's cousin. Although she emigrated to Canada with her husband, Archibald, in 1953, she still vividly recalls her life in the Dingle, as this interview, conducted in Toronto in 1984, shows. She also remembers that all of the neighborhood kids, including Ritchie, used to refer to her jokingly as "Auntie Nellie with the Wooden Belly."

GEOFFREY   What was Ritchie's family like?

AUNTIE NELLIE   Well, his mother, Elsie, was quite nice, as was his father, Dickie. He was a dockworker and had it very hard indeed. They were just a typical working-class family, though, who would often get together with friends and family and tipple a good bit.

GEOFFREY   How did his parents get along?

NELLIE   At that time very well, though of course some years later they did divorce. Generally speaking, though, all the Starkeys were very close with their wives and children.

GEOFFREY   What do you remember about Ritchie's birth?

NELLIE   I can remember Elsie being pregnant and little Ritchie being born, but Ritchie was never really a well child. His parents looked after him, though, and protected him. He was always very clean and tidy, even if his clothes were a little worn.

GEOFFREY   Your daughter has a funny story about Ritchie as a baby, doesn't she?

NELLIE   Oh yes. One day when Ritchie was just a few months old, my daughter Dorrie and I went round to the Starkeys to see the baby properly for the first time and have a little chat with Elsie. Now in Liverpool it's considered a very great honor for a kid to be allowed to look after a newborn baby. So Elsie told Dorrie that she could take the child for a little walk around the neighborhood and gave her a threepenny piece for her trouble. Naturally, Dorrie was delighted and hurried off with the pram to Barton's Sweet Shop on Mill Street. Well, she had her sweeties and then ran back home, happy as a little lark. As she came in the front door, however, I suddenly realized that something was wrong. "Where is Ritchie, dear?" I said to her. "Oh, he's just outside the door in his pram, mummy,"

Little Ritchie and his mother, Elsie, in the doorway of their Admiral Grove council house.

The Empress pub, one of the Starkey family's old haunts.

she replied. "No, he's not," I said. "Oh dear, I've left him outside the sweet shop, I'm sure," Dorrie cried out. "Well, you'd better get round there and have a look, young lady!"

GEOFFREY   So was he there?

NELLIE   Yes, he was. Fast asleep with a silly little grin on his face. He'd been lying there for almost two hours just as pretty as you please.

GEOFFREY   Were you very good friends with his mother?

NELLIE   Just casually, you know. We spoke quite a good bit, and we sometimes used to do our shopping together. However, Dickie and my husband were very close; they worked together on the docks for a long time.

GEOFFREY   The Starkeys were a rather large family, weren't they?

NELLIE   Oh yes, Ritchie's father came from quite a big family. He had two brothers called Billy and Georgie, and then there were his sisters Angie, Lily, and May.

GEOFFREY   What can you recall about Ritchie's early life?

NELLIE   Well, his parents always used to push him round the neighborhood in his pram. And of course he was called Ritchie — they never did call him Dickie after his dad. I can remember him running around the neighborhood with the other little boys, but he wasn't really a ruffian because he was so sickly. He was a good kid, a little rough and tumble maybe in his manner, but really just your average Liverpool scouser.

GEOFFREY   Were there any early signs of Ritchie's interest in music?

NELLIE   Oh yes, he was always musically inclined. You know, in Liverpool they used to have something called the Orange Day Parade. When Orange Day came along, the Starkeys all paraded. Their homes were decorated, the streets were decorated, and they all marched in the band. I can remember seeing Ritchie playing a little tin drum and marching along just as pretty as you please. Also, he played the accordion. You see, in Liverpool it was generally passed down from father to son, but Ritchie was a member of the accordion band at the Orange Hall. He learned there.

GEOFFREY   How do you think Ritchie might feel today about his early upbringing in Liverpool?

NELLIE   Ritchie doesn't seem to me to be the type to ever forget where he came from. I think he'll always be there in Liverpool with the other boys, laughing and larking about in his heart of hearts. I'm sure he has some wonderful memories, and so do I.

Shortly after the death of John's Uncle George in 1953 his mother, Julia, re-entered his life. Although John had heard very little about her whereabouts over the years, he had often wondered about her and secretly wished that he could see her again. Then when he found out that she lived

Richard "Ringo" Starkey, scruffy-looking even by early Liverpool standards, just before Brian Epstein made him shave off his mustache and beard to conform to the Beatles' early "mop top" image.

John Lennon and friends – the Quarrymen.

just a few short miles away in Allerton with her common-law husband, John Dykins (whom John preferred to call "Twitchy"), and their daughters, Julia and Debbie, he was thrilled. John remembers: "I started cycling up to see her occasionally, and soon she became rather like a young auntie to me. As I grew older, I began to have some nasty rows with Mimi. So I used to run away and stay with Julia for the weekend or maybe a few weeks at a time." Julia encouraged John in whatever he wanted to do. But most of all it was Julia's knowledge of popular American music that turned on John and his pals. "I started off with a banjo at fifteen which my mother taught me how to play," says John. "My first guitar cost ten pounds. It was one of those advertised in the paper you sent away for. Julia got it for me. I remember it had a label on the inside which said, 'Guaranteed Not to Split.' My mother used to say she could play any stringed instrument there was, and she really did teach me quite a lot. The first tune I ever learned to play was 'That'll Be The Day' by Buddy Holly."

In early 1956 John and his friends Eric Griffiths, Len Garry, Colin Hanton, Pete Shotton, and Rod Murray got together and formed a skiffle group they called the Quarrymen. Named in honor of Quarry Bank Grammar School, the group played its first gig at the annual Empire Day celebrations on Rose Street. The boys played from the back of an open lorry and were paid nothing. But the day went well, and soon the Quarrymen were appearing regularly at local parties and weddings, but most of all just for fun.

Meanwhile, having long since swapped the old trumpet his dad had given him for a guitar, Paul McCartney was making progress. Always the perfectionist, he practiced everywhere — in the lavatory, in the bathtub, on the bus — even at school. A fellow classmate, Ian James, also took up the guitar, and soon the two were cycling around Liverpool with their instruments strapped to their backs, looking for places to play. Much to Jim McCartney's dismay Paul had taken to wearing the sort of clothes a guitar-picking teddy boy might choose. With his long, slicked-back hair piled high over his forehead, narrow drainpipe trousers, and white, sparkly sports coat, he might even have managed to fool a few people! That is, if it wasn't for that perpetually innocent, choirboy face of his. At fourteen Paul McCartney was far from being a tough Liverpool teddy boy, but he was also a long way from being the proper schoolboy Jim McCartney would have preferred.

Ivan Vaughan, an old schoolmate of John's, had recently met and befriended Paul McCartney. On June 15, 1956, the two boys went together to see the Quarrymen perform at an outdoor party at the Woolton Parish Church. Paul was impressed with what he heard and remembers John singing the Del Vikings' "Come Go With Me." "John didn't really know all the words, though, so he made up his own," says Paul. "It was something like 'Come on go with me, down to the penitentiary . . .' I thought, 'Wow, he's great. That's a good band there!'" After the performance Paul met the

The Quarrymen as country gentlemen shortly after Paul joined the group.

A young George takes time off school to practice with his mates John and Paul. Unable to afford real "ciggies," the three lads used to fill Paul's father's pipe with Typhoo Tea and puff away during their impromptu rehearsals.

group in the church hall. He recalls his first encounter with John Lennon: "I played him 'Twenty Flight Rock' and a few other tunes I'd learned. Then he played me all of his stuff, and I remember he seemed a little bit drunk. Quite a nice chap, but he did smell rather beery."

About a week later Paul took a spin over to Menlove Avenue to visit Ivan. On the way home he happened to meet Pete Shotton, who informed him that John had been impressed with his guitar work and wouldn't mind if he wanted to join the group. "Sure, okay," said Paul. "Cheerio then, Pete." His first public performance with the Quarrymen was at a dance held at the Conservative Club in Broadway. After the dance was over, Paul played John a couple of numbers he'd written himself. One of them was called "I Lost My Little Girl." Not to be outdone, John soon started thinking up his own tunes and bouncing them off Paul. And so began, very casually and with no apparent fuss, the greatest two-man songwriting partnership of this century.

George Harrison's initial interest in the guitar came about slowly. Mrs. Harrison remembers that one day she started finding sheets of paper covered with drawings of guitars among his school things. Soon afterward she bought George an old secondhand box guitar from one of his classmates for three pounds. "George tried very hard to teach himself to play," recalls his mother, "but progress was very slow and painful. I told him to just dig in and keep at it if he really wanted to learn. And by God, he did. Sometimes he'd sit up all night and practice until his fingers bled."

George's dedication to his music gradually paid off. As his fingers became increasingly nimble, he began putting together the simple, flowing rhythms that were to become his unique musical signature. In 1956 George formed his own group, the Rebels. With his brother Peter and Arthur Kelly on guitars and two other friends on the tea chest and mouth organ, they played a dance at the Speke British Legion Club for the whopping sum of ten bob each.

Talk of George's newfound musical accomplishment soon reached the ears of Paul McCartney, who would often go around to George's, lugging along his guitar for an impromptu jam session. Then in early 1958 Paul introduced George to the Quarrymen and, more important for music history, to John. "I listened to George play and asked him if he knew the song 'Raunchy'," says John. "Well he did, and so I had to make the decision whether or not to let him in the group. Finally I said, 'Okay, you're in, mate.' And then it was really just the three of us from that day on."

By the time George became a bona fide member of the Quarrymen, things had begun to look up for the band, but personally John Lennon was undergoing difficult times. On July 15, 1958, his earthy, free-spirited mother was knocked down by a car and killed while crossing Menlove Avenue. "She got killed by an off-duty copper who had been drinking," John recalls.

Number 3 Gambier Terrace, John and Stuart's first home away from home.

"I was just sixteen at the time, so that was another big trauma for me. I lost her twice, and it made me very bitter. I cried a lot about not having her anymore, and it was torture. Still, being so much on my own at that age gave me a certain awareness of myself and a sense of independence I might not have otherwise developed."

Around this time John left his aunt's pleasant, decidedly middle-class home and moved into a very shabby one-room flat at 3 Gambier Terrace with his good friend Stuart Sutcliffe. John remembers his life there: "We lived rough all right. It was a dirty old flat. I think we spent about four months there, practicing and painting. It was just like a rubbish dump. The others tried to tidy it up a bit, but I didn't bother. I left all my gear there when we went to Hamburg."

John was now attending classes at the Liverpool College of Art and soon began playing occasional lunchtime sessions with his group, renamed the Silver Beatles, in the student lounge. After tiring of being known as the Quarrymen, the group had been briefly called Johnny and the Moondogs. John and Paul even performed a few gigs under the unlikely name of the Nurk Twins. Although John's friend Stuart was a talented artist, he had little appreciable musical ability, but that didn't stop John from inviting him to join the group. Besides, Stuart had just earned sixty pounds from the sale of one of his paintings and could afford to buy his own first-class bass guitar.

By this time the group had gone through a succession of different drummers and had finally settled on a quiet, strangely good-looking fellow from West Derby by the name of Pete Best. Pete was born in 1941, the oldest child of Mona and Johnny Best. His father, an ex-Liverpool boxing promoter, met his wife in her native India during the Second World War. Pete was a good-natured but rather shy little boy who grew up to be an excellent student, easily passing five subjects at the O level and entering the Sixth Form near the end of his school days. "I got good and fed up with being at school as time went by," says Pete. "I'd been thinking of going on to teachers' training college but left just before sitting for my A levels. Paul McCartney, an old acquaintance, rang me out of the blue one day and asked me if I'd like to become their drummer and go to Hamburg with them. The pay was fifteen pounds a week, which was a lot of money in those days. Anyway, it was definitely much better than going to a training college for the rest of my life."

Allan Williams, an aggressive, fast-talking scouser with a keen eye for a fast buck, was the first real promoter to take an interest in the Silver Beatles. He liked the Boys personally and figured they might one day even have a shot at becoming professional. Acting on their behalf, he negotiated a deal for them to appear in Hamburg at Bruno Koschmeider's Indra Club. The Beatles played Hamburg twice during a short period — from August to December 1960 and from April to July 1961. George Harrison recalls: "In my opinion our peak for playing live was in Hamburg. You see, at that time we weren't so famous, and people who came to see us were drawn in simply by our music and whatever atmosphere we managed to create. We got very tight as a band there, as most nights we had to play for over eight hours. We were at four different clubs altogether in Germany. Originally we played the Indra, and when that was shut down, we went over to the Kaiserkeller and then later on to the Top Ten. That was a fantastic place, probably the best one on the *Reeperbahn*. There was even a sort of natural echo on the microphones — it was really a gas. The Star Club was very rough, but we enjoyed ourselves there as well. We developed quite a big repertoire of our own songs but still played mainly old rock 'n' roll tunes. Back in England all the bands were getting into wearing matching ties and handkerchiefs and were doing little dance routines like the Shadows. We were definitely not into that bit, so we just kept on doing what we felt like, and ultimately I guess it worked out okay."

If the Beatles' music underwent a powerful, positive transformation in Hamburg, so did the Boys themselves. Stuart met and fell fiercely in love with a beautiful German photographer named Astrid Kirchherr. She and two friends, illustrator Klaus Voorman and fellow photographer Jurgen Vollmer, were among the first from the artistic community to appreciate the potential that the Beatles' vibrant music and charismatic personalities might hold for a mass audience. Soon both Astrid and Jurgen were photographing the Beatles as a group and individually in various locations around the *Reeperbahn*.

Meanwhile John, Paul, George, and Pete were busy soaking up what they could of Hamburg's notorious nightlife. As well as sampling the strong German beer, they also became enamored of an over-the-counter amphetamine called Prellys, which delivered an occasional burst of artificial energy to the overworked musicians and also gave them their first taste of the joys of illicit self-medication. On the *Reeperbahn* drugs were an easily obtained, two-bob, ten-hour vacation from a crazy world of unending sensory overload. The buxom, accommodating fräuleins of the *Grosse Freiheit* also packed some surprises for the five basically naive scousers. Once, legend has it, while John was groping one of the more heavily made-up patrons of the Top Ten, he discovered to his horror that "she" was outfitted with an extra piece of decidedly *un*feminine physiology. There were probably at least one bloody nose, one very red face, and countless belly laughs among the Boys over that little indiscretion!

Tony Sheridan, a popular, transplanted English singer with a large, faithful following among the Germans, was regarded by many as the "performer in residence" at the Top Ten, one of the best clubs in Germany. Because Tony was really a solo artist, he often used whatever band happened to be playing the club as his backing group. In April 1961, during the Beatles' second trip to Hamburg, Tony used them at Polydor recording sessions produced by the well-known German orchestra leader Bert Kaempfert. Although the Beatles had recorded a few times before, once as

Auntie Mimi's favorite warning to her nephew set into a photograph of John and Stuart taken by Astrid Kirchherr in Hamburg, 1961.

A guitar's all right John but you'll never earn your living by it.

Stuart's grave, kept up today by a few faithful fans.

Paddy Delaney, the Cavern's big-hearted bouncer. Liverpool 1984.

The Silver Beatles, backed by Pete Best, rip it up at one of the Cavern's lunchtime sessions.

the Quarrymen in a Liverpool friend's basement studio and then in the fall of 1960 at Akustik studios in Hamburg, these were their first professional sessions. They recorded eight tunes, six backing Tony and two others, "My Bonnie" and "Cry For A Shadow." Years later these recordings became pivotal in a lawsuit brought by Tony Sheridan against the Beatles and Apple Records, but for now the sessions were an important milestone for the Boys. No longer were they simply another scruffy rock band posing as professional; however rough and uneven the finished product may have been, the Beatles had finally made a record!

Stuart did not join the others at the Sheridan recording sessions. He was becoming far too absorbed in his relationship with Astrid and in his painting. Although he wished them all well, he realized that his days as a Beatle were finished. He would stay in Hamburg and marry Astrid. However, the months of sleeping rough in the cramped, dirty digs provided by the club owners, the unrelenting eight-hour sessions onstage, and the careless pill-popping and drinking eventually took their toll on the young artist. Time was rapidly growing short for the only true fifth Beatle, and the rest of the lads would soon have to resign themselves to let it be. Stuart Sutcliffe passed away on April 10, 1962, of an apparent brain hemorrhage. Astrid was with him right until the end.

Paddy Delaney, a former Royal Guardsman and the original bouncer at the Cavern during the first heady days of pre-Beatlemania in Liverpool, remembers his past easily and with an obvious sentiment bigger than the big man himself. Paddy still spends a lot of time around Mathew Street. Only now, instead of tossing people out of the Cavern, he's more likely — such as during this interview in 1983 — to invite you in for a bacon butty, a cup of tea, and a lively chat about the good old days.

GEOFFREY   What is your first memory of the Beatles?

PADDY DELANEY   Well, their initial appearance on the scene occurred on March 21, 1961. The first one I ever saw was George Harrison. In those days hairstyles were very strict and tidy, but George's hair was down to his collar. He was very scruffy and hungry-looking. I remember him ambling down the middle of the street, and for a minute I didn't think he was coming in the Cavern. I stopped him at the door and asked him if he was a member. Of course I knew he wasn't, and he said no, he was with the Beatles. Now we'd heard a lot about the Beatles over the previous weeks, and I knew the Beatles were on that particular night, so I let him in even though he was wearing blue jeans — which were strictly banned from the club. About fifteen minutes later Paul McCartney tumbled down the street with John Lennon in close pursuit. Paul was carrying his bass guitar, and John had his hands dug deep into his pockets. I had an idea they were with George because they all had the same sort of hairstyle. It wasn't quite a Beatle haircut then, but it was still well past their collar. A little while after

29

The newly restored stage at the Cavern club on Mathew Street, where the Beatles played 292 times.

they strolled in, a taxi pulled up in front of the club and out came their drummer, Pete Best. He was carrying the Beatles' first sound system, which consisted of two cheap chipboard speakers and a beat-up-looking amplifier. He also had a set of old drums, which he unloaded and took down the stairs. This is how the Beatles first arrived at the Cavern club.

GEOFFREY   What was their attitude in those days?

PADDY   They had a certain animal magnetism and a raw vibrancy to their music. There was an air about them that seemed to say, if you didn't like them, too bad — they couldn't care less.

GEOFFREY   How affected were the Beatles by their early success?

PADDY   Well, shortly after they recorded "Please Please Me," Brian Epstein was giving them a weekly salary of only eight pounds. I remember one night Paul went over to the snack bar to buy himself a Coke and a cheese sandwich. Now he had enough for the Coke but not for the sandwich, so he asked me for a loan, and I said, "Yeah sure, but don't forget me when you're at the top." Well, he winked at me and said, "Don't worry, Pat, I won't forget."

GEOFFREY   What about George, who was a bit younger than the others?

PADDY   George was always a big-hearted lad. I remember him once coming down Mathew Street driving a spanking new second-hand car which he had just bought with the first little bit of money that he'd made from the Beatles. As he stepped out of his car and locked it up, I happened to be arguing with two girls who didn't have enough money to get in. Now this was a big night at the Cavern club. The place was packed, and these poor girls were just standing outside in the street in tears. Well, George pushed past the two and into the club but paused at the top of the stairs and motioned for me to come over. "What's the matter with those two, Pat?" "Look, George, I'm sorry, but they haven't got enough money to get in." Chuckling, he pulled a pound out of his pocket and told me to give it to them but to make sure they didn't find out who it was from. Well, I had to make up a story very quickly, so I went outside into the street and told them, "Look, there's nothing I can do about it, girls. If you haven't got the money, how can you expect to get in? Oh, for Christ's sake, I'll tell you what. I've got a pound here — you go ahead and take it."

GEOFFREY   Did they really fall for that?

PADDY   Not a bit. "George gave you that, didn't he?" they shouted. "No," I said. "What makes you think George would do a thing like that?" Well, the next thing I knew they both started sobbing their hearts out and crying for George. "Take it or leave it," I said. "We'll pay him back!" they screamed. "You'll pay *me* back on Friday." And that, my friend, is what I had to put up with for the Beatles and their girls. Now here's a story that's never been told before about the Beatles. It happened during one of their last gigs at the Cavern. We were almost filled to capacity, but there were

Rory Storm and the Hurricanes, one of Liverpool's most popular bands, featuring a bearded Ringo Starr on drums. The band's good-looking front man, Rory Storm (*center*), was never able to accept the world-shattering success of his rivals, the Beatles, and he and his mother ended their lives in a bizarre suicide pact in their comfortable Merseyside bungalow.

"Father" Tom McKenzie in Liverpool in 1984, almost twenty years after the fact.

still dozens and dozens of people lined up outside hoping to get in. As I walked outside to tell everybody that we could only let in just a few more, a group of teenage girls handed me a toilet paper roll! "Now, what the bloody hell is this all about?" I said. "Unroll it, Paddy!" the crowd was all shouting. So I did, and my God, the kids had very carefully unrolled the damn thing, all signed it, and then rolled it back up again. They just passed it from one end of the line to the other. "Would you mind giving it to the Beatles, Pat? And please, tell them that we love them." They knew they could never all get in, so I guess this "love letter" they wrote to the Beatles was the only way to let the Boys know how they all felt. That spelled out very clearly the real success of the Beatles to me, mate.

Over and over again one point is made — what a big part just *being* from Liverpool played in making the Beatles. And Liverpool is mostly about people — basically honest, sincere, hard-working, nice people. "Father" Tom McKenzie is all of this and more. As the Beatles' compere during the two years they made fairly regular treks out of town to perform at various county fairs, workingmen's clubs, or wherever else they might find a paying gig or a receptive audience, "Father" Tom was there, taking tickets, arranging transportation, fending off out-of-control teenyboppers, and, most important, hosting the manic shows. This interview was conducted in Liverpool in 1983.

GEOFFREY   Why are you called "Father" Tom McKenzie?

TOM McKENZIE   When I was in the antiaircraft squadron in Coventry during the war, I felt somewhat jinxed because there always seemed to be an air raid whenever I was on sentry duty! You see, if there wasn't a raid, you could go to sleep, but if they attacked, you had to stand guard in the sentry box. Well, I was so fed up with being dragged out of bed when I'd just gone to sleep that I deliberately stayed awake darning my socks at night just to give me something to do. I told the Beatles about that once, and they thought it was very funny. And I think when they wrote "Eleanor Rigby" they had not forgotten me. They always used to say that I treated them just like a father when I compered their early shows.

GEOFFREY   And how did that come about?

TOM   In 1962 I began to work with the pop and rock groups that were coming along then. People like the Dakotas, the Bachelors, Tom Jones, the Rolling Stones, Cilla Black, and Gerry and the Pacemakers were all just starting out. There were also a lot of lesser-known but still very popular groups playing for us, like the Hurricanes and the Cruisers. Now in February of 1962 the Beatles came to the hall where I was working for the first time. I remember someone saying to me, "This is a very different type of group, Mr. McKenzie. They wear black leather and are very wild onstage."

GEOFFREY   So this was a very early appearance for them?

TOM   Yes. Actually, they went down very well, but they were still only in the second spot to a band called the Hollies, who, by the way, were about equivalent to the Beatles in popularity then. I did a memorable show with them in July of 1963. I'd asked them if they would please come down and crown our local carnival queen. I remember I hired John to print up the

34

Paul chats up a young fan backstage at the New Brighton Tower with Faron of Faron and the Flamingoes.

programs, and I had them picked up in a little van at his Auntie Mimi's house. It was a hot, muggy day, and the Boys had to wait until the procession traveled completely around the town. It took the parade about an hour longer than it should have, and by then the Beatles had been waiting in their van from one o'clock until four in the steaming heat. When the procession finally got back to the park, we had sold every ticket and program, which came to about ten thousand in all! You know, this was the first time the Beatles ever got any national publicity, because the story was printed up in the Sunday papers the next morning. Incidentally, on the Saturday before Brian Epstein came down and asked me to please keep playing "Love Me Do" all day long over the loudspeakers! Well, we finally got the Beatles onstage and Paul put the crown on upside down, and because we were so short of time we couldn't afford to let him make any long speeches, so he just said, "I would like to crown Miss Millington your new Carnival Queen."

GEOFFREY   So how did the Beatles' day at the fair end up?

TOM   Oh, the Beatles had a hectic time that night. They only did one set, and I think they were paid sixteen pounds for the evening. Now this particular night the Boys had to rush out the stage door before the fans could catch up with them. After they left I drifted into the dressing room, only to find George Harrison still in the toilet. "What's up, George?" I said. "Oh, Tom, I've got a dreadful bellyache," George called out. "Sorry, son, but the other Boys have already left. It looks like you're stuck here," I said. "Let me see what I can do." Well, I opened up the outside door, and there were literally hundreds of people shouting and wanting autographs. So I said, "Hold on," went around the back, and happened to spot a bus driver and called out to him, "Excuse me, but I'd like to see you about your bus for a moment, if you don't mind, and you'd better come in here." So he did, and then I said to him, "Look, mate, lend me your hat and coat, will you? I have George Harrison of the Beatles stuck in here, and I've got to get him out." Anyway, I put the hat and coat on George, we quietly walked out to the bus, and lo and behold, nobody noticed that it was him at all. Everyone thought it was just the bus driver coming back out again. About two hundred yards or so up the road the rest of the Boys were waiting in their car for George, so we just kind of ambled out of sight of the crowd and ran up to the car. Now when the other Beatles saw George, they almost pissed themselves with laughter. I mean, the poor sod was a funny sight. The bus driver was a rather stocky fellow, and of course George was mostly skin and bones anyway, so with the big coat on and the hat falling down over his ears, he looked absolutely ridiculous. So anyway, while the Boys were hooting away at George, they all signed an autograph for the driver, and off they drove down the road in their beat-up car. And that, sadly, was the last time I ever saw them.

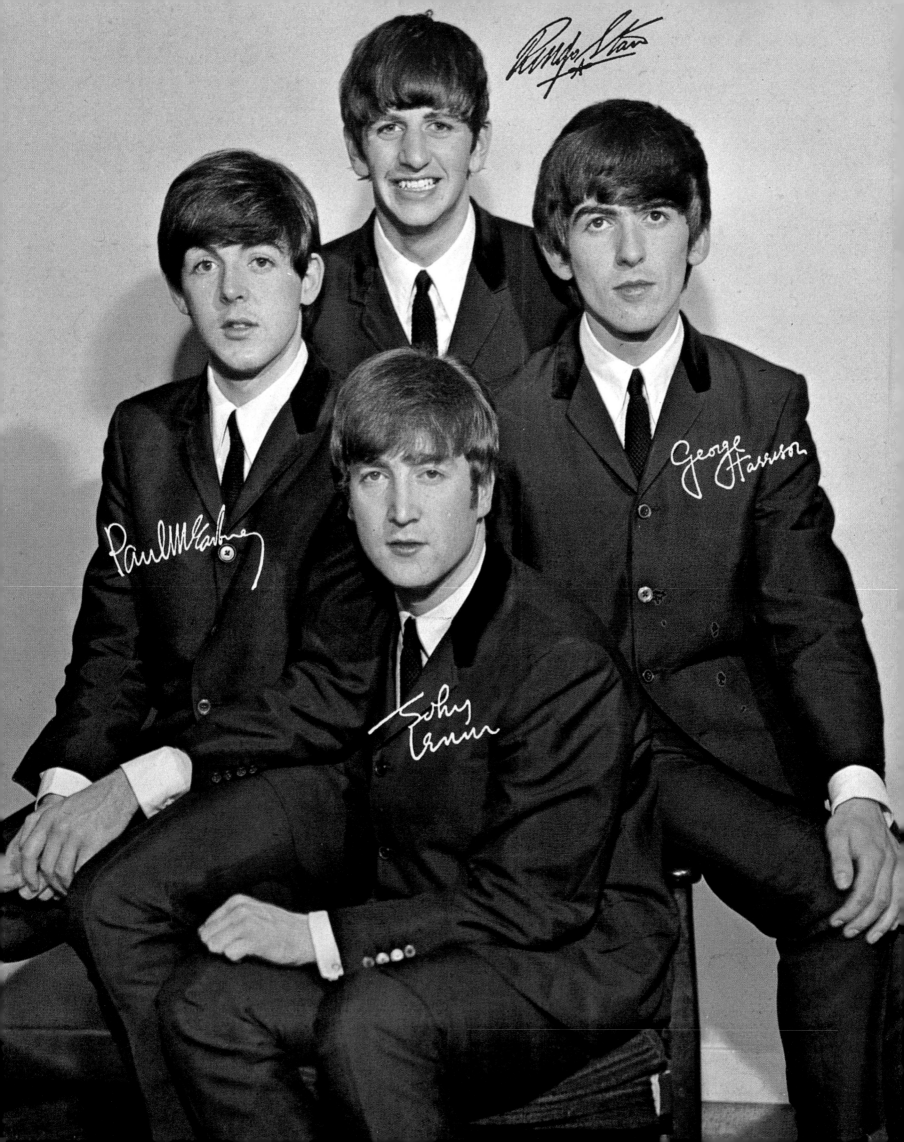

2 | Hot As Sun | *The World Goes Mad*

"They were generally regarded as clean-living, forthright chaps during the years they were getting themselves established. And they were certainly responsible for taking an awful lot of kids off the street. Their effect on Liverpool was positive. For a while the city almost seemed to lose the inferiority complex it had always had." SIR HAROLD WILSON

"That was a great period. We were like the kings of the jungle then." JOHN LENNON

The Beatles after dying their hair red to appeal to Lucille Ball.

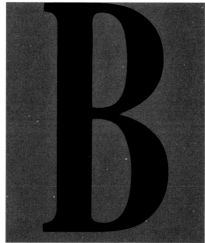

rian Epstein had never paid too much attention to pop music before. Pop was traditionally the kind of sound young housewives enjoyed listening to on their radios while doing the washing up. In its rawest, rockingest form it provided entertainment for the hordes of common street toughs who roared up and down Liverpool's back alleyways with their tiny transistor radios strapped to the handlebars of their big, greasy motorbikes. Not exactly the kind of music a gentleman with Brian's refined tastes was apt to enjoy. However, on October 28, 1961, an eighteen-year-old Huyton boy named Raymond Jones changed all that forever. He called in at the Epsteins' Whitechapel department store, NEMS, to ask about a record he'd heard of by the Beatles called "My Bonnie." He mentioned that it was probably an import from Germany, but beyond that he knew nothing. Brian was dumbfounded. He had always prided himself on the fact that any inquiry made by a customer should ultimately result in finding the desired item, but in this case he drew a complete blank. What's more, none of Brian's numerous contacts in the import business had ever heard of the record or the group. The situation was further aggravated by the fact that within the week two or three other requests for the same disc came across Brian's desk. Later, when he heard that the band was coincidentally playing only a couple of blocks away at some place called the Cavern on Mathew Street, he decided he'd better check things out.

A little after noon on November 9, 1961, dressed in his usual immaculate three-piece suit and carrying a slim, black leather briefcase, Brian descended for the first time the long, narrow stone steps of Liverpool's best-known cellar. Brian later remembered what he found: "Inside the club it was very black, dank, and smelly, and I immediately regretted coming. I chatted for a moment with one of the two hundred or so teenagers standing around the dance floor when suddenly there, on a platform high at the end of the dimly lit tunnel, stood the Beatles. They were certainly not very tidy or even very clean, but I had never in my life seen anything remotely like them! They smoked, ate, and joked amongst themselves as they played and all in all gave a most honest, captivating performance."

After the session Bob Wooler, the club deejay, announced over the loudspeakers that "Mr. Brian Epstein of NEMS is in our audience today, friends" and encouraged the sweating, wound-up kids to "please give him a warm Cavern welcome." This obvious attempt to patronize the prominent businessman embarrassed even Brian, who felt woefully out of place among the rocking teenyboppers. He later admitted that he was "really more than a little diffident" by the time he actually fought his way to the stage to speak to the Beatles about their record. After a brief, fairly confusing first encounter with the Boys Brian invited them all to come to his office at 4:30 P.M. on December 3, "just for a chat." Ten days after that John, Paul, George, Pete, Brian, and his personal assistant, Alistair Taylor, met at Pete's house and formalized an agreement for NEMS Enterprises to assume management of the Beatles. Although the original contract was signed by all four Boys and then witnessed by Alistair, Brian never actually put down his name. After all, he was a gentleman, and his good word was his bond.

The oldest child of Harry and Malka ("Queenie") Epstein, Brian was born on September 19, 1934, in a private nursing home on Rodney Street in Liverpool. His mother recalls that he was a beautiful baby with a natural curiosity who "always wanted to know everything." The first school he attended was the Beechanhurst Kindergarten, where he vaguely remembers spending an afternoon hammering various multicolored shapes into a wooden board. In 1940 the Epsteins were evacuated to Southport to wait out the merciless Nazi bombing of Liverpool. Brian was enrolled in Southport College, but he felt miserable and out of sorts with the other boys from the start. In 1943 the family returned home to Liverpool, and Brian entered prestigious Liverpool College. A year later, charged with impertinence to his masters and failing badly in just about everything, he was expelled at the ripe old age of ten. Eventually he wound up at a Jewish prep school near Tunbridge Wells called Beaconsfield, where he took up horseback riding and developed an interest in art. He was unfortunately unable to go on to a Headmasters' Conference private school because he failed the common entrance examination.

"Brian always had extraordinary taste in everything."

One of the Boys' lunchtime sessions at the Cavern.

Pete Best with legendary producer Bob Gallo.
New York, October 1965.

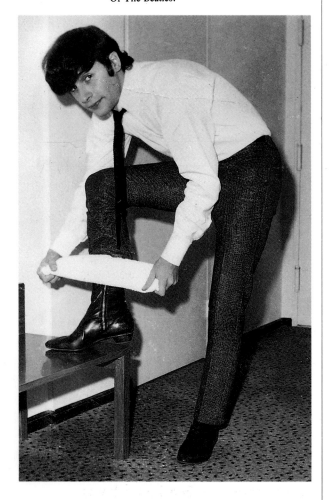

In the fall of 1948 his father managed to pull a few strings, and on his fourteenth birthday Brian was admitted to Wrekin College in Shropshire. There he became interested in acting and had a starring role in a production of *Christopher Columbus*. Despite his relative success at Wrekin he left just two years later, determined to put school behind him forever and find himself a job. Although keen to try his hand at women's fashion design, Brian was finally persuaded to accept a five-pound-a-week position as a furniture salesman in the family's Walton store.

Happily, he settled in very well with his new work. "Brian always had extraordinary taste in everything," recalls Queenie. He also took an active interest in redoing the traditional window displays that had soberly graced the Epstein shop for many years. On December 9, 1952, however, Brian was unexpectedly called upon to serve in Her Majesty's Armed Forces, a prospect that frankly frightened him to death. He joined the Royal Army Service Corps and was stationed at the esteemed Albany Barracks in Regent's Park, London. After completing only a year of his national service, however, he was discharged on medical grounds.

Returning home to Liverpool, Brian went back to work at the family store and soon became friendly with two young actors from the Liverpool Playhouse, Brian Bedford and Helen Lindsay. He appreciated their theatrical, energetic approach to life, and his own interest in acting was renewed. A few weeks later he applied for admission to the Royal Academy of Dramatic Art in London and was accepted after only a brief audition. But this dream, too, was destined not to be. Shortly after beginning his fourth term at RADA, Brian quietly packed his bags and boarded a train for Liverpool, swearing never again to forsake the comfortable lifestyle his birth afforded him for anything so uncertain and fickle as show business.

Under Brian Epstein's careful management the Beatles were gradually transformed from a scruffy band of somewhat amateurish beat musicians into a reasonably smart ensemble of professional entertainers. The cheap, black leather jackets and trousers from Germany were replaced by stylish matching suits, white shirts, yarn ties, and highly polished Cuban-heeled boots. In addition, the Boys were forbidden to eat, smoke, swear, or drink onstage. The ever-rebellious John Lennon found these restrictions particularly irksome.

One real bone of contention between the Beatles and their fans was the replacement on drums of Pete Best by Ringo Starr. It was no secret that Pete and Paul had never got on that well, and now that things had taken a turn for the better, the time seemed right for a change. "It was late one night when the first tiny hint of trouble reached me," remembers Pete. "I was helping Neil pack up the equipment after a gig at the Cavern when a call came through that Brian wanted to see me the next morning in his office at NEMS. So early the next day Neil shot by my place, and we headed into town to see what was up. When we arrived, Brian was sitting behind his

Tony Mansfield as he is today.

desk looking very white-faced and nervous. He said hello, tried to smile, then asked me how I thought I was getting on with the group, and did I feel everything was okay? 'Yeah, great,' I said, 'as far as I know. Why?' 'Well, Pete,' he said, 'I'm sorry to say that the Boys want you out of the group and Ringo in.' I couldn't believe it, but after a few moments of complete shock I finally asked him why. 'First and foremost, you're not really thought to be a good enough drummer,' said Brian apologetically. 'I'm sorry, very sorry indeed, Pete.' Then for almost another full hour Brian sat there trying to come up with other possibilities that he thought would please me. He even suggested that a new group could be formed around me if I liked, which he would be more than happy to manage. Or perhaps I'd prefer replacing another drummer in one of his other groups? At the very least, he wanted to keep me on the NEMS payroll for a few more weeks until I could come up with something else. But I just turned everything down. Neil drove me home, and for about five or six days I just couldn't bear to go out for fear I might accidentally have to face one of them."

Tony Mansfield, born in Salford on May 23, 1943, received his first drum kit at thirteen as a birthday present from his mother. As a schoolboy Tony was a great jazz fan who dreamed of one day drumming for a big Basie-style orchestra. In 1960 he was offered a gig playing with a well-known Manchester ballroom group, but he reluctantly agreed to join his father's growing confectionery business as a trainee baker. Months later, while vacationing at Butlin's Pwllheli Holiday Camp, he met and became acquainted with Ringo Starr, who was drumming for Rory Storm and the Hurricanes. It was this chance encounter with the cheery, hard-rocking Ringo that ultimately decided the young man's future. That September Tony formed his own fledgling group with guitarist Robin MacDonald and christened it the Dakotas after the roving tribe of American Indians. Some time later they were joined by singer Pete MacLaine and in February 1962 became fully professional.

It was around this time that the Dakotas first played the Cavern along with the Beatles and were observed by their future manager, Brian Epstein. A year or so later Brian took over the popular, hard-working group and dropped front man Pete MacLaine in favor of his newest solo singing discovery, Billy J. Kramer. Now known as Billy J. Kramer with the Dakotas, they spent their first month together playing Hamburg's Star Club. On their return to England they recorded their first Lennon-McCartney hit, "Do You Want To Know A Secret," for EMI producer George Martin. The Dakotas then embarked on a series of successful European tours, backing up the Beatles along with other NEMS favorites: Cilla Black, Gerry and the Pacemakers, the Remo Four, and singer Tommy Quickly. (Tony Mansfield's sister, the popular British singer Elkie Brooks, also toured with the Beatles during the early sixties.)

Pete Maclaine and the Dakotas. An early press shot.

Ringo, Rory, and the Hurricanes at Butlin's Holiday Camp in North Wales. Summer 1961.

John, Paul, George, and *Jimmy*? Ace drummer Jimmy Nicol fills in for an ailing Ringo Starr on the first leg of the Beatles' 1964 world tour.

Today a successful businessman with a string of small companies on both sides of the Atlantic, Tony Mansfield has remained friends with few from the golden days of "Merseymania," but he still keeps in touch occasionally with Ringo Starr. Recorded here for the first time, during an interview conducted in Toronto in 1983, are his remembrances of the inner workings of Brian Epstein's famous "NEMS Stable of Stars" and his private thoughts on the Beatles' meteoric rise from Liverpool's smoky basement clubs to the absolute zenith of the music industry.

GEOFFREY   I understand that you've been friends with the Beatles, and Ringo in particular, for many, many years now.

TONY MANSFIELD   Well, he wasn't a Beatle when I first met him — he was just plain Ritchie! It was the summer of 1961, and he was playing Butlin's in North Wales. He was the drummer for Rory Storm and the Hurricanes, and they were working the Rock and Calypso Bar every night. It was a very laid-back encounter. I got up and sang a song called "Donna." I was only fifteen, and Ritchie was a bit older than me. The next time I met him was a couple of years later at the Cavern. My band had just finished doing a lunchtime session, and I was packing up my drums. In fact, they were shooting some publicity photographs of the Beatles that day. I remember he had these silly knitting needles for sticks, so I asked, "What the bloody hell have you got them for?" "Well, I sometimes play too loud, so they told me I should use lighter sticks," said Ritchie. "Who are you playing for now, then?" "Oh, haven't you heard? I'm playing in the Beatles." Now the next one I met was George. He was hanging around the Cavern, as he'd been sent back home from Germany because he was under eighteen and didn't have a proper work permit.

GEOFFREY   What do you remember about their early gigs?

TONY   Well, the first time I actually saw the Beatles play was with Pete Best at the Cavern. They were doing a lunchtime session. We'd heard about the Beatles and seen a photograph of them. I remember the comment we all made at the time was, "Oh my God, the drummer's got an old Premier kit. Hey, look at that funny bass this guy's got!" It was Paul's old Hoffner violin bass, you know. They all looked very different from us, that's for sure. We were all into wearing suits and being clean-shaven like Cliff Richard and the Shadows. But they were playing for the fans, you see, so they dressed like their fans. They were very artistic, you know, especially John and Stuart.

GEOFFREY   What kind of numbers were the Beatles doing in those days?

TONY   A lot of Chuck Berry, Arthur Alexander, and old tunes like "Shot Of Rhythm And Blues" and "If You Got To Make A Fool Of Somebody" by James Ray. I heard them play "Love Me Do" a few times, which was completely different, as Pete Best was still with the group and his drumming was not at all the same as Ringo's. When I first met the Beatles, they

The Beatles in living, painted plastic.

had already written a lot of their own numbers. They used to do an awful lot of rock 'n' roll as well — "Hippy Hippy Shake," "Mr. Moonlight," "Ooh My Soul," and "Long Tall Sally," among others. They were very entertaining, especially on the lunchtime sessions, because it was so much more laid back. Many people were out of work, and I'll always remember John walking up onstage with a bacon butty in one hand and a cup of tea in the other, coming out with comments like, "I've got to finish me butty first before we play, luv." The girls would shout requests to John, and he would continually come out with all these crazy wisecracks. They used to do television commercials too, you know. I remember them doing one for Omo. (*He sings*) "Omo washes not only white, not only bright, but clean!" They were just fooling around, but it was a good laugh.

GEOFFREY   Were you on your own with any of them much?

TONY   Oh, Ritchie and I were quite friendly. I think drummers usually are, and I always liked his playing. I watched him play a lot, and sometimes John would stand offstage and watch me play. It was a nice turn, I admit. And it certainly inspired me to play a little bit better. They were a very good band live, even though the kids were constantly screaming, which pissed them off because they couldn't concentrate. It didn't matter what they played, you know. As soon as George shook his head or Paul winked or waved his hand, all the girls used to go bloody crazy anyway! Of course everyone was capitalizing on the Beatles, trying to make themselves some easy money, including our band. Our second record, "Bad To Me," was written by John and Paul, who came down to Abbey Road with the lyrics scrawled on the back of a Senior Service cigarette pack.

GEOFFREY   Did they ever rehearse with you to show you how the numbers went?

TONY   Well, they always showed us the chord structures on acoustic guitar. Altogether we had six records written for us by John and Paul. The first was "Do You Want To Know A Secret," with the B side entitled "I'll Be On My Way." Then of course "Bad To Me" was a monstrous hit for Billy, and the B side of that was "I Call Your Name." The Beatles later recorded that themselves. Then there was "I'll Keep You Satisfied," and "From A Window" was the final one.

GEOFFREY   Were you assured of a big hit simply because the Beatles wrote the tune for you?

TONY   No, nothing was ever assured. It was like living on a balloon, and we were all just waiting for it to burst.

GEOFFREY   Do you think the Beatles felt the same way? That maybe it wasn't going to last all that long?

TONY   Yeah, everybody thought that way. Brian worked us all an awful lot.

GEOFFREY   Now the Beatles had the number-one hit in the country, and

The Beatles, George Martin, and Eppy cop yet
another distinguished award. 1964.

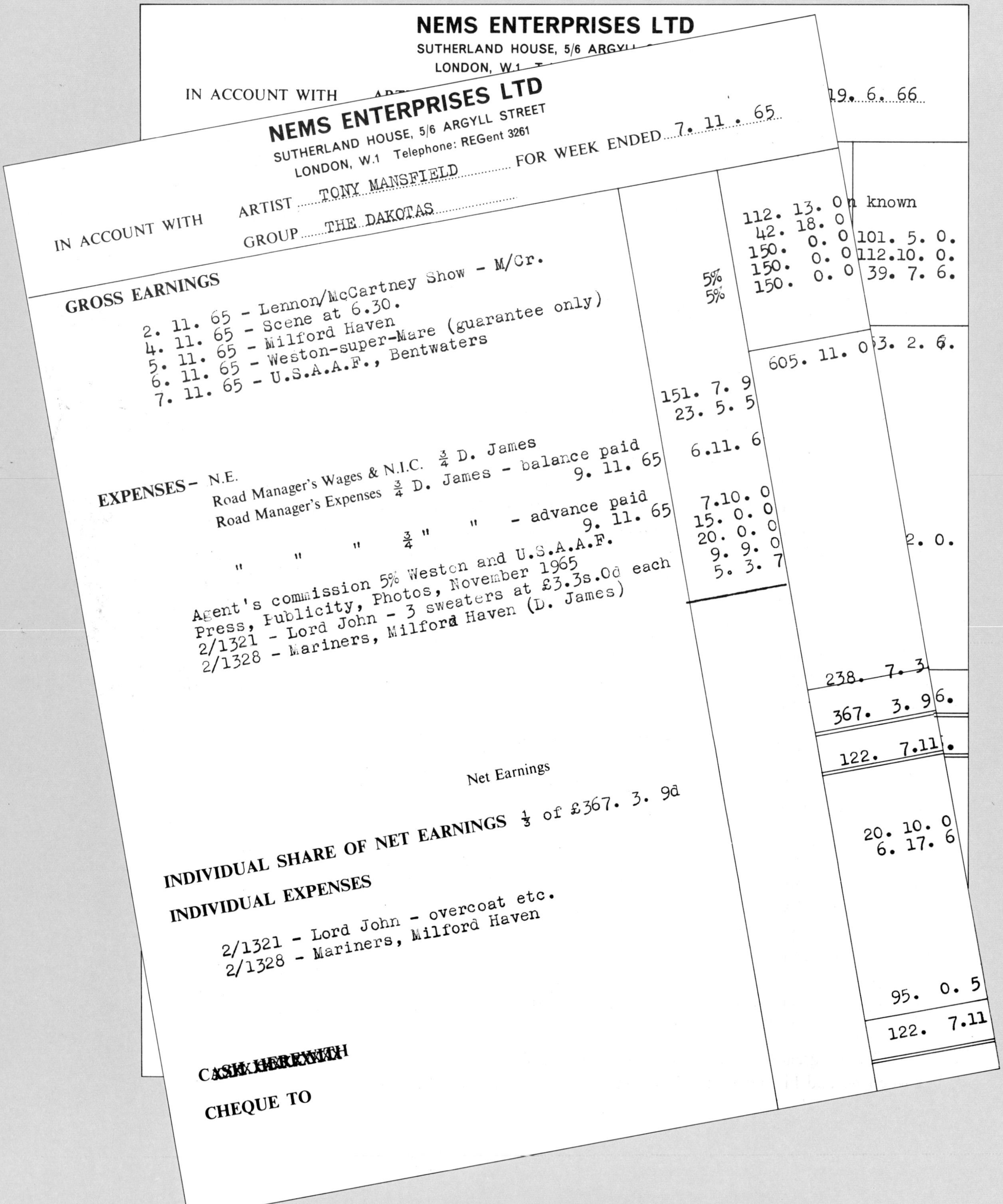

NEMS ENTERPRISES LTD
SUTHERLAND HOUSE, 5/6 ARGYLL STREET
LONDON, W.1 Telephone: REGent 3261

IN ACCOUNT WITH   ARTIST ...... TONY MANSFIELD ...... FOR WEEK ENDED .. 7 . 11 . 65

GROUP ...... THE DAKOTAS ......

GROSS EARNINGS

    2. 11. 65 - Lennon/McCartney Show - M/Cr.
    4. 11. 65 - Scene at 6.30.
    5. 11. 65 - Milford Haven
    6. 11. 65 - Weston-super-Mare (guarantee only)
    7. 11. 65 - U.S.A.A.F., Bentwaters

	112. 13. 0	n known
	42. 18. 0	
5%	150. 0. 0	101. 5. 0.
5%	150. 0. 0	112.10. 0.
	150. 0. 0	39. 7. 6.
		605. 11. 0

EXPENSES - N.E.

Road Manager's Wages & N.I.C. ¾ D. James   151. 7. 9
Road Manager's Expenses ¾ D. James - balance paid 23. 5. 5
                                        9. 11. 65   6.11. 6
     "   "   "   ¾ "   "   - advance paid
                                        9. 11. 65   7.10. 0
Agent's commission 5% Weston and U.S.A.A.F.   15. 0. 0
Press, Publicity, Photos, November 1965   20. 0. 0
2/1321 - Lord John - 3 sweaters at £3.3s.0d each   9. 9. 0
2/1328 - Mariners, Milford Haven (D. James)   5. 3. 7

                                                   238. 7. 3
                                                   367. 3. 9
                                                   122. 7.11

Net Earnings

INDIVIDUAL SHARE OF NET EARNINGS ⅓ of £367. 3. 9d

INDIVIDUAL EXPENSES

    2/1321 - Lord John - overcoat etc.   20. 10. 0
    2/1328 - Mariners, Milford Haven   6. 17. 6

                                                    95. 0. 5

                                                   122. 7.11

~~CASH HEREWITH~~

CHEQUE TO

NEMS ENTERPRISES LTD
SUTHERLAND HOUSE, 5/6 ARGYLL
LONDON, W.1

IN ACCOUNT WITH   ARTI   19. 6. 66

Pay statements from NEMS Enterprises to Tony Mansfield.

you guys were just a working band not really making all that much money. How did you feel about that?

TONY   Fabulous — because we really enjoyed their music. In fact, we often played "Please Please Me" in Germany.

GEOFFREY   Were you ever jealous?

TONY   No, no, we were very proud of them. It looked good on all of us that they were so successful. I mean, we were all fellow musicians, and while I can't sit here and say that John and I were bosom buddies, we certainly had respect for each other. I know that John always liked my playing, and vice versa. As a matter of fact, he would often yell out to me from backstage, "Tony, kick ass! Kick ass, man!"

GEOFFREY   I wanted to ask your impression of Brian as a person, because there has always been so much cheap talk about him. The Beatles were very protective of him, weren't they?

TONY   They were indeed. And although he was gay, I don't think even Brian knew what he *really* was sexually. He was a very frustrated man, completely torn in two over his homosexuality, I think. Also, with the normal caliber of personal manager running around at that time being the typical fast-talking, cigar-smoking type of guy, Brian was a real gentleman. The business wasn't used to a Brian Epstein, and they didn't always know how to treat him.

GEOFFREY   Was he a good businessman?

TONY   Well, people say he wasn't particularly good, but he certainly seemed to be running NEMS properly.

GEOFFREY   Did Brian dote on the Beatles particularly?

TONY   Yes, Brian was very infatuated with the Beatles. They were his whole life, really.

GEOFFREY   How did Brian's interest in the Beatles manifest itself on a day-to-day basis? I suppose he always made sure everything was absolutely perfect for them?

TONY   No, they worked very hard! I remember doing a week in London with them once, and they would rehearse all day at the theater because we were doing a Royal Variety Show, which as you know was a very important gig. We didn't party much because we were always too damn tired. And when we did do a week in one place, it gave us some time to catch up on our sleep!

GEOFFREY   How about some tasty one-liners on the following people? Neil Aspinall.

TONY   Neil's a great guy. The Beatles always called him "Nell." I remember when he had his old Bedford van and was still hauling the Beatles' equipment around.

GEOFFREY   John Lennon.

TONY   Nice guy. Whenever I met him he was always *very* funny. He had

RINGO

lots of balls and was a great rocker with a very good voice. I never rated him highly as a guitar player, but he always put on a terrific show.

GEOFFREY   George Harrison.

TONY   Well, he was always the Quiet One. Very polite and funny at times, too. When we would go into the Beatles' dressing room after a show, they always had their own silly little words they used all the time, their own personal "Beatles terminology," you might say. But despite all that they made us feel very comfortable.

GEOFFREY   Ringo Starr.

TONY   He had a very good way about him, and he's a very solid drummer as well. He always had a nice word to say to everybody, and he was so funny. He's often used my kit, and I've used his. I remember using his Premier kit at the Cavern once and even knocking his bass drum off the end of the stage!

GEOFFREY   Paul McCartney.

TONY   Good musician, lots of energy, and he always listened to you when you were talking, or he *seemed* to anyway.

GEOFFREY   He was a real diplomat, wasn't he?

TONY   Yes, very much so, and he was a very good businessman. Whenever we were in the studio with John and Paul, we generally had to learn their tunes on the spot. So it was certainly never boring, I will say that!

GEOFFREY   George Martin.

TONY   Oh, George was a fabulous guy to work with. He was a gentleman, very professional and enthusiastic. You know, he wrote an instrumental for our band called "Magic Carpet" once, but it didn't do anything — it just flew away! He had a lot of charisma. You listened to George, you didn't swear in front of him or anything. You treated him with great respect.

GEOFFREY   Mal Evans.

TONY   Mal was a bundle of fun. He helped me out many times when we had trouble on the road touring with the Beatles.

GEOFFREY   Norman Smith, the recording engineer who worked with the Beatles.

TONY   Fabulous. I'll always remember Norman with his little cigarettes. He used to roll his own, and he smoked them right up to the bitter end. Good lad — he was always worrying about how the drums were going to sound and was generally very concerned with doing a good recording.

GEOFFREY   Billy J. Kramer.

TONY   Billy and I never got on together, we had lots of rows. He had virtually no confidence onstage and would often take it out on me personally.

GEOFFREY   How did you feel as the years rolled by and you realized the place in history the Beatles had made?

TONY   It makes me very proud that I was once associated with them. On a musical basis, having had them write songs for our band and also being

Brian Epstein's personal Christmas cards and a telegram sent to Tony Mansfield for his twenty-first birthday.

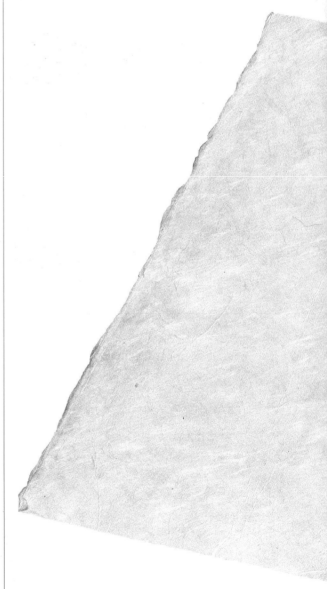

48

HAPPY BIRTHDAY TO YOU

✦   MR 383   SRL 6 (TS777/J141) BH6   2.25

REGENT TS 21 BIRTHDAY

PENNY MANSFIELD 117 CAVENDISH RD SALFORD-6 =

GOOD LUCK BEST WISHES CONGRATULATIONS

MANY MANY HAPPY BIRTHDAYS =

JOHN PAUL GEORGE AND RINGO +

✝

Happy Everything

Tony,

and good luck
in the future.

Brian

24 Chapel Street · London SW1

THIS COMING FRIDAY LUNCHTIME

Special Double Bill
ON STAGE

12·20 P.M.
THE BEATLES

1·00 P.M.
PETE MACLAINE & THE DAKOTAS

1·40 P.M.
THE BEATLES

→ Come Along Early !

Paul waves to the ever-present paparazzi on one of the Beatles' early European tours.

The only known surviving hand-painted poster advertising the Beatles at the Cavern. A unique collector's item, it has been appraised at over $20,000.

The Beatles between takes during the shooting of their first feature film, *A Hard Day's Night*.

MEET JOHN LENNON
Vital Statistics:
Birthday—Oct. 9, 1940
Birthplace—Liverpool
Hair—Brown
Eyes—Brown
Height—5'11"
Weight—159
Favorite Color—Green
Favorite Food—Corn Flakes
Hobby—Writing
Favorite Singer—Shirelles
Likes—Cats
Favorite Type of Girl—His
Wife
Brothers & Sisters—2 Step-
Sisters

involved with their recording manager, George Martin, was absolutely fantastic. I love listening to the old Beatles records even today, and to the Dakotas, of course!

Once it got going, Beatlemania swept across the British Isles with an intensity and momentum far beyond anything Brian or the Boys could have envisioned. It was hard to believe that when he first took over the Beatles, Brian had been unable to interest any of the major record labels in them and that it was only by the luckiest of coincidences that he landed a deal with Parlophone. Now everywhere the Beatles went, they were pursued by hordes of screaming, crying, swooning young women. And by a ruthless British press, who faithfully reported every successive outbreak of Beatle-mania with the kind of coverage usually reserved for "lesser" news events, such as the outbreak of world war! Still the Beatles remained dissatisfied. Locked up by themselves for days on end in one lifeless hotel room after another, they talked of only one thing — conquering America!

Midway over the Atlantic on board Pan Am flight 101 to New York, the Beatles were feeling more than a little anxious about what sort of reception they would find on landing. But all doubts were swept away when at 1:35 on the afternoon of February 7, 1964, they touched down on the icy runway of Kennedy Airport. As the plane slowly made its way toward the terminal, the shrill sound of over ten thousand teenage voices chanting and screaming for the Beatles penetrated the hull of the aircraft. Peering out of the frozen windows of the DC-10, the Beatles saw for the first time what America had in store for them. "Every kid from Broadway to the Bronx was there," remembers one seasoned veteran of the quizzical New York press corps. "They were all wearing buttons that said 'I LIKE THE BEATLES' and waving banners and placards they'd made up at home. Little girls were fainting, cops were sticking bullets in their ears to help drown out the screaming, and the poor Beatles were just standing there at the door of the plane completely and utterly in shock. No one, I mean no one, had ever seen or even remotely suspected anything like this!" The Boys were led to the airport press lounge, where they held the largest, wildest press conference in the history of New York City. John Lennon yelled at everyone to shut up, and the entire room applauded! Beatlemania now held the entire world in its grasp as an untold number of hustlers, con men, and copycats all clamored to jump on board the bandwagon.

QUESTION   Ringo, why do you wear two rings on each hand?

RINGO   Because I can't fit them through my nose.

QUESTION   Do you think it's wrong to set such a bad example to teenagers, smoking the way you do?

RINGO   It's better than being alcoholics.

QUESTION   What do you think of the criticism that you are not very good?

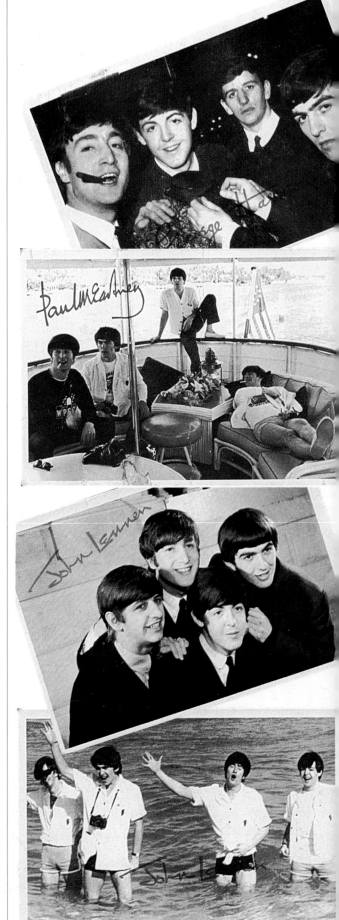

GEORGE We're not.

QUESTION What do you believe is the reason you are the most popular singing group today?

JOHN We've no idea. If we did we'd get four long-haired boys, put them together, and become their managers.

QUESTION What do you miss most now that your fame prohibits your freedom?

RINGO Going to the movies.

GEORGE Having nothing to do.

JOHN School, because you don't have much to do there.

PAUL Going on buses.

QUESTION What do you do when you're cooped up in a hotel room between shows?

GEORGE We ice-skate.

QUESTION How did you find America?

RINGO We went to Greenland and made a left turn.

QUESTION Would you like to walk down the street without being recognized?

JOHN We used to do that with no money in our pockets. There's no point in it.

QUESTION How do you keep your psychic balance?

RINGO The important thing is not to get potty. There's four of us, so whenever one of us gets a little potty, the other three bring him back to earth.

QUESTION Does all the adulation from teenage girls affect you?

JOHN When I feel my head start to swell, I look at Ringo and know perfectly well we're not supermen.

QUESTION How do you feel about the invasion of your privacy all the time?

RINGO The only time it bothers us is when they get us to the floor and really mangle us.

QUESTION Do you speak French?

PAUL Non.

QUESTION What's the secret of your success?

JOHN We have a press agent.

QUESTION Do you have any special advice for teenagers?

JOHN Don't get pimples.

QUESTION What would you do if the fans got past the police lines?

GEORGE We'd die laughing.

QUESTION What will you do when the bubble bursts?

GEORGE Take up ice hockey.

George

Ringo

DELL PUBLISHING CO., INC.

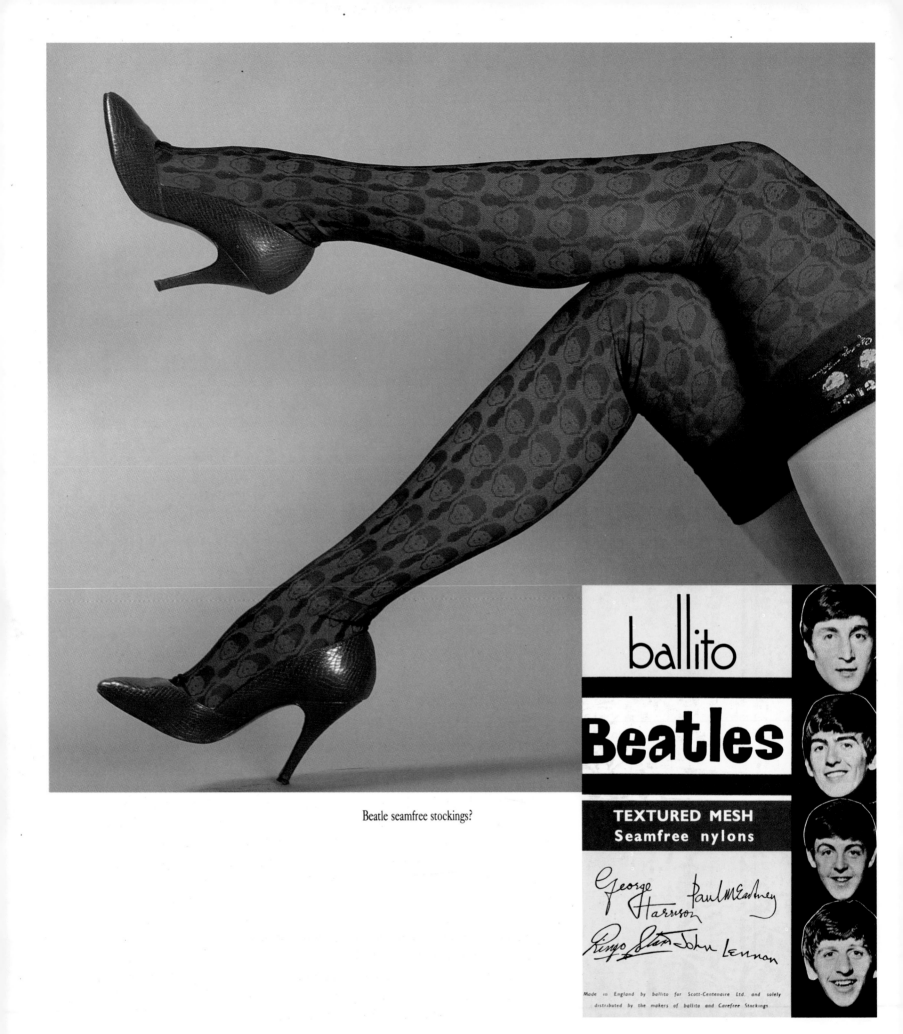

Beatle seamfree stockings?

ballito

Beatles

TEXTURED MESH
Seamfree nylons

George Harrison   Paul McCartney

Ringo Starr   John Lennon

Made in England by ballito for Scott-Centenaire Ltd. and solely
distributed by the makers of ballito and Carefree Stockings

"This cute and talented group of young girls has developed its own unique sound in the true Beatles tradition. We think its name will last long after the Beatles are gone. . ." From the liner notes of the Beatle Buddies' first and only LP. A product of Synthetic Plastics, Newark, New Jersey.

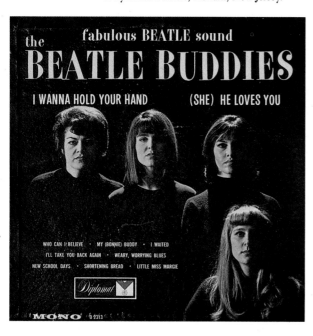

An original dayglow plastic Beatle guitar complete with its own carrying case (not shown).

PAUL   Play basketball.

QUESTION   Has success spoiled the Beatles?

JOHN   Well, you don't see us running out and buying bowler hats, do you? I think we've pretty well succeeded in remaining ourselves.

PAUL   The great thing about it is that you don't have big worries anymore when you've got where we have, only little ones — like whether the plane is going to crash.

QUESTION   What is the biggest threat to your careers, the atom bomb or dandruff?

RINGO   The atom bomb. We've already got dandruff.

After the press conference the Beatles were ceremoniously driven into New York City and installed in a palatial suite of rooms at the Plaza Hotel. George didn't like the food, but this didn't really bother the management, because it didn't especially care for the Beatles and their fifteen thousand or so screaming fans tearing up the hotel. This it rather ungraciously made known to the entire world by offering the Beatles to any other four-star hotel that would have them. The fact that New York's innkeepers lacked a sense of humor, however, was no indication that the rest of the nation wasn't ready for a good, hearty "Yeah, yeah, yeah." Even Elvis Presley, the Beatles' rock 'n' roll hero, acknowledged their impact on the music scene by sending them a congratulatory telegram following their first appearance on the "Ed Sullivan Show." In fact, many newspapers were already calling for the "King" to abdicate his throne. The New York *Daily News* wrote, "The Presleyan gyrations and caterwauling of yesterday are but lukewarm dandelion tea in comparison to the 100-proof elixir served up by the Beatles." And so it seemed that John Lennon's longtime wish that the Beatles might one day be bigger than Elvis was finally coming true.

Despite their many triumphs, however, as the Beatles toured the United States the pattern of lunacy that constantly surrounded them began to take its toll. John and George, in particular, became very cynical about the fact that the Beatles seemed to have become an excuse for kids to run wild in the streets, smashing up phone boxes and climbing up elevators shafts in hopes of catching a brief glimpse of one of their idols. Plopped down in the middle of Anytown, U.S.A., the Fab Four were forced to perform in outdoor sports arenas with virtually no acoustics, proper amplification, or adequate security. "The bigger we got, the more unreality we had to face," says John. "It was all just a bad joke to me. One has to completely humiliate oneself to be what the Beatles were. I didn't know, I couldn't foresee. It just happened gradually, bit by bit, until you're doing exactly what you don't want to do with people you simply can't stand! The people you hated when you were ten." Still the tours lumbered on, each city melting into the next, each performance more meaningless than the one before. Their ever-faithful road manager, Mal Evans, remembers they even faced being

John and Paul on the "Ed Sullivan Show."

electrocuted by their own instruments when they were forced to continue performing at outdoor gigs when it began to rain. "What could we do?" he muses. "If we'd stopped the show, the kids would have stampeded and probably torn us limb from limb!" A plane carrying the Beatles was shot at by a jealous boyfriend, and Brian became the victim of an extortion attempt after a shadowy love affair with a New York construction worker. But what was worse — what made it absolutely impossible for the Beatles to continue touring for an extended period of time — was the undeniable reality that in the midst of all this chaos, the audiences had forgotten the music. Everyone was still applauding, but no one was really listening anymore.

From February 2, 1963, to August 29, 1966, the Beatles played over 225 live shows in almost every country and continent of the free world. They performed for millions of hysterical teenyboppers, were pelted by rock-hard jelly beans, and were constantly harassed by fans looking for souvenirs — everything from personalized autographs to bits of their hair, clothes, and even fingernails. Crippled children were wheeled into the Boys' dressing rooms in hopes that a dose of their mysterious power might restore or straighten lifeless limbs and twisted bodies. Airport terminals were continually soiled by young women who wet their pants on catching up with their favorite Beatle.

This was, all in all, quite a lot of madness for four provincial young men from the north of England to endure. And so, when the Beatles laid down their instruments after their last number at Candlestick Park in San Francisco in August 1966, they said good-bye to public performing forever. From now on John, Paul, George, and Ringo would devote themselves exclusively to working their magic only in the privacy and sanctity of the recording studio.

THE BEATLES

JOHN LENNON   PAUL McCARTNEY   GEORGE HARRISON   RINGO STARR

WATCH THEM GROW THEIR OWN HAIR
LIVE IN YOUR OWN ROOM!
Yes, Can You Imagine, You Can Even Give Them Haircuts!

You can actually have the fabulous BEATLES GROWING IN YOUR OWN ROOM! YES! Watch, RINGO, GEORGE, PAUL AND JOHN grow their famous hairdoes right before your very eyes. Give them any style haircut, any time you like.

A scientific wonder that will amaze you and your friends

Yes, due to a fantastic scientific method, these miniature BEATLES will GROW BIGGER AND BIGGER, FASTER AND FASTER EACH AND EVERY DAY. Imagine the look on your friends faces when you take them to your own room and show them your very own LIVING BEATLES. See them gasp with awe and delight as you give your BEATLES their Haircuts. All you have to do is lead them to a cup or glass of water and give them a drink.

- Actually cut their hair
- A wonderful gift for kids
- Not available in stores
- Live in your own room from 6 to 60 anywhere

These delightful BEATLES are available only through this advertisement. They are not in stores anywhere, so rush your order now!

NOVEL PRODUCTS, CORP.   31 Second Avenue, Dept. HP-1   New York, N. Y. 10003
Gentlemen:
Please RUSH me the following:
☐ 1 Set Only $1. plus 25¢ Postage & Handling   ☐ SPECIAL! 3 Sets only $3. post paid.
☐ 2 Sets Only $2. plus 25¢ Postage & Handling   ☐ _____ Amount enclosed. SORRY NO C.O.D.'s

Name ....
Address .... City .... Zone .... State ....

Milton Bradley's celebrated Flip Your Wig game.

A hand-printed serigraph advertising a little-known movie trailer.

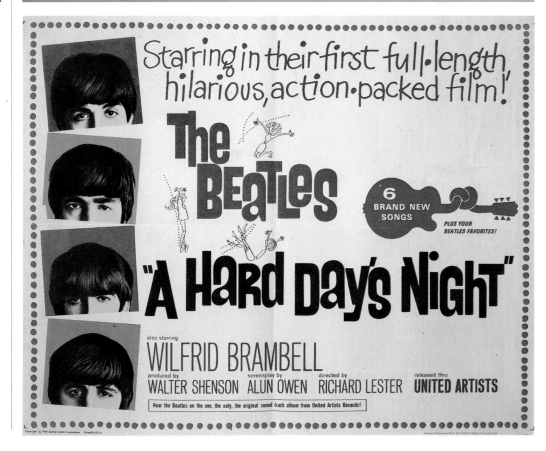

Maple Leaf Gardens, Toronto, September 7, 1964.

A vintage 1964 authentic Beatle wig.

The Beatles arrive in San Francisco for their last concert at Candlestick Park.

A vivid example of early San Francisco psychedelia. This rare graphic heralded the end of the Beatles' performing career.

The *crème de la crème* of Beatle collectibles — the rubber REMCO dolls.

An example of the many attempts to exploit the Beatles' name.

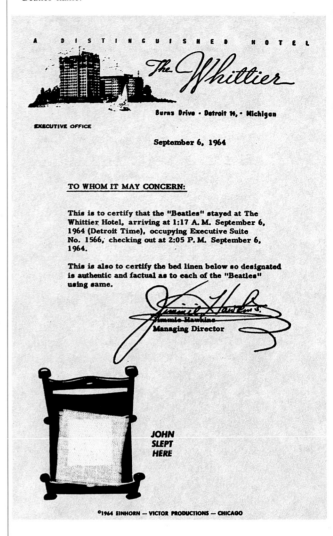

Programs from the Beatles' 1965 and 1966 concerts.

A 1965 scandal sheet.

Britain's Top Pop Group Confesses

A Different Girl Every Night

THE NATIONAL

Insider

Informative • Provocative • Fearless • Entertaining

★★★★★ (See pages 2-3)

SPECIAL WEEKLY FEATURE **15¢**

Vol. 7, No. 13 — Sept. 26, 1965

The Cop Who Led The Raids Tells All!

BEATLES BEDROOM SCANDAL

Police Find A Sexy Blonde Teen in Paul's Room!

3

All Together On The Wireless Machine

The Studio Years

"The Beatles didn't really come up with anything new. They just heralded the change in consciousness that was happening in the sixties." GEORGE HARRISON

"We became technically efficient recording artists because we were basically competent people, and whatever media you put us in, we could generally produce something worthwhile." JOHN LENNON

A surreal collage of the Beatles from the time of the "white" album.

rian Epstein's first attempts to secure a recording contract for the Beatles relied heavily on family connections. With a couple of smartly placed phone calls he was first able to interest Decca Records and arranged for an A & R representa-
tive to come up to Liverpool to view for himself, as Brian modestly put it, "England's newest pop phenomenon in the making." The fellow's name was Mike Smith, and he liked what he saw. As a result an audition was scheduled for January 1, 1962, at Decca's Hampstead studios in London. The Beatles recorded fifteen songs that morning, including "Like Dreamers Do," "The Sheik Of Araby," "Three Cool Cats," "September In The Rain," and "Besame Mucho." Everyone was very nervous, but by the time the session was over, Smith seemed genuinely pleased with the results and enthusiastically told Brian to expect a call from his boss, recording manager Dick Rowe, in the very near future.

Weeks later, when that call had not yet come, Brian decided to take the bull by the horns and ring up Rowe himself. "Unfortunately, Decca turned us down cold. Rowe told me that they hadn't liked the Beatles' sound all that much and that groups featuring guitars were on the way out! I assured him that my Boys would soon be bigger than even Elvis and that, in our opinion, Decca wasn't the right sort of company to handle an act of this magnitude anyway." Despite the bravado, though, Brian was crushed. What would he say to the Boys? And after all his big talk at home about how easy it was going to be to secure a recording contract for them, what would his parents think? Unfortunately, he would have plenty of opportunity to perfect his apologies, as the Beatles were also turned down by Pye, EMI, and a host of smaller companies.

All this time Brian had been taking tapes of the Beatles' music around to various record companies. After one or two interviews with potential backers during which the tapes couldn't be played for technical reasons, he decided it would be more convenient and impressive if he were to have a few records made. So tapes in hand, he headed down to London yet again in one final, all-out effort to pull something together for the Boys. Coincidentally, a friend at the HMV Record Centre introduced him to a small music publisher named Syd Coleman, who thought the tapes were terrific and wanted to sign the Beatles to a long-term publishing deal immediately. He even offered to hawk them to George Martin, a friend of his and a producer at Parlophone, a small but reputable offshoot of the vast EMI empire. George readily agreed to meet with Brian, but after listening to the tunes said that while the music was indeed interesting, the band was still quite rough and would need a lot of grooming before he could seriously consider taking them on.

Still, they arranged for an audition on June 6, 1962, at the EMI studios on Abbey Road in St. John's Wood, London. The Boys went through almost their entire repertoire while Martin listened very carefully and jotted down notes on a thick yellow pad balanced on his knees. "Right then, fellows," he said when the session was finished. "I'll let you know. Thanks very much for coming down." Crashing down the stone steps of EMI, Brian and the Boys assumed the worst.

This time, however, the untold hundreds of hours spent pulling together their unique sound in the seedy cellars and nightclubs of Hamburg and Liverpool more than paid off. Toward the end of July Brian received word from London that Parlophone had decided to give the Beatles their shot. A formal recording session was set for September 11. Martin chose two songs for their first single, "Love Me Do" backed by "PS I Love You." By this time Ringo Starr had replaced Pete Best on drums. Martin was very concerned about this change and engaged the services of session drummer Andy White just in case he might be needed. When the Beatles arrived, Martin greeted them warmly and encouraged them to let him know immediately if there was anything they didn't like. "Well, for a start, I don't like your tie," said George Harrison, only half joking. Rude as it may have been, this little crack helped break the ice, and after a hearty laugh all around the session proceeded without further ado.

The single was released on October 4, 1962, and "Love Me Do" crept slowly up the pop charts to number seventeen. Brian Epstein and George

A record player with the Beatles' picture on it is worth $500-plus today.

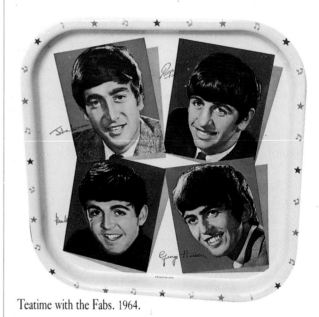

Teatime with the Fabs. 1964.

The Beatles as everyone's father wanted to see them in the mid-sixties.

64

A collection of rare Beatle tour programs from the early sixties plus a special invitation to the press showing of *A Hard Day's Night*.

Martin were pleased, but not overwhelmed. They had much bigger things in mind for the Beatles, for now nothing but a full-fledged, number-one smash hit would do! And that's what "Please Please Me" gave them. Recorded at EMI on November 26, 1962, but not released until mid-January 1963, the Beatles' second single topped the charts only one month later, making this happy, bouncing teenage love call one of their greatest achievements. In four weeks it climbed, in the words of a deliriously joyful John Winston Lennon, "right up to the toppermost of the poppermost!" At last John, Paul, George, and Ringo had the biggest hit in the country!

The Beatles' kindly, good-natured, quietly brilliant record producer, George Martin, was born in 1926 in Muswell Hill, North London. His father, a carpenter by trade, was hit hard by the Depression and was eventually reduced to selling newspapers on the street in London's Cheapside. His mother, a devout Roman Catholic, doted on young George and made sure that both he and his older sister, Irene, were suitably educated within the stringent domain of the church.

By the age of eight George had enthusiastically taken up the piano, but after he had attended only a few lessons, his mother had a row with the instructor, a distant relative, and no further musical training was made available to him until he was well into his teens. At sixteen George sought to express his musical interests by playing one or two nights a week in a dance band called the Four Tune Tellers. Made up of friends from a local church, the band specialized in pleasant, lilting standards like "The Good Night Waltz" and "The Way You Look Tonight." After the war broke out, George joined the Fleet Air Arm and did very well, reaching the rank of lieutenant and working as a release officer. Never anyone's fool, and using the full force of his rank, he released *himself* from His Majesty's Armed Forces early in 1947 and went home, now in Bromley, Kent. Awarded a respectable government grant of £160 a year, George applied to the Guildhall School of Music in London. In September 1947 he became a full-time student there, concentrating on piano and studying the oboe as his second instrument.

In January 1948 George married his Navy sweetheart, a lovely, quiet young woman named Sheena, and together they moved into a cheap cold-water flat in Acton. He stayed at Guildhall for three years, eking out a living between classes by scoring bits of music for people and working evenings as a freelance oboe player. He earned only two pounds ten shillings per performance, so life was pretty hard for the young couple. Then in September 1950, out of the blue, George received a letter from a man named Oscar Preuss offering him a job with EMI's Parlophone in Abbey Road as an assistant A & R man. He accepted with pleasure. Oddly enough though, as the years went by, George created a niche for himself by producing not the classical music that had always been his passion, but the recorded wit of such outlandish comedy groups as Beyond the Fringe

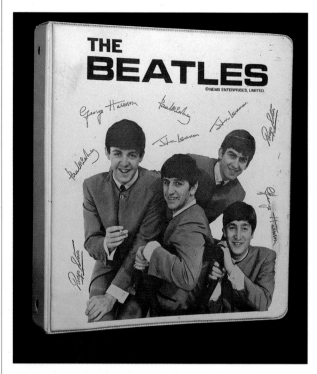

A three-ring notebook.

Left Pete Best's only serious attempt to launch an independent recording career. *Right* Perhaps the world's first Beatle bootleg based on the Tony Sheridan recordings in Hamburg.

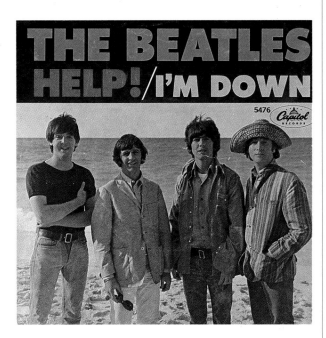

(with Peter Cook and Dudley Moore) and the Goons (with Peter Sellers, Spike Milligan, and Harry Secombe).

Later on, as the homegrown skiffle craze grew and the English rock scene expanded to include popular artists like Lonnie Donegan, Gene Vincent, Little Richard, and Elvis Presley, Parlophone began to consider producing some commercial, youth-oriented music. By May 1962 it had been looking around for a suitable group for some time and was delighted at the prospect of finally landing its very own rock 'n' roll band.

The resounding success of the Beatles' chart-topping single, "Please Please Me," led in April 1963 to the release of their first full album. Sensibly titled after their big hit, "Please Please Me" the LP remained on the charts for a full six months, spawning in its wake "From Me To You," another number-one tune for the group. From that time on the Beatles racked up an astounding list of worldwide number-one singles, more than any other band in the history of popular music, including "She Loves You," "I Want To Hold Your Hand," "Can't Buy Me Love," "A Hard Day's Night," "I Feel Fine," "Ticket To Ride," "Help!," "Paperback Writer," and "Yellow Submarine." The Beatles also released several successful albums during those years that reached the highly coveted number-one position: "With The Beatles," "A Hard Day's Night," "Beatles For Sale," "Help!," "Rubber Soul," and the prepsychedelic chartbuster, "Revolver."

The Beatles' retreat from public life into the studio gave them greater scope to express themselves musically and reduced the pressure of having to crank out one top-selling hit after another. After so many years of hustling to reach the top, the Beatles reveled in their newfound artistic freedom. One of the first and most significant manifestations of this change in direction was their concentrated effort to write better, more meaningful songs. John explains: "Beatlemusic is when we all get together, you know. Of course, we really don't write songs together that much anymore. Now it's just occasional bits, a line or two. We used to write a lot when we were touring, mainly out of sheer boredom. But today the Beatles just go into the studio, and it happens! See, I remember our early meetings with Dylan where he'd constantly go on about the words. Well, I naturally play with the lyrics anyway, but I suppose I made a more conscious effort to be 'wordy à la Dylan' after that. When I started out, you see, rock 'n' roll itself was the basic revolution to people of my age. We needed something loud and clear to break through all the un-feeling and repression that had been coming down on us kids. Rock makes good sense, but then again, so does pure sound. Paul has always said that in the end we'll all probably be writing one-note pop songs, and he's right. But for now we're still working with the concept of 'sound pictures' — that is, creating visual images through the medium of sound. There's still a lot to be learned in this area as well."

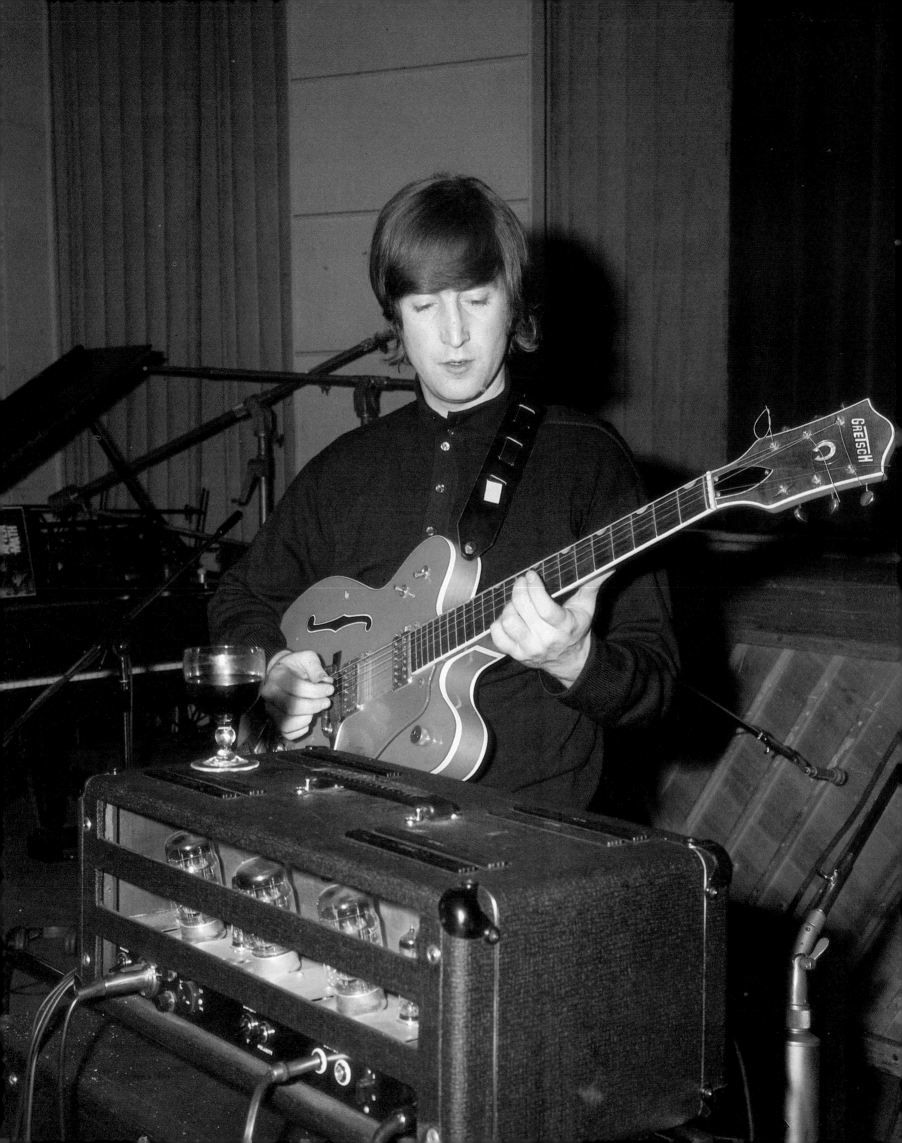

In the studio working on Paul's soulful "Fool On The Hill."

The Beatles meet the press following a Toronto gig. 1966.

John in the recording studio. 1966.

Albums like "Rubber Soul" and "Revolver" certainly shook up the Beatles' musical image with their innovative use of classical orchestrations, lofty, intricate lyrics, and the virtually unheard-of addition to popular music of sound effects. And although they were all very successful, they were little more than brief, though thoroughly engrossing, sideshows to the main event, "Sgt. Pepper's Lonely Hearts Club Band."

The album was recorded with great enthusiasm at the EMI studios between December 1966 and April 1967. The project started off with the recording of "When I'm Sixty-Four" on December 10. Written chiefly by Paul, it also featured him on lead vocals, piano, and bass. Strongly influenced by the old-time music hall sounds of English vaudeville, this song typifies the extended repertoire the Beatles had worked to develop. The second tune committed to tape, the epic "A Day In The Life," was initiated on January 19. Using a forty-one-piece orchestra and backed by a dreamy montage of vocal harmonies by John, Paul, and George, it is the longest song on the album, clocking in at five minutes, three seconds.

John and Paul recall the inspiration for the work. "I was writing the song with the *Daily Mail* propped up in front of me on the piano," says John. "I had it open at the 'News in Brief' section or whatever they call it. Anyway, there was a paragraph about four thousand holes in Blackburn, Lancashire, being discovered, and there was still one word missing in that particular verse when we began to record. I knew the line should go, 'Now they know how many holes it takes to . . . the Albert Hall.' It was a nonsense verse really, but for some reason I just couldn't think of the bloody verb! What did the holes *do* to the Albert Hall? It was actually Terry Doran who finally said, '*Fill* the Albert Hall, John.'" Paul McCartney remembers: "There'd been a story about a lucky man who'd made the grade, and there was a photograph of him sitting in his big car, and when John saw it he just had to laugh! That's all just a little black comedy, you know. The next bit was another song altogether, but it happened to fit well with the first section. It was really only me remembering what it was like to run up the road to catch the school bus, having a smoke, and then going into class. We decided, 'Bugger this, we're going to write a real turn-on song!' This was the only one in the album written as a deliberate provocation to people. But what we really wanted was to turn you on to the *truth* rather than just bloody pot!"

Another remarkable tune on the album is George's "Within You Without You." Recorded in mid-March, the basic tracks were done by George with a little help from Neil Aspinall on the tamboura. Indian session musicians were brought in to play the exotic dilruba, sword mandel, sitar, and tablas. George Martin helped out as overall producer-arranger as well as conducting and coordinating the eight violinists and three cellists brought in to add texture and mood to the track. George remembers how it all got started: "Klaus Voorman had a harmonium in his house, which I hadn't played before. I was doodling on it, playing to amuse myself, when 'Within You' started to come. The tune came initially, and then I got the first line. It came out of what we'd been discussing that evening."

The other ten songs on the album — "Lucy In The Sky With Diamonds," "Sgt. Pepper's Lonely Hearts Club Band," "With A Little Help From My Friends," "Being For The Benefit Of Mr. Kite," "She's Leaving Home," "Fixing A Hole," "Getting Better," "Good Morning, Good Morning," "Lovely Rita," and the "Sgt. Pepper Reprise" — were all exquisitely crafted songs, as compelling and ingenious in their lyrical inspiration as they were revolutionary in style and innovative in production techniques.

The trendy, elaborate uniforms made for the "Pepper band" were the creation of the well-known London theatrical costumers, Bermans, with more than a little input from the Beatles themselves. At first the Boys were going to dress in ordinary Salvation Army–style outfits, but when one of the tailors from the agency dropped by the studio with some fabric for them to examine, the Beatles immediately chose the brightest patterns from a pile of satin samples. Four pairs of outrageous orange and yellow patent leather shoes were ordered, and arrangements were made for John, Paul, George, and Ringo to nip into Bermans to be measured and fitted for their costumes.

There they sifted through mountains of frogs, braids, medals, hats, and trinkets to find just the right accents for their pseudomilitary fantasy. Finally, the instruments the Beatles would hold on the cover were hired and collected by Mal Evans, who spent over four hours polishing them in preparation for the photo shoot. The montage of famous faces and figures forming the backdrop for the band was assembled by Peter Blake and Jann Haworth and photographed by Michael Cooper. This was a gargantuan task in itself and took months of painstaking work. Moreover, the plain, white paper sleeve that normally holds the record was replaced by a swirling red- and wine-colored inner wrapper designed and executed by a trio of Dutch designers called the Fool. "Sgt. Pepper's Lonely Hearts Club Band" was released on June 1, 1967, to a flood of acclaim from just about everyone who owned a record player. And it still stands today as the Beatles' crowning achievement; from then on rock 'n' roll was no longer just teenage dance music — it was art.

The idea for *Magical Mystery Tour*, the Beatles' first TV movie, was conceived by Paul McCartney, and filming began on September 11, 1967. (It would have been produced sooner, but the Beatles' participation in the global satellite telecast "Our World" caused a delay.) The concept was quite simple — the Beatles would invite a select group of close friends, fan club secretaries, character actors, midgets, and circus freaks to travel around the English countryside with them in a rented coach and just see what happened. Ringo, listed in the credits as "Richard Starkey MBE," was ostensibly director of photography, and although all the Beatles contrib-

"The Dreamweaver" in the studio during sessions for "Sgt. Pepper." 1967.

The original, unused logo for Sgt. Pepper's bass drum.

A rare advertisement for "Our World."

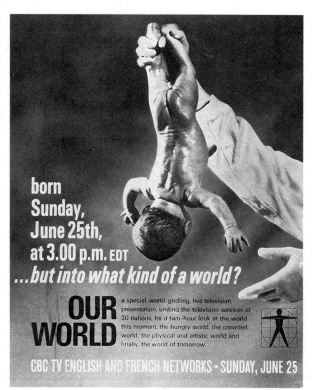

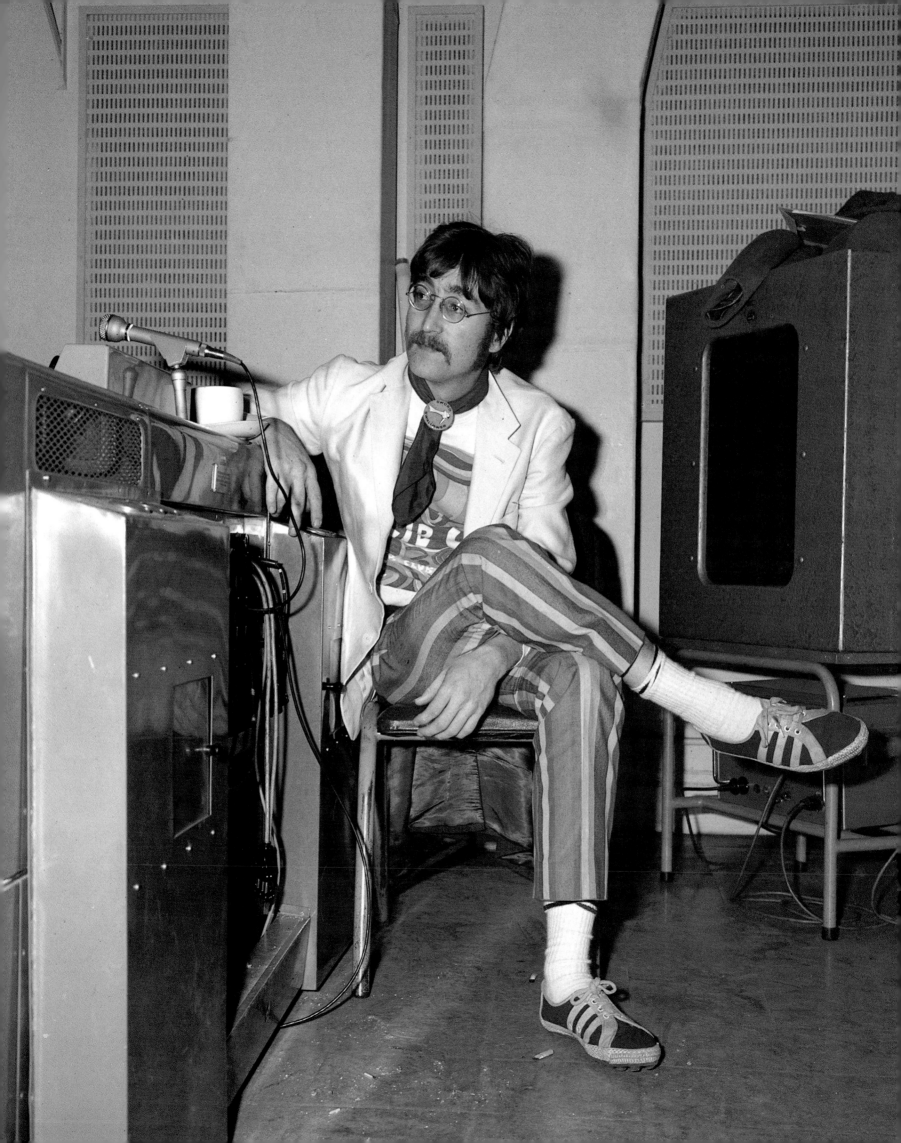

Paul and Ringo tackle the all-important drum
tracks for "Sgt. Pepper." 1967.

Working out a new arrangement for one of John's
tunes. 1967.

An overview of the original "Sgt. Pepper" set. Note the grinning Mahatma Gandhi peering out of the ferns at a radiant Diana Dors. The figure of Gandhi was later taken out when EMI bigwigs decided that it might offend record buyers in India. Similar representations of Elvis Presley, Jesus Christ, and the Führer were also removed before the final photo was taken for reasons of either copyright or propriety.

John and Ringo chat with Neil Aspinall and Mal Evans backstage at the "Pepper" photo shoot. Cynthia Lennon is in the background.

Remember is The Beatles

New Parlophone LP on sale now

Parlophone PMC 7027(m) PCS 7027(s)

The original Magical Mystery Tour coach fully restored by Beatle City.

uted to the final editing of the film, it was Ringo and Paul who looked after the overall production. Unfortunately, the film was not very well received by either the critics or the public after its premiere on BBC-1 on Boxing Day 1967. The London *Daily Mail* called it "blatant rubbish," while the *Los Angeles Times* reported, "Critics and Viewers Boo: Beatles Produce First Flop with Yule Film." Paul McCartney was definitely not amused and quite rightly commented that if the film had been shown in color as originally intended, rather than black and white, it might have made more sense. Nevertheless, American network officials canceled their option to broadcast the film in the United States. It is interesting to note, however, that today the film has attained cult status among collectors and is heavily traded on video cassette on the underground market.

But public acceptance of the film's soundtrack was a different matter. Released in England as a deluxe double EP (complete with a lovely, twenty-four-page souvenir booklet) and in America as a straight twelve-inch LP, it immediately went straight to number one in both countries. Six tunes were written especially for the project — "Magical Mystery Tour," "The Fool On The Hill," "Flying," "Blue Jay Way," "Your Mother Should Know," and "I Am The Walrus." In the United States, West Germany, and a few other countries five "filler" tracks were added to round out the album — "Hello Goodbye," "Strawberry Fields Forever," "Penny Lane," "Baby, You're A Rich Man," and "All You Need Is Love."

The Beatles' famous "white" album, released on November 22, 1968, was the first official group project to be released on their newly formed Apple Records. Recorded under the working title of "A Doll's House," it featured a stark, all-white cover designed by artist John Kosh with the title, "The Beatles," embossed on the front and an edition number stamped in gray ink just below. Inserted inside the double album were four 8″ × 10″ head shots of the Boys and a freaky, collage-style poster (that doubled as a lyric sheet) by Richard Hamilton. Most of the thirty-odd tracks were written during the Beatles' stay with the Maharishi Mahesh Yogi in early 1968, when they were still in their transcendental meditation phase. This album showed just how far the Beatles' widely diverse songwriting ability and increasing prowess in the studio had developed, as evidenced by two prominent tunes, "Glass Onion" and "Happiness Is A Warm Gun," both written by John.

He remembers their inception: "With 'Glass Onion' I was just having a laugh, because there had been so much gobbledygook written about 'Sgt. Pepper'. People were saying, "Play it backwards while standing on your head and you'll get a secret message, etc. Why, just the other day I saw Mel Torme on TV saying that several of my songs were written to promote the use of drugs, but really, none of them were at all. So this one was just my way of saying, 'You're all full of shit!' As for 'Happiness Is A Warm Gun', I consider it one of my best. It's a beautiful song, and I really like all the things that are happening in it. It was put together from bits of about three

different songs and just seemed to run the gamut of many types of rock music. I pulled the title straight off the cover of a gun magazine George Martin showed me. I thought, 'What a fantastic, insane thing to say.' A warm gun means that you've just shot something."

By now faint cracks were beginning to show in the Beatles' inner circle. John and Paul were often at odds over problems arising in the studio, and Ringo and George were getting fed up with a lot of the nonsense that went with being a Beatle. Still, fans the world over thought the "white" album was great and pushed it to the very top of the charts.

"Yellow Submarine," the soundtrack album of their animated feature film and released on January 17, 1969, contained only four "new" songs — "Hey Bulldog," "Only A Northern Song," "It's All Too Much," and Paul's rather thinly veiled plea for greater unity within the group, "All Together Now." This recording project, while reasonably popular with the fans, wasn't really much fun for the Beatles. John has said that he found it embarrassing to be working on something as "lightweight" and "poppy" as "Hey Bulldog" during Yoko's first visits to the studio to watch him record. His personal standards about what tunes he would allow himself to do were very strict, and this song was only borderline material at best. Conversely, George's two contributions to the album, "Only A Northern Song" and "It's All Too Much," were both strong, striking tunes, heavily introspective and deeply engrossing in their spacey, mantra-like melodies. Two other previously released recordings were added to the package to further emphasize the movie's swinging, upbeat message: "All You Need Is Love" and of course the wild undersea fantasy sung by Ringo, "Yellow Submarine." Side two, an entertaining medley of incidental music from the film, was composed by George Martin and performed by his own orchestra. However, the album climbed to only number four in the *Melody Maker* charts and didn't really do much better in America.

"Let It Be," originally called "Get Back," was the Beatles' last official release as a group. Designed as a way to help them return to their original rock 'n' roll roots, it was promoted as a "new-phase Beatle album," but the truth was, it was their last hurrah. By the time the sessions for "Abbey Road" rolled around six months later, they had all but decided to go their separate ways.

John remembers: "In a nutshell, it was getting to be time for another Beatles movie or something, so Paul thought up the idea of us just playing live somewhere and then filming it, raw, as it happened, with no icing on top. But where? Someone mentioned the Colosseum in Rome, and I think originally Paul might have even suggested a bloody boat in the middle of the ocean. As for me, I was rapidly warming up to the idea of an asylum! He also had the mistaken impression that he was going to rehearse us. Of course by that time we'd been playing together for about twenty years or something, and we just couldn't get into it. So anyway, we laid down a few tracks, but nobody was really into it at all. It was just such a very, very

The finale of *Magical Mystery Tour* — the rehearsal and the real thing.

George and Ringo chow down in the studio control room. 1968.

Outside Apple.

Valuable examples of original artwork from the animated feature, *Yellow Submarine*.

The Corgi Yellow Submarine.

Pattie and George in Manhattan. June 1968.

dreadful feeling being there in Twickenham Studios at eight o'clock in the morning with some old geezer pointing a camera up your nose expecting you to make good music with colored lights flashing on and off in your face all the time. To me the whole thing ended up looking and sounding like a goddamn bootleg version of an eight-millimeter home movie, so I didn't want to know about it. None of us did." George later declared, "I couldn't stand it! I decided, this is it! It's just not fun anymore; as a matter of fact, it's very unhappy being in this band at all!"

The unfinished tapes were ultimately turned over to legendary rock producer Phil Spector, who did his best to whip them into shape in time for designer John Kosh to complete the ambitious visual package Apple had approved for the project. "Let It Be" was to be issued with a lavish, oversize paperback portfolio of photographs from the sessions (taken by Ethan Russell) complete with a classy all-black exterior set off by four head shots of John, Paul, George, and Ringo recording the album. (In the end only a few select countries in the British Commonwealth received the whole package; everyone else just got the record.) Although none of the Beatles bothered to attend the London premiere of *Let It Be*, the fans gathered anyway and screamed and jostled each other for one final cinematic peek at their idols.

The following interview with George Harrison took place in the Apple offices at Number 3 Savile Row in the latter part of 1969, a particularly uncertain and volatile period in the personal and professional lives of the Beatles. Tottering on the brink of their dissolution as a group, they found themselves flung headlong into a series of combative, unpleasant business trials, management problems, marital difficulties, and musical differences. Even so, the sessions for their last album together were proceeding faithfully in the hope that, above all, it would be the music that would save them. This conversation, a reflective, unhurried, sideways look at the first five years of the Beatles' extraordinary time together, examines George's all-consuming interest in Indian music and philosophy and gives a candid, blow-by-blow account of the recording of the Beatles' eclectic swan song, "Abbey Road."

QUESTION   I was talking to Keith Richards the other day, and he told me he felt that the Stones were more of a performing group, whereas the Beatles were simply a good recording band.

GEORGE HARRISON   Well, no, we performed a lot until that last tour we did. That was our whole thing, really. We gigged before we were famous as well, right there at school — we performed all the time! In Germany we used to do things like "Money" and all the tunes that weren't really popular but were actually quite heavy. We did lots of Chuck Berry, Little Richard — all the standard rock 'n' roll things. And then when the Hamburg thing died out, we came back to England and were regarded as sort of a new

A tasteful, one-sheet promotional poster for "Let It Be."

The lavish "Let It Be" boxed set.

John and George put the finishing touches on the dramatic ending of "Being For The Benefit Of Mr. Kite." 1967.

band! That period was particularly good, but then we started to get famous doing our own songs, and so we went out on the road. Of course we had to constantly play our own hit tunes in order to promote them. Which led right up to the last tour we did, where it just became a bloody rut. We played the same stuff to different people all over the place!

QUESTION   Wouldn't it have been nice to be able to turn around and just say, "Let's do anything out of the blue and have some fun?"

GEORGE   It was a very slow process. At first it was really nice to be booked some place and know that people were coming simply because we always had new songs to promote. But when we really got big, we also got very bored. We had to do "She Loves You" all the time, which wasn't really bad at first, but then we trapped ourselves because we couldn't play any-thing other than our own songs, and the concerts just got bigger and bigger. Did you see the Shea Stadium gig?

QUESTION   No, but I certainly heard about it.

GEORGE   Well, when I look at the film, I know we tried to have a good time, but the show we did there was really for ourselves. The people were miles away and were basically on their own scene. I mean, they were buzzing around, leaping up and down, and we were just playing very, very loudly. But the sound was always so bad. We'd just be joking with each other to keep ourselves amused, and it became very impersonal. With so many police and kids flying around it was more like a political thing, you know, especially with John's remarks about Christ. I was just so sick of it — I think we all were. We were absolutely nervous wrecks, getting thrown around to press conferences everywhere we went. It was just too much, man.

QUESTION   You're much happier now, I suppose, just recording when you all feel like it and following the other interests you've developed for yourselves?

GEORGE   We also got involved with this big business thing, you know. Maybe people think it's a drag that the Beatles are doing business, but remember, we were always involved in it. We just didn't notice because Brian Epstein always did it for us, but when he died we suddenly realized that a lot of people had contracts with us, and it was just becoming ridiculous. We had to try and solve these problems and sort it all out.

QUESTION   Was Brian's death a very great loss to the group? Looking back on it now, do you think it would have changed much?

GEORGE   In a way, but I think that it had to happen. I can't imagine where we'd be if he *hadn't* died, because we suddenly had to find out what was happening and be responsible for *ourselves*. We were anyway, but the business side of it was always rather abstract to us because we'd always imagined, "Well, Brian does all that, and everything is fine," even when it wasn't fine. With nobody there it was directly up to us to work out what we had to do, and consequently we found out all these bizarre things were going on, to our absolute horror.

An obscure promotional poster for "Abbey Road."

The Beatles 1968. Happy after their brief encounter with the Maharishi.

Paul and long-time girlfriend, Jane Asher, leaving for Rishikesh, India.

Derek Taylor sports a mask at George's home in Henley, Friar Park.

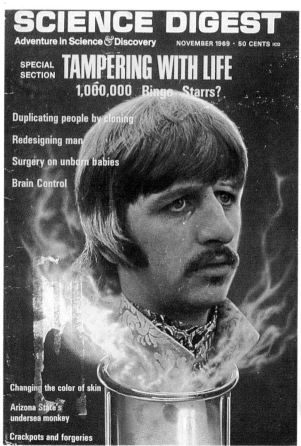

QUESTION   Are you happy with the way Apple is going at the moment?

GEORGE   Quite happy. But if you say to the wrong person, "such and such," and he says it to somebody else, by the time it comes back to you it usually has nothing to do with what you originally said. That's the main problem with Apple as I see it, and I'm sure it's the same with any big business. That's the really difficult thing. If you say to somebody, "Okay, now here, do this," and it comes back just slightly different, it really takes up a lot of your time to fix things. As Derek says, "Apple is really just for our whims." Derek, how did you describe Apple?

DEREK TAYLOR   It's an organization which has developed without anyone really planning it this way, as a service which exists to implement the whims of the Beatles which, fortunately, often turn out to be very commercial. However, if they didn't, we'd still have to do it, and that's okay as well. That's the gig. The gig is not Apple, the gig is working for the Beatles! You come here and you work for the Beatles. Now the latest whim is to take the world's worst minority religionist cult in England, the Hare Krsnas, and get them a top-thirty record within ten days! It's nothing else, you know, and that's what it will ever be.

QUESTION   George, what about the new album ["Abbey Road"]? Why don't we start off with a rundown of the lineup?

GEORGE   Well, "Something" is a very nice song, I think. It's probably the nicest melody line I've ever written. "Maxwell's Silver Hammer" is just something of Paul's which we've been trying to record for ages. We spent a hell of a lot of time on it, and it's one of those instant, whistle-along tunes which some people hate and other people really like. It's quite like "Honey Pie," I suppose, a fun song, but actually it's pretty sick because Maxwell keeps on killing everyone! "Oh! Darling" is another of Paul's songs, which is a typical 1950, 1960s period song because of its chord structure.

QUESTION   "Happiness Is A Warm Gun" too — there was a similar kind of feel for that in there as well.

GEORGE   Yeah, that's it, but this is really just Paul singing by himself. We do a few things in the background which you can barely hear, but it's mainly just Paul shouting. "Octopus's Garden" is Ringo's song. It's only the second song Ringo has written, mind you, and it's lovely. Ringo gets bored with just playing the drums all the time, so at home he sometimes plays a bit of piano, but unfortunately he only knows about three chords! He knows about the same on guitar too. This song gets very deep into your consciousness, though, because it's so peaceful. I suppose Ringo is writing cosmic songs these days without even noticing it! The last tune on side one is "I Want You (She's So Heavy)," and it *is* very heavy. John plays lead guitar and sings, and it's just basically an old blues riff he's doing, but again, it's a very original John-type song as well. John has an amazing thing with his timing — he always comes across with very different time signatures, you know. For example, on "All You Need Is Love," it just sort of skips a beat here and there and changes time. But when you question him as to what it is he's actually doing, he really doesn't know! He just does it naturally, and once you try and pin him down, forget it. It's a very good chord sequence he used on this particular one. On side two "Here Comes The Sun" is the other song which I wrote especially for the album. It was written on a nice, sunny day early in the summer in Eric Clapton's back garden. The Beatles had all been through hell with various and sundry business trips, you know. It had been very heavy, but on that particular day I just felt as though I was sagging off from school. It was such a great release for me simply being out in the sun, and the song just came to me. The next tune, "Because," is a bit like "If I Needed Someone" — you know, the basic riff going through it is somewhat the same, but it's actually quite a simple tune. It's a three-part harmony thing which John, Paul, and myself all sing together. John wrote the tune, the backing is a little like Beethoven, and the three-part harmony goes right the way throughout.

QUESTION   To me it seems more like a Paul McCartney song than one of John's.

GEORGE   Yeah, well, that's because of the basic sweetness of it. Paul usually writes the sweeter tunes, and John writes more of the rave-up–type things, all the freakier songs. John just wants to write twelve bars all the time, but I can't deny it, I think this is possibly my favorite one on the album because it's so damn simple. The lyrics are uncomplicated, but the harmony was actually pretty difficult to sing. We had to really learn it, but I think it's one of the tunes that will definitely impress most people. Then begins the big medley of Paul's and John's songs all sewn together. "You Never Give Me Your Money" you have to actually hear because it does two verses of one tune, and then the bridge is almost like a different song altogether, so it's quite melodic. "Sun King" is John's thing which he originally called "Los Paranoias." "Mean Mr. Mustard" and "Polythene Pam" were both written in India about eighteen months ago. "She Came In Through The Bathroom Window" is a very strange song of Paul's with terrific lyrics, but it's hard to explain what they're all about! Anyway, "Golden Slumbers" is another very melodic tune of Paul's which is also quite nice. In fact, "Carry That Weight" keeps coming in and out of it at different times. "The End," of course, is just the end. Maybe when we get the album finished and in the sleeve, I'll be able to get a real impression of it, but so far no. With "Sgt. Pepper" and the "white" album I was able to gather an overall impression, but with this one I'm kind of at a loss. People have said it's a bit more like "Revolver," and maybe it is, but it still feels rather abstract to me. I can't yet see it as a whole or really get a complete image of the album.

QUESTION   George, I think it might be possible now for you to make some comment about the last album. There was generally a very mixed reaction to it.

Paul cops a kiss from a friendly fan following a late-night remix for the "white" album. 1968.

George and Pattie in the Haight-Ashbury district of San Francisco.

John listening to a playback of "Strawberry Fields." Late 1966.

GEORGE   The "white" album, you mean?

QUESTION   Yeah. I guess you saw a lot of the reviews — some people called it the best thing since "Sgt. Pepper," and other people panned it. How do you see it?

GEORGE   Well, I think in a way it was a mistake doing four sides, because it's just too big for most people to really get into. Maybe now that people have bought it and have really listened to it, they have their own favorites. I think there are a couple of things we could have done without on the album, and maybe if we'd made it more compact, only fourteen songs, say . . .

QUESTION   Which tracks do you feel could have been left out?

GEORGE   Well, it's only my personal thing in a way, but "Revolution Number Nine" wasn't particularly like a Beatles number.

QUESTION   A lot of people put the album down purely because of that track.

GEORGE   Then again, it has some very good points, because "Revolution Number Nine" worked quite well in the context of all those different songs. I mean, that was the great thing about it. If people actually care to spend enough time listening to it, then they'll find there are many, many different types of music woven in and out of it. There was actually nothing really shocking about it, you know. I don't think there was anything particularly poor about it either, but it was a bit heavy! I find it heavy to listen to myself — in fact, I don't, really. I listen mainly to side one, which I like very much, "Glass Onion" and "Happiness Is A Warm Gun" being my particular favorites.

QUESTION   "While My Guitar Gently Weeps" I thought was a great track. Tell me how that one came about.

GEORGE   I wrote it at my mother's house in the north of England. I had my guitar with me, and I just wanted to write a song. I do this off and on, if I haven't got a particular idea for a song. I believe in the *I Ching* which says, "Everything at that moment is relative to that particular situation," so "My Guitar Gently Weeps" was very typical of that. I just opened an old book that was lying around, and the first thing I looked at actually became the song. It just said something about "gently weeps," and from there the whole thought started coming to me, and I simply wrote the song. You know of course that Eric Clapton played guitar on that one. Some people wrote letters to me saying, "You've really got a very good blues feel the way you played that guitar, man." We didn't exactly publicize it, but we didn't keep it a secret either. Eric is a good friend of mine, and I really dig him as a guitarist and as a person.

QUESTION   What about the Indian scene — are you still very much committed to it?

GEORGE   Do you mean musically or generally?

QUESTION   Intellectually and any way, really.

GEORGE Yeah, it's my karma. It's like saying, Brian Epstein did die and we did go to America and we did get Apple. Everywhere you go you've got a number of choices. There's a crossroad and you can go left or right, but if you just follow yourself, your natural instincts, you don't have to decide too much. You'll naturally go down one of them. There's always choices and many different ways to go, but if you keep following yourself and what you feel, then you will automatically go down the right road. It happened with me just through constantly experiencing action, reaction, action, reaction. I got into Indian music, which was very remarkable, because the first time I ever heard it was on a Ravi Shankar album, which of course it had to be really, looking back. I played the music, and although it's very intellectual, it is technically and spiritually the most amazing music I have ever heard! I listened to the music, and even though I didn't understand it, I felt within myself as though I knew it back to front. It just seems so obvious and logical to me. Ravi Shankar is probably the person who has influenced my life the most up to this point. Maybe he's not aware of it, but I love Ravi, and he's been like a father figure and a spiritual guide to me. Later I realized that Indian music was like a stepping stone to spiritual life, because I also have a great desire to know about the yogic path. I always had a feeling for that, and the music led me right there. I got involved with Hinduism because Ravi Shankar was a Hindu and because it just happened that it came my way, so I went off to India. I like India a lot; it was a very natural involvement for me. I got to understand what Christ really was through Hinduism. So I have a greater respect for Indian music, history, and philosophy now. Down through the ages there has always been a spiritual path, and if anybody ever wants it in any age, it'll be there. It just so happens that India was the place where the seed of it was originally sown. The Himalayas were generally very inaccessible to people, so they always had real peace there. The yogis are the only people who can make it out there, you know. It may be something to do with my past lives, but I just felt a great connection with it all. In this age the East and West are becoming closer, and we can all benefit so much from each other. We can help them with all our material attributes, and they can help us with the spiritual side of things. We need them both. You need the outer aspect of life as well as the inner, because the outer is empty if you don't have any spiritual side to life, and vice versa. The western people needed to go through this material life. Well, they've been through it, and we've got so many material things now, it's got to evolve into the other side of things, you know? We can give to each other. It's all a part of our overall evolution, taking the best from both sides.

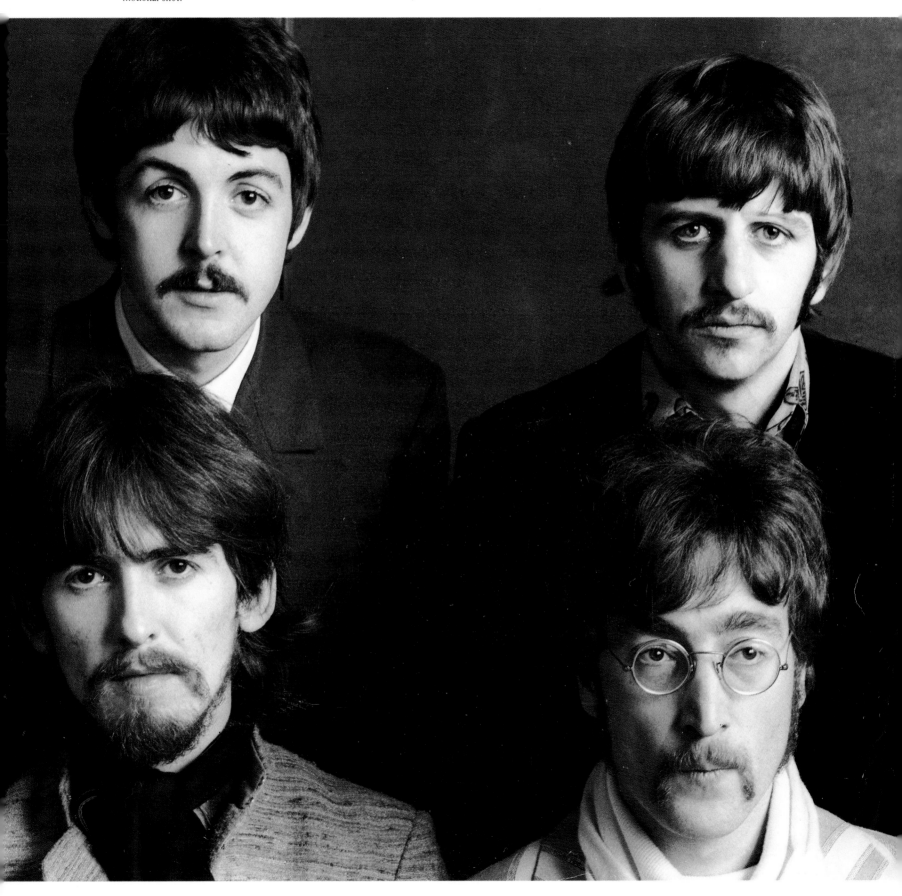

The Fabs looking rather serious in this 1967 promotional shot.

4 The Innerlight *In Search of Meaning*

"My life belongs to Lord Krsna now. I'm just the servant of the servant of Krsna. I've never been so humble in all my life, and I feel great!" GEORGE HARRISON

"You're just left with yourself all the time, whatever you do anyway. You've got to get down to your own God in your own temple. It's all down to you, mate." JOHN LENNON

"God is everything. God is in the space between us. God is in the table in front of you." PAUL McCARTNEY

"The four of us have had the most hectic lives. We've got almost everything money can buy, but of course that just means nothing after a time. But we've found something now that really fills the gap, and that is the Lord." RINGO STARR

The author's colorful vision of the Beatles in India.

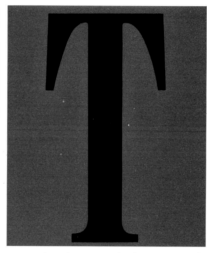

he Beatles' first encounter with marijuana was on New Year's Eve 1962 on Shaftesbury Avenue, near Trafalgar Square in London. They were in town auditioning for Decca when they met someone who had a little pot and wanted to borrow their van to toke up in. "Forget it," said John. "This band has enough problems without getting mixed up in anything like that!" Despite their rough-and-tumble, teddy boy appearance, they were still basically four homespun schoolboys from the North country who were frightened to death of anything even remotely connected with drugs. And although they had always enjoyed the mildly stimulating alcoholic effects of a few too many bevies, they were more than a little sceptical when, in Hamburg, they were first offered amphetamines.

After they made it big, however, the pressure to maintain their exalted position was tremendous, and the natural restraint they had shown as youngsters soon gave way to the unnatural excesses of pop stardom. "I've always needed a drug to survive," declared John in his now-famous quote. "Of course the others did too, but I was always the worst. I wanted more of everything because I'm probably crazier than the rest!" With pot, pills, sex, and booze, the Fabulous Foursome razzled with an intensity few performers in sleepy Londontown could match. "It's not something you can go on and on doing, though," says John. "With drink or anything, you've got to come to terms with it. And you've got to try and get out of it too, if you can." If the Beatles found the long-term use of recreational drugs physically and mentally harmful, they were soon to be knocked out of their dayglow socks by LSD. Introduced first to John, George, and their wives, Cynthia and Pattie, by their dentist, their first trip was a nightmarish avalanche of distorted sensation and hallucinatory perception.

"It was just insane going around London," John explains. "We ended up at this nightclub, only we all thought it was on fire! We ran about cackling in the streets, and someone was yelling, 'Let's break a window!' Somehow or other George managed to drive us home in his Mini. We were only going about ten miles an hour, but it seemed like a thousand. God, it was just terrifying, but it was also fantastic! I was pretty stoned for a month or two." George recalls the evening with similar enthusiasm: "It was like I had never tasted, smelled, or heard anything before. For me it was like a flash. It just opened up something inside of me, and I realized a lot of very heavy things. From that moment on I wanted to have that depth and clarity of perception all the time."

Paul and Ringo tried it later, and they too became ardent devotees of Dr. Leary's wonder drug. "It opens up some of the hidden parts of your brain that you don't normally use," said Paul. "I've had many realizations through acid." Creative inspiration also seemed to be one of the more advantageous side effects of the drug, and the Beatles soon learned how to incorporate its freaky, multidimensional imagery into their music. "Revolver," "Sgt. Pepper," "Magical Mystery Tour," the "white" album — in fact most of the Beatles' songs written after the summer of 1966 — owe at least part of their inspiration to LSD. Like every trip, though, their's had to come to an end, and when it did, they were left feeling even more uncertain and edgy about the future than before. They were only in their mid-twenties, yet they had the entire world at their feet. But what did it all mean?

From the first eerie twang of the Indian sitar in the motion picture soundtrack of the Beatles' second feature film, *Help!*, George Harrison was hooked forever. From that moment on all things Hindu — philosophy, diet, fashion, literature, and art — held their transcendent sway over the young devotee, who shuttled his revelations across the Indian Ocean into the appreciative arms of a turned-on generation of seekers. Suddenly, in tiny bedrooms and cluttered crash pads around the world, young people were ripping down their tattered Escher posters in favor of brightly colored representations of an array of multiarmed, benevolent demigods from Buddha to Brahma. And at the very hub of this spiritual revolution was George's friend and mentor, sitar virtuoso Ravi Shankar.

"I met him at a friend's house in London for dinner," recalls George, "and he offered to give me some instruction on the basics of sitar. It was

The infamous Beatles butcher cover, 1966. This outrageous Robert Wittaker cover shot of the Boys dressed as butchers, surrounded by decapitated baby dolls and slabs of red meat, caused an uproar among Capitol Records officials in the United States, who immediately ordered all 750,000 albums, as well as promotional material, destroyed. A few copies made their way into the hands of collectors, however, who value them highly and regularly sell them off at up to $500 each. The album was later released with this rather innocuous replacement shot.

Property of United Artists Corp. Ltd. Leased for restricted use only. Must be returned to United Artists Corp. Ltd. and must not be sold, leased, or given away by any other party. Permission is hereby granted to newspapers, magazines and other periodicals to reproduce this illustration. Printed in England.

THE BEATLES in " **HELP!** " Ⓤ also starring **LEO McKERN** · **ELEANOR BRON** · **VICTOR SPINETTI**
ROY KINNEAR Produced by **WALTER SHENSON** Directed by **RICHARD LESTER** **EASTMANCOLOR** Released thru **UNITED ARTISTS**

Ravi Shankar at his comfortable Bombay home sitting before a painting of his musical guru, affectionately known as "Baba."

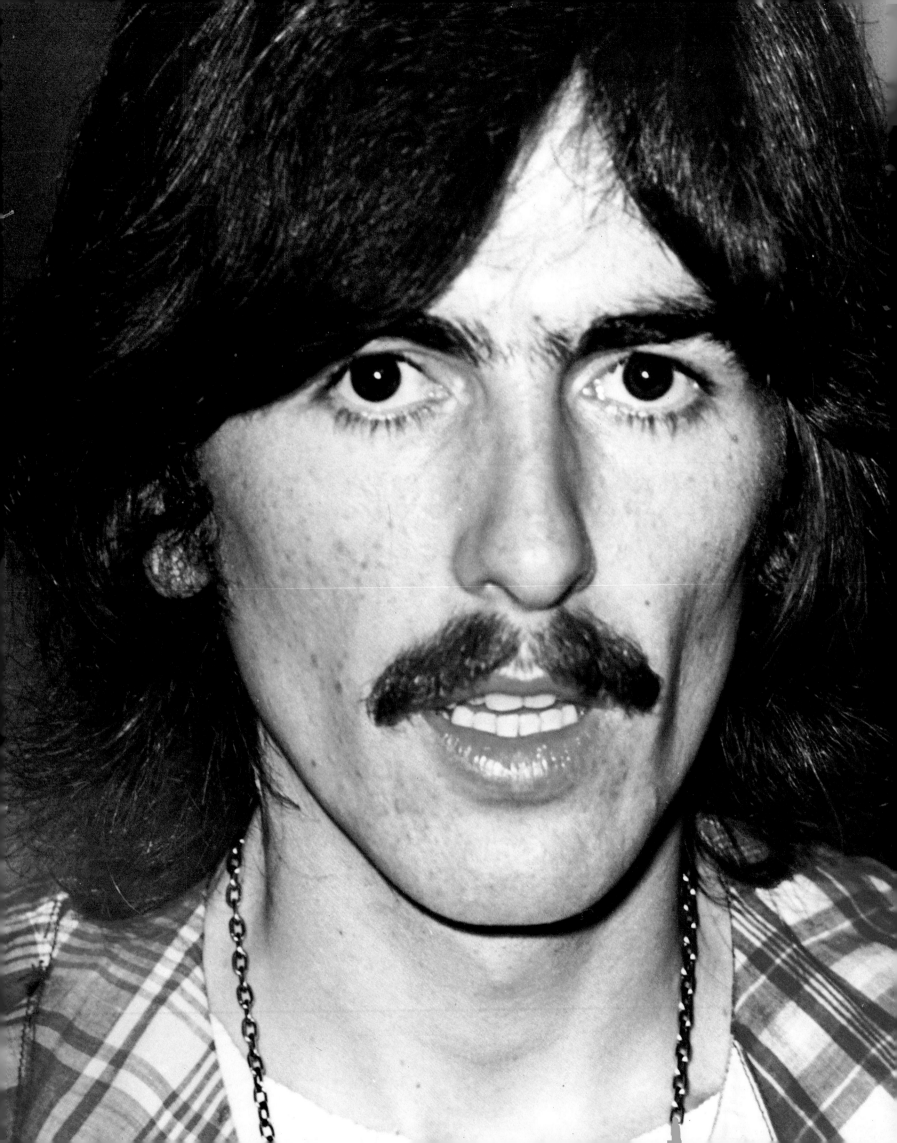

British actress Rita Tushingham visits George in a Bombay recording studio during the making of his first solo album, "Wonderwall Music."

Sessions for "Wonderwall" in Bombay's EMI studios. Shambu Das is holding the stopwatch.

George in India. 1966.

the first time I'd ever actually approached music with a bit of discipline. Then later I started really listening to Indian music, and for the next two years I hardly even touched the guitar, except for recording. Having all these material things, however, I still wanted something more, and it suddenly all came to me in the form of Ravi Shankar." In the early summer of 1966 George humbly requested that Ravi accept him as his student (or *shishya*). It was a big step for George, but he applied himself admirably and came away with a newfound knowledge and respect for Hindu culture.

"I went over partly to try and learn the music, but also to absorb as much of the actual country as I could. I'd always heard stories about these old men in the Himalayas who were hundreds of years old, levitating yogis and saints who were able to be buried underground for weeks and live. Now I wanted to see it all for myself. I'll tell you one thing for sure — once you get to the point where you actually believe that you're doing things for *truth*'s sake, then nobody can ever touch you again, because you're harmonizing with a greater power. And the farther into spiritual life I go, the easier it is to see that the Beatles aren't really controlling any of it, but that *something else* has now taken us firmly in hand."

Ravi turned over the daily task of tutoring the youngest Beatle to Shambu Das, his right-hand man. He talks glowingly of his protégé: "Shambu Das was born in Banaras, India. His musical training, inspired by his father, began at the very early age of six with the study of Indian classical singing and an instrument called the israj. Later he learned tabla and sitar from different teachers but has been an advanced pupil of mine since 1959. His devotion as a student brought him into a very close relationship with me, and he stayed at my home in Bombay until the middle of 1970. Regarding his music, he is a very talented musician — hardworking and most sincere. He was appointed a sitar teacher at my Kinnara School of Music in Bombay in 1962 and has proved himself thoroughly capable in that capacity as well. Apart from teaching, he is a well-known international performer of our classical music and has attained a level of excellence rarely seen."

In December 1967 Shambu once again worked with George, as co-producer and arranger on the Indian music sections of George's newest recording project, the soundtrack of the avant-garde movie *Wonderwall*. Released in Britain on November 1, 1968, "Wonderwall Music" was the first album issued on Apple Records as well as George's first solo venture. Here, from an interview conducted in Toronto in 1982, are Shambu's exclusive memories of his time with the Beatles and especially of his good friend and former pupil, George Harrison.

GEOFFREY How did you meet George?

SHAMBU DAS I first met him in Bombay in 1966. He came around with Ravi Shankar. I guess all the Beatles were great admirers of Ravi from listening to his records. George told him he wanted to learn to play the sitar. At the time I was looking after some of Ravi's business affairs, so I advised George to please come along and study if he wanted to. I was teaching regularly at Ravi's music school in Bombay, and he suggested that I personally look after George's progress. Once in a while, however, Ravi would come in just to see how the lessons were going and occasionally would even teach George himself.

GEOFFREY Was this his first real exposure to the sitar?

SHAMBU Yes, and he loved it. Earlier, of course, he had put some sitar sounds on the Beatles' music, but later, when he really started learning to play, he became very serious about it. He knew the rigorous technique involved, so he became very sober. Ravi used to come by once in a while, and we would all sit down and practice together. Oh, we had a fantastic time. Pattie, his first wife, was there as well, and she was very friendly to everyone. We used to visit some old Hindu temples in the area, and then we'd come back home and practice some more.

GEOFFREY Was he a good student?

SHAMBU He was very intelligent. He used to put in seven or eight hours a day of very concentrated practice. Later, after he left, he started writing to me about how much he enjoyed his visit to India. He wanted to do this "Wonderwall" soundtrack and requested some help from me, as he wanted to record it almost entirely in India. So I was taking care of all the musical arrangements — that's what I was mainly responsible for. I personally played sitar on "Wonderwall," and a few of my friends played several other Indian instruments too. George and I were consulting together on a lot of things in those days, how should we do this or that — you know, just throwing ideas back and forth. Anyway, we recorded for almost an entire week, and while he was there he started to use his hands to eat. We'd sit on the floor and eat Indian-style together. He loved it; he was a very good friend. Anyway, that was during his second visit. The third time all the Beatles came.

GEOFFREY To India?

SHAMBU With the Maharishi for training in transcendental meditation. At the time I was busy with Ravi's movie *Raga*, and there was a whole crew from New York that came over. I think it was Columbia Pictures and Apple Films that were doing it. At the same time George wanted me to visit him in Rishikesh. So I went, but I couldn't stay for very long. I was only there about four days, but the Maharishi became very close to me, because George wanted me around, I think. And one day as he was sitting around talking to the Beatles, he suddenly said to me, "We would like you to do some special work for us." But I knew that Ravi Shankar was in a different pot, philosophically, so I was very confused.

GEOFFREY How did George feel about that? He has said that he always felt that Ravi Shankar was like a father to him, yet he went off to study with the Maharishi.

SHAMBU That is what I'm trying to say. They both had a very different view of life in those days, but I stayed for a while anyway.

George and Pattie arrive in Paris for the premiere of *Wonderwall*.

Lakshmi Shankar, Pattie, Ravi, George, and Shambu visit an ancient Hindu ruin.

Three letters from George to Shambu Das written during the mid-sixties as well as a telegram arranging the particulars of the "Wonderwall" recording sessions.

INDIAN POSTS AND TELEGRAPHS DEPARTMENT
TELEGRAM
00071
SHAMBHU DAS VILL MANORAMA SWAMI
VIVEKANANDAROAD BANDRA BOMBAY 15

XF 1622 BR 282 LONDON LG 29 OCS P 1/50 85/84
WILL YOU BE FREE FROM TUESDAY NIGHT THROUGH TO FRIDAY 12TH
FOR RECORDING WITH MUSICIANS STOP TWO OR THREE SHANAI THREE SITAR
AND ONE DHA SHANAI STOP PLEASE CONFIRM IF THEIS IS POSSIBLE SO I CAN
BOOK EMI STUDIOS THROUGH LONDON OFFICE (((50))) STOP GRATEFUL IF YOU
WOULD ARRANGE APARTMENT FOR MYSELF AND ONE OTHER FOR PERIOD 7-15TH
INCLUSIVE STOP INFORM IF YOU NEED ANY MONEY AS DEPOSIT STOP PLEASE REPLY
NEMSTAFF LONDON STOP REGARDS -- GEORGE HARRISON -

Shambhu-Das.
Villa-Manorama
Swami Vivekananda Road.
Bandra.
Bombay - 50.
India.

30/11/67.

Dear Shambhu,
Thank you for your very quick reply.
At the moment I am having difficulty with the people from the film company and I cant go ahead now until that business is cleared up. I still think I will come to Bombay, but now maybe not until after 1st January. I will write to you again when I know the exact time I can come, and I will give you enough time to arrange these things, and also tell you how many musicians of each kind I will require. Can you tell me what the equipment is like in the

Esher —
Surrey - England

Dear Shambhu,
Sorry I have been so long replying and sending the records - but I am a naughty boy and very busy.
The shanais arrived and are very very nice indeed. Thank you so much for doing that for me - you are very kind. I hope you will like the record. and also the new little record
ALL YOU NEED IS LOVE.
from George + Pattie.
Prem + OM and love
I will write more soon.

Dear Shambhu,
IF it is possible, could you send me some special Durbar Agabathi please, as they are so beautiful and I dont know where else I can get them.
I have found these supers, but if you need some more please tell me.
Love from George.

95

Singer Lakshmi Shankar, George, and Shambu stroll on Juhu Beach, Bombay.

Srimati Radharani and Krsna, the transcendental couple that captured the hearts of John and George for a time.

George amid the Himalayas.

Arranging the particulars for the recording of "Wonderwall."

GEOFFREY Was this the Beatles' first trip to India?

SHAMBU I'm not sure. They may have passed through once or twice going to Japan on tour, but they stayed much longer with the Maharishi. He made a lovely space for them in his ashram on top of this very beautiful hill. Even the bungalow I was given was fully outfitted by American standards.

GEOFFREY How long did they stay?

SHAMBU They stayed, I think, for three or four weeks altogether. Then all of a sudden we got a cable saying that George was coming down to see us in southern India. He was apparently very disturbed for some reason, and I still don't exactly know what happened. He just wanted to talk with Ravi by himself. So Ravi took him off to some isolated place, and they spent a couple of days together, and gradually George started feeling better. Then everyone ran away from us, and I didn't know why!

GEOFFREY Why did the Beatles come to India at all? What do you think they were looking for?

SHAMBU Well, I always felt they were looking for something in their lives beyond reputation, beyond money. They were looking for some kind of lasting peace of mind.

GEOFFREY What did George confide to you about his involvement with the Hare Krsna Movement? Did you see any change in his life after he became friends with its founder, Srila Prabhupada?

SHAMBU He changed, I think. He certainly stopped smoking quite a bit. George really liked Prabhupada's philosophy. He was always talking about his spiritual life. He was definitely going in that direction. I guess of all the Beatles, he was probably the most serious about the spiritual side of things.

Mahesh Prasad Varma, born in India in 1918, graduated from Allahabad University with a physics degree in 1942. He soon abandoned his worldly aspirations, however, and spent the next thirteen years living the life of a Hindu ascetic uncovering the delicate mysteries of meditational yoga. During that time he took initiation from his spiritual master, or Guru Dev, and accepted the name Maharishi Mahesh Yogi. In 1959 he traveled to the West and soon established the International Meditation Society in London.

By the autumn of 1967 both George and Pattie Harrison had become absorbed in cultivating their spiritual life. They had already endeavored to teach themselves meditation from books but weren't making much headway. So when a girlfriend of Pattie's suggested she attend an introductory lecture on transcendental meditation at Caxton Hall, she readily accepted and afterward even signed up to become a member. Later, after she'd received some literature advertising the fact that the society's founder, the Maharishi, would be holding a ten-day conference in Bangor, North Wales, she decided she'd like to attend.

George, meanwhile, had alerted the other Beatles that the Maharishi was coming to town and that they could hear him speak at the Hilton hotel

His Divine Grace the Maharishi Mahesh Yogi holds court in his private quarters in Bangor, North Wales.

in London on August 24. They went and were quite impressed with the giggly Hindu fakir. Afterward the Maharishi met the Boys and invited them to go to Bangor with him on the train the next day. They readily agreed. Also accompanying them on the "Mystical Special" (as the *Daily Mirror* called it) were Mick Jagger, Marianne Faithful, and Pattie's younger sister, Jenny Boyd. The Beatles and company were very excited about the prospect of finally hooking up with an apparently genuine spiritual master, and the platform in Bangor was naturally mobbed by hundreds of screaming fans. The next day, after the Beatles had all been formally initiated into the society and were resting, some very distressing news suddenly came through from London: Brian Epstein was dead.

There hadn't really been much room in the Beatles' busy lives for Brian lately. They were all involved in their own work in the studio and were spending a lot of time with their new families. Consequently, Brian was unsure what he should do for them, and once they stopped touring, he remained their manager in name only. And although he still had quite an active social life in London, toward the end he was very lonely and unhappy. Always a tender and caring person, Brian had never been able to establish a stable personal relationship and therefore had to be content to find his affections when and where he could. This instability invariably led to disappointment and heartache for the rich young man, who often confided to his friends that he had felt cursed ever since he was a little boy.

Brian Epstein died in his bed on August 27, 1967, from a cumulative overdose of bromide mixed with large quantities of barbiturates and other antidepressants. An official inquest by the Westminster coroner's court proclaimed on September 8 that Brian's death was "accidental, due to repeated, incautious, self-administered doses of sleeping tablets." John recalls his reaction on learning the dreadful news: "We were just outside the lecture hall in Bangor when we heard. One of the press walked up to us and said, 'Brian's dead.' I was absolutely stunned — in fact we all were. I didn't really have any misconceptions about our ability to do anything other than play music, and I was scared. We all had complete faith in him when he was running us. We'd never have made it without him, and vice versa. We were the talent, but *he* was the hustler. I often miss him very much indeed." Eppy was buried in Liverpool's Jewish cemetery in a private funeral attended only by close friends and family. Because of the disturbance that might have been caused by their presence, the Beatles did not attend.

After the initial shock of Brian's death wore off, the Beatles went back to work in the studio and continued their meditational practices as directed by the Maharishi. In Bangor he had extended an invitation to the Boys and their entourage to travel to his International Academy of Transcendental Meditation in Rishikesh, India, to take part in his advanced teachers' training program, and on February 14, 1968, Mal Evans picked up the Beatles' luggage from their homes and boarded Qantas flight 754 from

Brian "Eppy" Epstein
September 19, 1934–August 27, 1967.

George and the Maharishi. London, August 12, 1968.

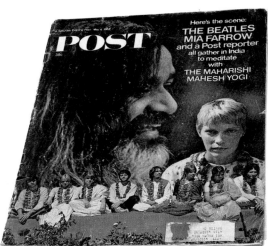

A revealing cover of the *Saturday Evening Post* shows the Maharishi looming large over a waif-like Mia Farrow.

Srila Prabhupada, Pattie, George, and Dhananjaya Dasa stroll through the grounds of Friar Park during the early seventies.

Part of the promotional campaign for the Radha Krsna Temple LP.

100

George and Pattie at the Maharishi's Rishikesh retreat.

Heathrow to New Delhi. A few days later John, George, Pattie, Cynthia, and Jenny Boyd flew in, and Mal was waiting at the airport for them. Meanwhile Paul, his girlfriend, actress Jane Asher, Ringo, his wife, Maureen, and a few members of the unshakable British press corps arrived at the Maharishi's comfortable mountain retreat late on February 19, completing the Beatles' inner circle.

Everyone seemed to relax as the initial excitement of the trip subsided, and their pent-up tensions began to slowly unravel under the magic spell of the meditation. Surprisingly, most days it was the normally sluggish John who was the first up, and after about a half hour's meditation he would go for a leisurely stroll around the compound with Mal or George.

"The Maharishi was a wonderful teacher," recalls Cynthia. "His lectures and talks were humorous, enlightening, and provided truly halcyon days. John and George were in their element. They threw themselves totally into the Maharishi's teachings, were happy, relaxed, and above all had found a peace of mind that had been denied them for so long." Paul, too, became very much absorbed in the Maharishi's philosophy, but Ringo didn't particularly like the simple Indian food or the many insects and complained that the stifling midday heat was keeping him from meditating properly.

Many of the Beatles' personal friends had joined them on the pilgrimage. There was Donovan, the eccentric Greek inventor, "Magic Alex," Beach Boy Mike Love, Mia Farrow, and her sister, Prudence. All in all, it was as perfect and peaceful an interlude as anyone could hope to experience. That is, until a few nasty rumors rocketed through the camp about the Maharishi making a play for the all too earthly affections of the famous Ms. Farrow. The Beatles, shocked and disillusioned, confronted the swami, whose vague, evasive explanations seemed to confirm, at least to John, that the rumours just might be true. But that was all it took, and the very next morning the Beatles packed their bags and departed Rishikesh for London.

Now where were they to turn? Brian was dead, the drugs had turned out to be as hollow and debilitating as they'd been warned, and now even their blossoming faith in the Lord had been severely shaken by the Maharishi's rather "ungodly" behavior. John and George, especially, were absolutely adamant that somewhere out there a *real* spiritual master must be waiting.

A. C. Bhaktivedanta Swami Prabhupada, the founder and guru of the much misunderstood Hare Krsna Movement, first met the Beatles during his initial visit to England in September 1969. In his twenties Srila Prabhupada developed a sincere desire to dedicate his life to propagating the transcendental message of the Lord Sri Krsna. At Allahabad in 1933 he was formally initiated into the charismatic cult of the great Bengali prophet Sri Chaitanya Mahaprabhu, and in September 1965, at the advanced age of seventy, he traveled to America to try and fulfil his master's sacred mission.

Almost immediately he was successful, and right up until his death on November 14, 1977, he attracted thousands of people, young and old, to spiritual life. As part of his legacy to his disciples, Prabhupada (as he was later affectionately known) established over one hundred Krsna Consciousness Centers around the world and wrote over eighty scholarly books on Vedic philosophy and culture.

From the moment they first met the benevolent guru in "the Temple" at Tittenhurst Park, John's palatial country home in Ascot, on that cold, rainy autumn day in 1969, the Beatles were confident that here at last was a sincere and knowledgeable advocate of the mystical science that so attracted them. Even today George still embraces many of the basic tenets of Prabhupada's philosophy, and according to Yoko so did John, right up until he died.

George performs a half lotus at the press party for the official launch of the Radha Krsna Temple album.

Mukunda Das Gosvami, an American-born devotee of Krsna now in the renounced order of life (*sannyasi*), has been a friend and adviser to George Harrison for over fifteen years. He is one of Srila Prabhupada's original disciples and currently heads up the Public Affairs Office of the International Society for Krsna Consciousness (known in the sixties as the Radha Krsna Temple) in Los Angeles. He is listed on the Radha Krsna Temple's Apple album as arranger and is a talented musician in his own right. He has written two books on the Beatles' involvement with the Hare Krsna Movement, *Search for Liberation/Lennon '69* and *Chant and Be Happy*, and has edited scores of other books, magazines, and periodicals on everything from reincarnation to evolution. Always busy, he has recently designed and implemented a free-food-distribution program, Food For Life, that feeds daily over 100,000 homeless, poor, and underprivileged people around the world. Although he rarely discusses his relationship with George, he graciously consented to an interview in Toronto in 1982 to clarify a few discrepancies regarding Harrison's longtime involvement with the devotees.

GEOFFREY   Mukunda, who was your first link to the Beatles?

MUKUNDA DAS GOSVAMI   Syamasundara happened to meet George Harrison while we were living on Betterton Street in London. He came down to the temple about a month later, and sometime after that we were all invited to his home in Esher for a feast. George had a very nice vegetarian meal prepared, and afterward we all chanted with him and Billy Preston. It was a long session. I would say that we chanted for somewhere between two and four hours. Billy was playing an early type of Moog synthesizer, George was playing his guitar amplified, and we were playing drums and kartals. I remember us doing a bit of cooking together that night, and I think he may have played us a Lenny Bruce record.

GEOFFREY   How did your personal experience with the Beatles compare to the popular images of them projected by the media?

MUKUNDA   Well, George was the one we really knew the best, and he

George contemplating the course his solo career should take in London during the mid-seventies.

actually seemed to fit pretty closely what we had thought about him prior to our meeting.

GEOFFREY   Did George strike you as sincere in his spiritual yearning?

MUKUNDA   Yes, he did. Obviously he was sincere. He was naturally that way even before he met us. Of course he'd been to India, and he used to talk about how he had always wondered and thought about God. As far as Pattie went, she was friendly, but she didn't really exhibit any kind of overtly spiritual characteristics.

GEOFFREY   What about George's involvement with the Krnsa book?

MUKUNDA   Prabhupada asked him to donate some money for it, and he did.

GEOFFREY   Whose idea was it for George to write the introduction?

MUKUNDA   It may have been Prabhupada's, I'm not sure. Once the idea was there, however, George was definitely into it.

GEOFFREY   Did George chant regularly?

MUKUNDA   He did at one time, but I wasn't keeping tabs on him. Syamasundara was the one who spent the most time with him and taught him how to chant properly.

GEOFFREY   Tell me about the devotees' participation in John and Yoko's Montreal bed-in.

MUKUNDA   The devotees were featured on their record "Give Peace A Chance." They were very well received, and John and Yoko seemed to like their presence. The media noticed them and liked them as well. They gave a nice flavor to the whole affair.

GEOFFREY   Did Lennon ever chant much that you know of?

MUKUNDA   No, not to my knowledge. He never chanted mantra except when he was singing with George.

GEOFFREY   Does George visit the temple much today?

MUKUNDA   Infrequently he comes by. He came to see Prabhupada quite a few times, but he's not a regular by any means.

GEOFFREY   How about his second wife, Olivia, and son, Dhani — have they changed him much?

MUKUNDA   Well, I think people change each other when they become husband and wife. He certainly seems to be happier than he was before. George and Olivia seem to be very domesticated. They really vibrate on the same wavelength, I think.

GEOFFREY   Is there a spiritual mood at George's home, Friar Park, today?

MUKUNDA   I think so, yes. I would say so.

GEOFFREY   What has Prabhupada said about the Beatles' past lives?

MUKUNDA   There was a letter from Prabhupada that said something about John Lennon being a prominent, charitable businessman in Calcutta in his last life.

GEOFFREY   Anything to say about George's apparent disillusionment with some of the Hare Krnsa devotees over the years?

MUKUNDA   George knows the philosophy is greater than anybody's particular frailties, so I wouldn't really call it disillusionment. I'd say he's got a pretty good knowledge of how the Hare Krsna Movement works.

GEOFFREY   I heard that at one time there actually was a temple set up at Friar Park.

MUKUNDA   There probably was when the devotees were staying out there. They maintained it, though. I don't know, he may have had a little marble Krsna or something.

GEOFFREY   Is George a vegetarian?

MUKUNDA   Yes.

GEOFFREY   Did George ever offer to surrender to Prabhupada as a disciple?

MUKUNDA   No, no.

GEOFFREY   There's a famous story about it, you know. Apparently George offered to become a full-time devotee, but Prabhupada said, "No, it's better for you to continue with your singing and just help as you can."

John and Yoko with the Montreal devotees during their bed-in at the Queen Elizabeth Hotel, Montreal.

George sends out a message to the world with the ancient Indian hand sign (*mudra*) signifying spiritual bravery in the author's collage.

HARE BOL

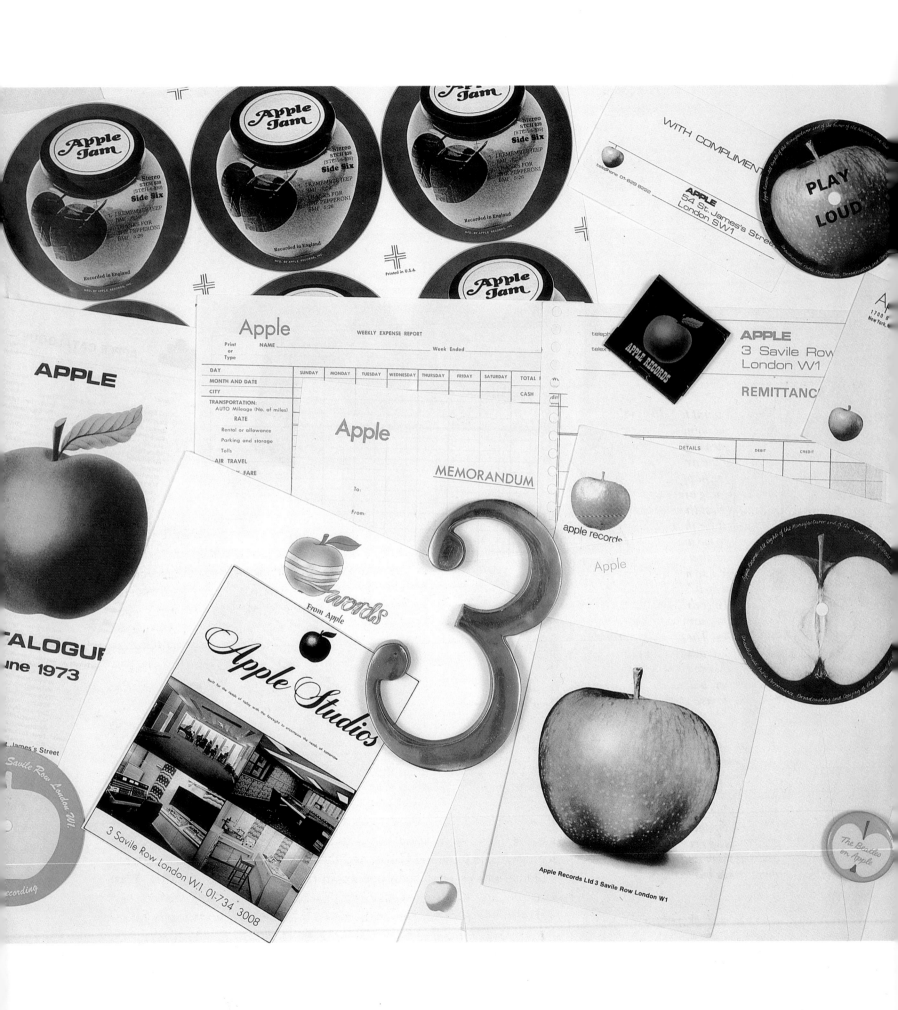

5 Swinging Days

Apple Corps Ltd

> *"We really want to help people, but without doing it like charity and just seeming like ordinary patrons of the arts. I mean, we're in the happy position of not really needing any more money, so for the first time the bosses aren't in it for the profit. If you come to see me and say, 'I've had such and such a dream', I will say, 'Here's so much money. Go away and do it.' We've already bought all our dreams, so now we want to share that possibility with others. There's no desire in any of our heads to take over the world — that was Hitler. There is, however, a desire to get power in order to use it for good."*
>
> PAUL McCARTNEY

> *"The aim of this company isn't really a stack of gold teeth in the bank. We've done that bit. It's more of a trick to see if we can actually get artistic freedom within a business structure, to see if we can create nice things and sell them without charging three times our cost."*
>
> JOHN LENNON

Relics from the Apple era often referred to by memorabilia dealers as "Apple Gold."

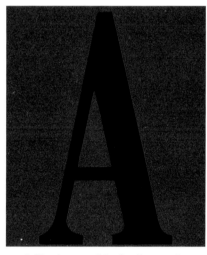

pple Corps Ltd, established in 1967 to manage and market the combined creative output of John, Paul, George, Ringo, and friends, first opened its doors to business at 95 Wigmore Street, London, in April 1968. Conceived by John and Paul as a kind of vast international consortium of what they termed "western communism," Apple took over the reigns from their previous management concerns: Beatles Limited, Seltaeb Inc., Subafilms, and the Beatles' Company. Among the various divisions set up by the Fabs (at a reported initial investment of over £ 2 million) were Apple Records, Apple Films, Apple Publishing, Apple Retailing, and Apple Electronics. In addition, several subsidiaries were later incorporated to expand the Beatles' business activities — Apple Wholesale, Apple Tailoring (civil and theatrical), Apple Studios, Apple Publicity, Apple Management, Apple Television, Apple Overseas, the Apple Boutique, and Zapple Records. Other branches discussed, but never really developed, were Apple Magazine, the Apple School, Apple Greeting Cards, and the Apple Express Courier Service.

Branch offices were soon opened in the United States, Canada, West Germany, Italy, France, Switzerland, Sweden, and the Netherlands. The original governing board of Apple, mostly old friends from the early Liverpool days (sometimes called the "Liverpool mafia" by the press), also

included a few new faces and was set up as follows: Presidents: John Lennon, Paul McCartney, George Harrison, and Richard Starkey; Managing Director: Neil Aspinall; Artist and Repertoire: Peter Asher; Assistant Managing Director: Malcolm Evans; Director of Public Relations: Derek Wynn Taylor; Director of Electronics: "Magic" Alex Mardas; Manager of Films: Dennis O'Dell; Division Head of Records: Ron Kass; Consultant: Brian Lewis; Beatles' Personal Assistant/Director of Social Events: Peter Brown; Art Director: Jeremy Banks; Apple Films Assistant/Record Publicist: Tony Bramwell.

The Wigmore Street offices soon became too small for the rapidly growing company, and on June 22, 1968, the London papers reported that Apple had purchased Number 3 Savile Row for over £500,000. It would become their new world headquarters. The first Beatle record to carry the Apple logo on the sleeve was "Magical Mystery Tour," but even Sgt. Pepper extended his thanks to the company on that back cover.

Apple's first public venture was the Apple Boutique at 94 Baker Street. It opened on December 7, 1967, with a gala celebration attended by John, George, their wives, and about two hundred more trendy people than could comfortably fit inside the store! John nicknamed it the "psychedelic Woolworths," and almost immediately it became *the* place to see and be seen in swinging Londontown. The exterior of the shop featured a far-out, acid-inspired mural by three Dutch designers called the Fool, who, after endearing themselves to the Beatles, proceeded to put their artistic touch to just about everything the Boys owned. Suddenly rainbow-colored designs showed up on George's living room fireplace and on one or two of his favorite guitars. John even commissioned a fancy new paint job for an antique upright piano. While the Beatles themselves were impressed by the flamboyant artists from Amsterdam, their neighbors on Baker Street were less favorably disposed and almost immediately petitioned city officials to have the offending "dreamscape" removed from the building. About eight months later the shop was closed down with the consent of the Beatles, and the entire contents were given away *free* to the public — that is, after the Boys stopped by to do a little last-minute shopping themselves.

Meanwhile Apple Records was doing extremely well plugging its first four album releases — "Wonderwall Music" by George, the controversial "Two Virgins" by John and Yoko, the Beatles' "white" album, and the "James Taylor" LP by the down-home, all-American country boy himself. Although the commercial success of Taylor's first Apple album was somewhat limited, he gained recognition within the industry and went on to become a very big star.

Another Apple artist who came from nowhere to gain international acclaim was the Welsh folksinger Mary Hopkin. But unlike James Taylor, Mary scored a number-one hit with her first captivating single, "Those Were The Days." She went on to record three best-selling albums for Apple — "Postcard," "Earth Song — Ocean Song," and "Those Were The

This album is so obscure that it isn't even listed in the official Apple Records catalogue.

A sampling of Apple Records' releases.

A 78 RPM by the obscure Sundown Playboys.

Originally called the Iveys but later renamed Badfinger — this is perhaps the hardest-to-find Apple record.

Billy Preston, an old pal of all the Beatles and an especially close friend of George's.

Days" — as well as another popular single, "Goodbye" (originally recorded, but never officially released, by the Beatles).

Apple's most successful discovery was probably the Swansea powerhouse, Badfinger. Formerly known as the Iveys, the four original members of the group — Pete Ham, Ron Griffiths, Tom Evans, and Mike Gibbons — were first noticed by Mal Evans at the Cavern, and he later arranged a recording deal for them with Apple. Their hits included "Come And Get It," "No Matter What," "Day After Day," "Maybe Tomorrow," and "Baby Blue." In 1969 they were commissioned by Commonwealth United Films to compose and perform much of the musical score for Peter Sellers's and Ringo Starr's hilarious antiestablishment spoof, *The Magic Christian*. By the time the Beatles broke up in 1970, a curious rumor had begun to circulate that Badfinger was actually the Beatles playing together incognito. Another interesting variation on the theme had Badfinger taking over the musical heritage created by the Fabs. One thing, however, is certain: the stories didn't hurt their record sales one little bit! The group recorded five popular albums for Apple: "Maybe Tomorrow" (as the Iveys), "Magic Christian Music," "No Dice," "Straight Up," and "Ass."

William Evert Preston was born in Houston, Texas, on September 9, 1946. He began his musical career early in life and was already considered a consummate R & B pianist, singer, and composer by the time he reached his mid-teens. Known to the world as Billy Preston, he first came to the attention of the public with his excellent keyboard work during the Beatles' "Let It Be" sessions. His relationship with the Fabs, however, began long before that, as Billy explains: "I was backing Little Richard in Hamburg, and the Beatles were among the fourteen other supporting groups on the tour." By 1969 George Harrison was the guiding light in Billy's steadily rising popularity and signed him to his recording contract with Apple. Billy's only two albums for Apple, "That's The Way God Planned It" and "Encouraging Words," unfortunately spawned no number-one single for the modest, good-natured American, but they showed off his unparalleled flair for funk and steady, soulful musicianship to an ever-increasing audience both at home and abroad.

Already a jazz institution in Europe and America when they came to Apple Records, the Modern Jazz Quartet had a firm, no-nonsense approach to their career and their art. "Gimmicks are great," says band member John Lewis, "but don't ever lose sight of what you're really selling." Their first album release on Apple, "Under The Jasmine Tree," gave the fans an early indication of what a noble experiment Apple really was — "every kind of music presented tastefully to its audience without unnecessary regard towards earning excessive profits." "Space," the quartet's second adventure in sound for the label, proved the theory once and for all. From now on Apple would content itself with occasionally going out on a financial limb for its artists as long as the music was good enough. In the case of the Modern Jazz Quartet, it certainly was.

Altogether Apple Records released 64 albums and 118 singles by an extremely wide range of artists, including the Radha Krsna Temple, Paul McCartney, Trash, the Black Dyke Mills Band, the Plastic Ono Band, George Harrison, Phil Spector, Ronnie Spector, Doris Troy, John Tavener, Ringo Starr, the Sundown Playboys, Ravi Shankar, the Hot Chocolate Band, Lon and Derrek Van Eaton, Chris Hodge, David Peel, Elephant's Memory, John Lennon, and Yoko Ono.

Zapple Records, an experimental offshoot of the Apple label, was the brainchild of John Lennon and his new girlfriend, conceptual artist Yoko Ono. It was introduced in 1969 to release spoken-word albums and music of a more esoteric nature. Well-known figures committed to Zapple releases included poets Richard Brautigan and Lawrence Ferlinghetti, poet-playwright Michael McClure, Kenneth Patchen, Charles Olson, Allen Ginsberg, and Lenny Bruce. But the only two actual releases were a John Lennon–Yoko Ono album, "Unfinished Music #2 — Life With The Lions," and an electronic-music album composed and produced by George Harrison and recorded with a Moog synthesizer called "Electronic Sound."

In the end Zapple will be remembered more for what it did *not* accomplish than for the little it did. The original idea behind the venture was laudable, but it never worked out. John had reasoned that while some records were designed to be played over and over again, others, especially more specialized ones, should only be listened to once or twice and then thrown away, like old magazines, newspapers, or paperbacks. Being mostly spoken-word albums, production costs would generally remain low, so they could be issued quickly and at a low price to meet the demands of any fast-breaking trend in the marketplace. But when the Beatles' new manager, Allen Klein, came on the scene, he decided that "there's no use in putting out anything that isn't up to par, even at a reduced price. From now on this company only concentrates on major releases." As a result Zapple Records folded quietly after operating for only about a year.

Apple Films, by contrast, fared a little better, although it wasn't able to live up to the lofty ideals on which it had been founded either. "The film division includes the creation, development and production of feature films, animated films, television programming and commercials," read the official Apple announcement. The first feature was the Beatles' self-produced, ill-fated *Magical Mystery Tour*. It was followed by *Yellow Submarine*, *Let It Be*, Ravi Shankar's autobiographical documentary, *Raga*, the 1971 spaghetti western–thriller, *Blindman*, starring Ringo, George's humanitarian epic, *The Concert for Bangla Desh*, Ringo's first directorial project, *Born to Boogie*, with Marc Bolan, his entertaining satire of old-time Hollywood horrors, *Son of Dracula*, with his chum Harry Nilsson, and *Little Malcolm and His Struggle against the Eunuchs*, produced by George. Apple movies that never made it past preproduction included *The Jam*, *Walkout*, *Gorgeous Accident*, and a film based on John Lennon's two books, *In His Own Write* and *A Spaniard in the Works*.

The graffiti-laden front door of Apple signed by fans from around the world. Photographed at Beatle City, Liverpool.

The Fool's foolish attempt at pop stardom.

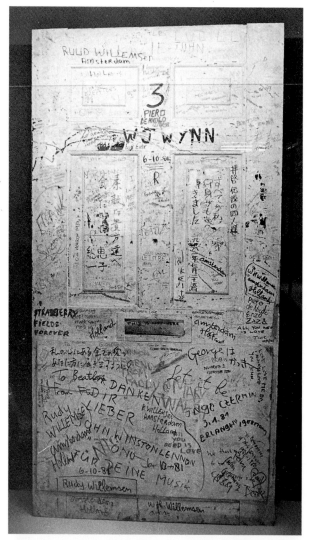

Promoting Zapple Records in the *Beatles'*
Monthly Magazine.

'Z' is for Zapple.

Introducing Zapple, a new label from Apple Records.

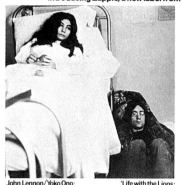

I'm interested in 'Zapple'. I'd like to know where my nearest stockist is. Also, could you please let me know what you'll be up to next before you get up to it.

Name

Address

Send this coupon to JACK OLIVER (ZAPPLE) APPLE RECORDS 3 SAVILE ROW, LONDON W.1.

John Lennon/Yoko Ono: (Zapple 01) 'Life with the Lions: Unfinished Music No. 2.'

A *Yellow Submarine* lunchbox. 1968.

An Italian promotional poster for *Yellow Submarine.*

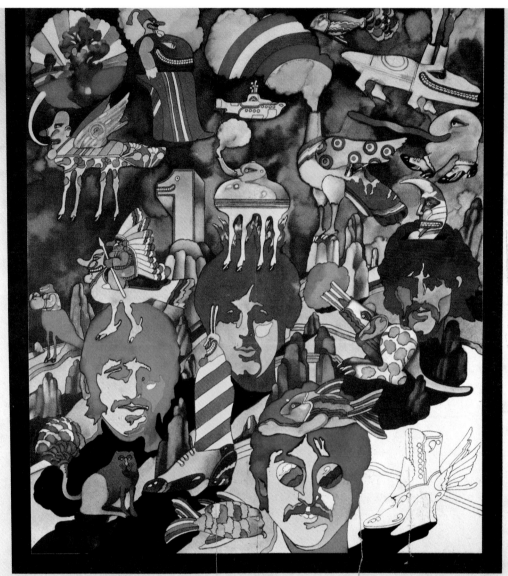

More merchandise inspired by *Yellow Submarine*.

John and Yoko Lennon as Mr. and Mrs. Claus at the Apple annual Christmas party. 1968.

The Apple boutique on Baker Street gets a shocking new coat of paint.

Apple Corps's most dramatic failure had to be its so-called electronics division, headed by the ambitious Greek inventor, "Magic" Alex Mardas. A close friend of all the Beatles but especially intimate with John, Alex promoted his whimsical creations to the Boys so well that Apple offered him full sponsorship to research and then manufacture prototypes of his wild inventions. "One evening after dinner as we were all sitting around the table, Alex suddenly set out a transistor radio which happened to be playing 'I Want To Hold Your Hand'," recalls a close friend of the Beatles. "Of course we assumed it was a tune off the radio. But we were wrong. Somehow or other he had hooked up the radio to receive sounds from a record player at the other end of the house, and all without any wires!" Another of Alex's infamous electronic gadgets was his "Nothing Box," which did absolutely nothing but run for a full five years switching on and off at random a row of twelve tiny lights set into the sides. He also brought in an electric Apple radio that pulsated several colored lights in time to the music. He even promised to produce a portable pocket force field that would allow the Beatles to go anywhere they liked, undisturbed by overly aggressive fans and curious onlookers. John had often complained to Alex that London's miserable weather bummed him out whenever he had to travel into town for a recording session. Alex suggested that work begin immediately on an artificial sun that would hang suspended over Savile Row, thus warming and illuminating the entire neighborhood!

Alex's biggest — and most expensive — fiasco was his $500,000 "renovation" of the Apple studios in the cavernous basement of Number 3 Savile Row. In those days most professional studios had sixteen-track recording, but true to form, Alex considered this inadequate for the Beatles' complex sound and set about designing a seventy-two-track system. The fact that the technology for such a setup didn't exist was of little concern to Apple, which tended to look on Alex with awe. Needless to say, the wonderful studio failed to materialize, and George Martin had to be called in at the last minute to supervise the installation of the new recording equipment. A few months later Alex's blueprints for the amazing seventy-two-track studio as well as his patents and designs for a hundred other magical inventions that had failed to see the light of day were delivered to Apple, where they collected dust in Allen Klein's desk for the next three years. Ironically, not one of Alex's space-age devices was ever commercially manufactured or marketed to the public.

Born in Bebington, Merseyside, Peter Brown, the Beatles' longtime personal assistant and close friend, began his career as a junior executive working first at Henderson's and then Lewis's, Liverpool's two most prominent department stores. Some time later he happened to meet Brian Epstein, who offered him a position managing the NEMS Charlotte Street record store. After the Beatles' initial success he joined Brian's office in London and quickly distinguished himself as a competent member of the

An impromptu jam session in the Apple boutique.

Beatles' management team. When Brian died, Apple hired Peter as one of its executive directors, and he became a kind of temporary substitute manager to the group until Allen Klein took over in 1969. He was on a twenty-four-hour-a-day alert for any Beatle-related emergency, with a special hot line for which only John, Paul, George, and Ringo knew the number. He acted as best man at John and Yoko's Gibraltar wedding and was remembered by John in the lyrics of the Beatles' 1969 hit tune "The Ballad Of John And Yoko." Peter's cool, cultured, diplomatic approach was a big asset to the Beatles' rather haphazard record company. He left Apple in 1970 for a high-ranking job with the Robert Stigwood Organization of America and opened his own consulting firm in New York a few years later. His best-selling controversial memoirs of his days with the Beatles, *The Love You Make*, received much critical acclaim and shed new light on many aspects of their incredible career. This interview was conducted in Toronto in 1983.

GEOFFREY   Mr. Brown, I understand there was a promotional film made of "A Day In The Life" that was never officially released.

PETER BROWN   No, it was a mess. The guy who was supposed to organize the thing was called Vic Sing; he was also involved with George's *Wonderwall*. It was Vic and Paul who set the whole thing up. They filmed the last session, which was the one with the London Symphony Orchestra, and as everyone arrived, they were given a sixteen-millimeter camera and a hand mike and told to film whatever they liked! But no provision was made by Vic Sing or Paul for any straight filmtaking, so everything that was done was just off the wall. There was nothing long enough — just people playing around with cameras. So instead of having one person doing the basic footage, there wasn't anything usable. There were a lot of people at that session — Mick Jagger, Marianne Faithful, Donovan. Mickey Dolenz of the Monkees was there. But I know nothing about what's happened with it. Neil has it all.

GEOFFREY   Do you feel there's any wisdom in bringing these things out? People are so hungry for Beatles products, why not go into the vaults and dig out the real gems?

PETER   The thing is that the "real gems" are only half-finished songs and things like that.

GEOFFREY   To your knowledge, did any of the Beatles ever consciously put backwards messages in their music?

PETER   Never.

GEOFFREY   About the Maharishi — is it true he was using the Beatles' name to promote his movement without their permission and that you went down with them to see him about it?

PETER   I went down on my own first, but I couldn't make any progress with him. The moment I started telling him to lay off of ABC Television he

Peter Brown, the Beatles' personal assistant.

would go all holy on me, so I went back and said to George and Paul, "You'll have to come with me and impress upon him the fact that he's not going to get you for an ABC special." The reason for taking Paul was that he was the charming, articulate one, and George was well known for being the one who was the most into TM, so it wasn't just Paul and me, the commercial end of the business, who were telling the Maharishi off. George came along as well, with the Maharishi knowing perfectly well he was his most loyal fan and disciple.

GEOFFREY Do you think the breakup of the Beatles could have been avoided or at least postponed for a few years?

PETER If Brian hadn't died, you mean?

GEOFFREY If any number of things hadn't happened — if Paul had been a little cooler and dug Yoko a bit more . . .

PETER Paul *tried* to dig Yoko, but it wasn't really possible to dig her at the time. She was just thrust at us, and there was no way you could take to Yoko much in those days.

GEOFFREY Is it true that in 1969, when Paul left the group, the three Beatles considered replacing him with Klaus Voorman on bass and Billy Preston on keyboards?

PETER No.

GEOFFREY Were you present for the "Sgt. Pepper" photo session?

PETER Yes, at the press conference. That's how Linda met Paul. I went to some of the cover assembly things as well, but I don't think I went to the final cover shoot.

GEOFFREY I wonder if you could say anything about John and Yoko's wedding in Gibraltar?

PETER The thing people don't realize is that John and Yoko were very hurt at that time, largely through their own fault. They'd made themselves the center of a media circus, and whatever they did was causing them derision in many ways. The romance relationship and love between them was *very* sincere, and they wanted to get married in a special way. John, particularly, had wanted to get married for quite a long time. I'd been in Holland one weekend when he called me up and said, "Hey, that's a great idea — you stay in Holland, and we'll come over and get married there," but I said, "No, you can't do that, John." And then when Paul tried to get married secretly, it became a media circus, so John and Yoko were all the more determined not to have to go through that. That's when he insisted to me, "Find somewhere fast that I can get married without any problems." Well, I tried *everywhere*, but then I discovered that Gibraltar was in the peculiar situation of being part of the British setup and remote enough that there wasn't any press corps.

GEOFFREY How did the death in 1977 of Mal Evans affect the Beatles?

PETER The only knowledge I have of Mal Evans's death is what John

The Bag O'Nails pub in London, where Paul Mc-Cartney and Linda Eastman *really* met.

Linda Eastman chats up Paul at the official press party for "Sgt. Pepper."

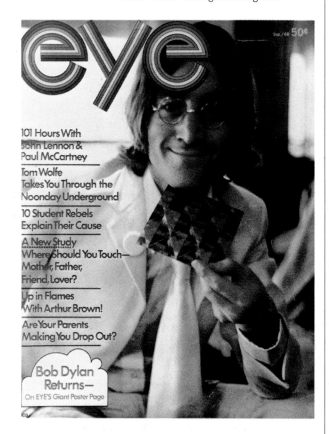

The September 1968 cover of Helen Gurley Brown's ill-fated underground magazine.

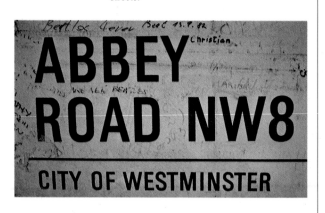

A road sign for one of the world's most famous streets.

Lennon told me. I went by for tea one day at the Dakota, and he said to me, "Did you know that Mal has been killed?" All Neil Aspinall did was to confirm John's story. Apparently Mal was getting into very bad shape and was shot by the Los Angeles Police Department, and his ashes were lost in the mail.

GEOFFREY   Was John upset about it? Was Mal a very close buddy of his?

PETER   Yes, he was very upset about it. But he also thought it was ironic that the ashes should be lost. He couldn't help but think that was funny. Poor Mal.

GEOFFREY   Was he at all like the image we've been given through the media over the years?

PETER   Oh yes, he was a lovely great bear of a man. He went from fixing phone transformer boxes to Shea Stadium — that's what Neil always said.

GEOFFREY   President of Apple Records for a time, wasn't he?

PETER   I don't remember that. Not while I was there! He signed a group or two, but everybody had discoveries during that period.

GEOFFREY   Would you ever in your wildest imagination see any combination recordings from Harrison-McCartney, Harrison-Starr, McCartney-Starr, etc?

PETER   No. Frankly, I think it's very unlikely because of their particular personalities.

Alistair Taylor, Apple Corps's conscientious office manager, was one of the few people in the Beatles' employ to bridge the gap between working for the group and actually becoming a close personal friend. Nicknamed the "Fixer Upper" by Paul, he was with them from the very beginning, even accompanying Brian on his first visits to the Cavern to see the Boys perform. It was Alistair who witnessed the signing of the Beatles' contract with NEMS in 1961, and right up until he left Apple in 1969, he worked diligently to help secure the Boys' often sporadic collective fortunes. Since that time he has tried his hand at managing a few unknown English pop groups, but he has not met with anything close to the success he experienced working with Brian and the Beatles. These days he is a frequent guest speaker at various Beatle conventions around the world and is writing his autobiography. During this interview, conducted in New York in 1984, Alistair looks back candidly on the "Beatle years" and shares the insights only a person on the inside of the phenomenon could have.

GEOFFREY   How did you first come in contact with Brian Epstein and the Beatles?

ALISTAIR TAYLOR   Well, I had a very boring job in an office. I happened to see an advertisement for a record shop assistant at NEMS in Liverpool. I applied, had an interview with Brian, and was offered a job as his personal assistant. Which, of course, I took. That was long before the Beatles! Then this guy, Raymond Jones, came in one day and asked us to get a

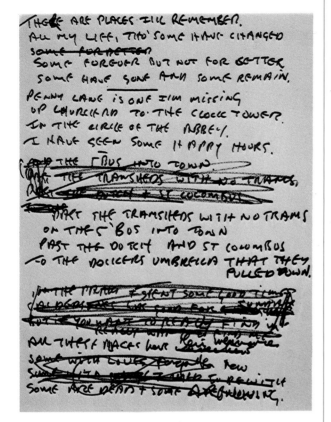

An early draft of "In My Life" in John's own hand.

record for him called "My Bonnie" by the Beatles, which we ultimately did, from Germany.

GEOFFREY   Were you there when the record came in?

ALISTAIR   Oh yes, I was there every day. At first we got a box of twenty-five, then another twenty-five. They kept selling as fast as we could import them. A few weeks later we went down to hear this group at the Cavern, and we just took it from there.

GEOFFREY   What was your initial reaction to the Beatles?

ALISTAIR   They were sensational! I hated pop music at that time; I was mostly into jazz and the classics. I still am, really, but they were just so *fantastic*. Not necessarily musically. As a matter of fact, they were bloody awful as musicians then!

GEOFFREY   So you and I couldn't have gone down to Woolton Village back then and found four other guys who had pretty much the same buzz about them?

ALISTAIR   Oh, Liverpool was full of guys like that at the time, but the Beatles had something else — charisma, or as I call it, "Ingredient X." I don't know what it was, but they certainly had it!

GEOFFREY   Was Brian enthusiastic about his discovery of the Beatles?

ALISTAIR   Yes, there's been a lot said about how he went around saying they were going to be bigger than Elvis. I don't remember it being as blatant as that. I mean, obviously we were enthusiastic. As a matter of fact, when we went for lunch the day we first met them, we sat down and talked about what we should do next. It was just something new and fun.

GEOFFREY   Brian's mother, Queenie, has said recently that if he were alive now and the Beatles had happened today, he might not have been as tortured a soul as he was, because now being gay is not such a big deal.

ALISTAIR   Right. He was a very complex man, and I think there's far more to it than his simply being gay. He wasn't happy at that, you know. In fact, he tried very hard *not* to be gay. Twice I had phone calls from him saying good-bye, he was committing suicide. I've often said that in many ways I might have been happier if he had.

GEOFFREY   You mean you don't think he did?

ALISTAIR   No. I *know* he didn't.

GEOFFREY   What happened then?

ALISTAIR   Accidental death, end of quote. That is one for *my* book.

GEOFFREY   Oh, you mean you have proof?

ALISTAIR   No. I mean I was *there*, at his house. Only thirty seconds behind the doctor.

GEOFFREY   But if he died accidentally and the family knows it, why is he buried way at the back of the Jewish cemetery in Liverpool like an outcast? Why would they allow that myth to be perpetuated when it's so hard on the family and on Brian's memory?

ALISTAIR   But they haven't, you see. The times I've been asked the question, "Why did he commit suicide?" Well, I want someone to tell me *where* it says he committed suicide! The verdict by the coroner's court was "accidental death," and the entire survey confirmed it. Remember, there were only two people in that room, the doctor and myself, right? I've never said it was suicide. Now, I've heard stories that there was a note found, but I certainly didn't find it.

GEOFFREY   Well, let's hope we can help put an end to the stories once and for all then. Now what about when the Beatles changed their public persona from four lovable little mop-tops to the psychedelic lords of London? What do you think changed them?

ALISTAIR   Look, if you weren't there, you can't begin to understand the pressures they were under and their way of life. I don't give a damn how many books you've read or how many people you interview, even I can't convey to you what it was like! I was very close to them, and I was under a lot of pressure. But I was not even remotely in their league. It was getting pretty unbearable, and they had to do something. Imagine not being able to walk down the street. You can't go out in a car, you can't do *anything* without literally being torn to shreds, day in, day out, night in, night out, for years! In the early days, possibly even before I knew them very well, they were on pills, but that was just youngsters experimenting. We've all done it, but later I think it was an escape. It was fun, they could afford it, and they mixed with people who said, "Hey, try this, man." Recently I've heard the statement that John Lennon was high almost every single day of the sixties! Well, when did he find time to compose songs, make movies, go on tour, do interviews, appear on television shows, or write his books?

GEOFFREY   There was a poster issued by Apple that shows you playing all these silly instruments like in a one-man band. What was that all about?

ALISTAIR   Well, that was Paul's idea. He was always very much the man with the ideas. Anyway, we had just set up Apple Corps, and we wanted to get some tapes and projects from unknown people. In fact Paul has cost me a great deal of money recently because I found, quite literally by accident, the original sketch Paul had done in my flat of the design for that ad you've just mentioned. It fell out of a book one day, and I thought, "Shit, this must be priceless!" I wrote Paul because I heard he was into Beatles memorabilia and offered him the drawing. I said, "Hey, I found this old sketch you did. Do you remember being in my flat? We were drinking coffee until two in the morning." We must have thrown dozens of these away, and I apparently used this one as a bookmark, and that's how I happened to find it. The next thing I know, his manager rings up from MPL to say that Paul wasn't interested. So I said, "Fine." Later Paul himself phones and dives straight in by saying, "It's not yours to sell and you've no right, you know!" Well, I haven't spoken to the guy for years and we were once very close, so I was a bit taken aback. I ended up by saying, "It *is* mine, it was in my house, you

A 1964 sales tag from the official Beatles line of clothing using an early Dezo Hoffmann shot of the Boys.

Promoting Apple Films' *Yellow Submarine*. Soho Square, London, 1968.

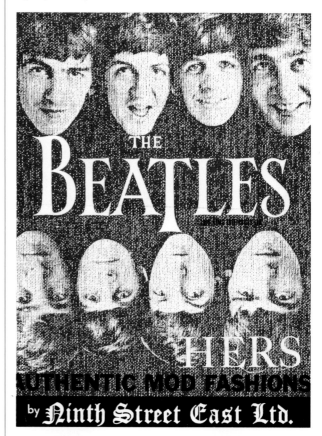

120

lost it and I need the money, so I'm going to go ahead and put it into Sotheby's." So he said, "You go ahead if you want to. It's up to you, I don't want to know about it." So I put it into Sotheby's, and the next thing I know there was an injunction from McCartney's lawyers blocking its sale, so I had to settle with him out of court.

GEOFFREY   One rumor is that he's stockpiling memorabilia and is going to do some kind of Beatles museum himself.

ALISTAIR   I don't know. I think he resents anyone making anything, however little, off him. He believes we milked him during the Apple years, but he forgets what we did for him!

GEOFFREY   Well, *someone* was certainly fiddling the till at Apple!

ALISTAIR   Sure, the Boys. We were all accused of ripping them off, and of course there *was* some nonsense going on. I tried to tell them this, and it was my idea to get Allen Klein in. I'm the guy who actually said to them one day, "Look, this is stupid. We cannot manage this business ourselves, you know."

GEOFFREY   They put John's old friend Pete Shotton in and gave him a big position, didn't they?

ALISTAIR   Let me tell you something now. One Sunday we were sitting in Hilly House, Brian's private office, having an Apple meeting. Just the Boys, myself, and Neil. Suddenly they picked up the phone and said, "Hey, let's get hold of Derek!" They rang up Derek Taylor, who was still working with the Beach Boys, and they said, "Pack your bags and come on over, man." Well, I said, "What's he going to do?" "Oh, well, we don't really know. I'm sure we'll find something." Later, when Derek arrived, he said, "Okay, let's get some kind of business up." At one time there was even talk about doing one of those express rider delivery services. "Now," said the Beatles, "who are we going to get to run publishing?" So Derek said, "Hey, there's this marvelous guy in the States." "Well, get him on the phone and bring him here!" They were just pulling people in and saying, "Oh shit, now what are we going to do with them? Oh, it doesn't matter. We'll think of something." So is it any wonder their money was flying out?

GEOFFREY   John once said, "Apple was like playing Monopoly, only with real money."

ALISTAIR   That's right. But you know, they've accused everybody else of ripping them off, but they personally gave *carte blanche* to just about anyone. People were buying genuine antique desks for their offices. Ron Kass had this incredible all-white office which must have cost the earth. Peter Asher had *real* Old Master paintings on the wall of his office. "The Beatles have plenty of money," they thought, "so let's spend." And we had this crazy idea of having two *cordon bleu* chefs in residence. Mind you, the idea was great. Here we were constantly entertaining people, spending a hell of a lot of money in posh restaurants, and so I said, "Look, this is much more sensible. We've got this beautiful house on Savile Row, so let's have our own cooks." But it was never used for that, you see. We still took people out to lunch, and the only folks that ever dined in at Apple were Peter Brown and Neil Aspinall. They were having eight-course lunches with vintage wine! There was this huge metal cabinet stocked full of wine and champagne. It was unbelievable!

GEOFFREY So what about this wonderful idea the Beatles had that Apple was going to save the world by giving all the young artists a break? What happened when you started getting millions of audition tapes by post?

ALISTAIR They collected dust in the corner! We just couldn't cope with it.

GEOFFREY Did you try?

ALISTAIR Yes, we tried. Obviously we got hold of a few good people — Billy Preston, Badfinger, James Taylor, and Mary Hopkin. The kids were sending all sorts of tapes and sheet music in constantly. Yeah, you'd come in in the morning, switch on the answering machine, and get some guy auditioning on the message tape! We used to send a lot of them around to the Grade Organization.

GEOFFREY Was there a time when they finally said, "Hey, I guess we're not going to save the world with Apple after all?"

ALISTAIR But it was never really meant to save the world! Let's put Apple into perspective, right? A lot of nonsense has been spoken about Apple. Apple was set up purely and simply as a *tax-saving* project. Instead of paying nineteen and six on the pound, we only paid sixteen shillings. In the beginning there was an executive board at Apple, so the Boys and Brian didn't want to know. It was Clive Epstein, myself, Geoffrey Ellis, a solicitor, and an accountant, and the idea was that we would quietly announce to the tax authorities that we would soon be opening a string of shops. That was the original concept, but when the Boys heard about it they decided that could become very boring — they didn't want their name above a string of ordinary shops! The original idea was greeting cards. Imagine Beatles' greeting card shops! Gradually they started drifting in on meetings, and Apple Corps as we know it evolved from there. Later it all turned into this silly philosophy, admittedly, but even then it was not really designed to save the world. All we wanted to do was to get rid of the hassle of big business. Why couldn't business be fun and pleasurable?

GEOFFREY Why do you think the Beatles broke up?

ALISTAIR Ah, I don't know. They broke up after I'd gone.

GEOFFREY Did they fight much?

ALISTAIR Come on, man, they were breaking up from about day one! More than once in the early days I had to go and find George. He'd just say, "I'm not doing this," and he'd piss off, you know. I think the pressures got so bad towards the end that I'm astonished they stayed together even as long as they did.

John and Paul perform "Hey Jude" on the "David Frost Show."

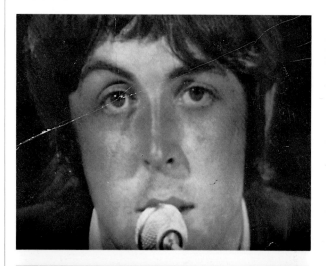

George and Paul attend a preconcert press conference in Germany on their final swing through Europe. 1966.

The lads take a rare back seat to Ringo while taping an appearance for a 1965 television special.

GEOFFREY   So how do you feel now about the Beatles and the way it all turned out?

ALISTAIR   I just find it sad.

GEOFFREY   Even though you haven't seen them in all these years, do you still feel close to them?

ALISTAIR   Oh yeah. You don't wipe out all those years together. You don't forget being close to a living legend, and you don't wipe out being a part of it and helping to create it. I've tried turning my back on it, but you find yourself name dropping when you've lived with someone like them. I literally worked twenty-four hours a day, seven days a week, for all of them many times. When you work for the Beatles, you *work* for them; you're on call constantly. I went on holidays with them, so we were friends — I wasn't just an employee. It was such an important part of your history, you find that you become rather self-conscious about it when you say things like, "Oh, I remember John and Paul telling me so and so," and people look at you as if to say, "Oh, big deal, name dropper!" You can't stop though, because that was your *life*.

6

Colliding Circles

The Breakup of the Beatles

"The Boys in their own way gave a great deal of their lives to us by being the Beatles, and now, happily, they have found their own individual selves. Jolly good luck to them." GEORGE MARTIN

"The whole Beatles thing is like a horror story, nightmare. I don't even like to think about it." GEORGE HARRISON

"It's just a pop band that's broken up, that's all. It's nothing really important." JOHN LENNON

"If I'd been Hitler's girlfriend, maybe things would have been different." YOKO ONO

The Beatles 1969.

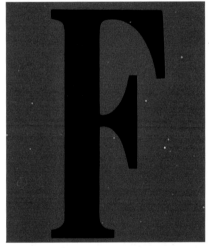

or John Lennon it was Brian Epstein's untimely death that precipitated the breakup of the Beatles. "After Brian died we virtually collapsed," said John at the time. "Paul took us over, though, and supposedly led us, but we only went round in circles. As far as I'm concerned, that's when we really broke up." For Paul, George, and Ringo, however, it may have been Yoko Ono's dramatic appearance on the scene that put the final nail into the group's coffin. Before Yoko no one had been able to penetrate the inner defenses of the four brotherly musicians, but Yoko's clear-cut ambition to succeed with her art *and* be with her man broke those defenses down.

Ringo, too, sorts out what was behind the breakup: "Because I left, because George left, because Yoko came in, because John left, because of the Apple business, because suddenly we all had individual things to do — millions of things. They're *all* part of it, you know. Little niggly things that cropped up because we'd been together for the past ten years and now wanted to do a few different things."

Another big problem for the Boys was the rapid disintegration of their multi-million-pound Apple empire and the inevitable squabbles that ensued over how to manage it properly after Brian died. Paul wanted to bring in his father-in-law, New York music-business attorney Lee Eastman, to help

125

The Beatles at one of their last photo sessions together.

A suitably macabre album cover subtly suggesting that Paul was indeed dead. 1969.

straighten things out, whereas John and the others were leaning toward hiring the Rolling Stones' manager, Allen Klein. Klein, a self-made music-publishing millionaire-turned-business-manager, was well known in American show biz circles for being an extremely shrewd negotiator as well as a clever organizer. More important to the class-conscious Lennon, however, was the fact that Klein hailed from a working-class background and never pretended to be anything other than what he was, unlike the upwardly mobile Eastman family. Ultimately, Klein did assume management duties for the Beatles and did a good job of streamlining the sorely flagging Apple Corps. His first order of business was to trim the executive office staff of several key members. Apple bigwig Ron Kass was the first to go, with Derek Taylor following shortly after.

Meanwhile the full impact of the financial mismanagement of Apple was coming to light. "Apple was always full of hustlers and spongers," says John. "The staff came and went as they pleased and were lavish with our money and hospitality. We have since discovered that two of Apple's cars completely disappeared and that we owned a house no one can remember buying! If Paul is suggesting that I was trying to rush him and the others into engaging Klein or pushing him down their throats, that is very wrong. Allen has always shown himself to be on top of the job. He is sometimes forceful to an extreme, but he gets results, and so far as I know he has not taken any commission to which he was not strictly entitled."

Paul, however, remained steadfastly unconvinced of either Klein's management abilities or his honesty and stubbornly held out his slice of the Apple pie for the Eastmans to handle. At one point the feud reached such ridiculous proportions that Paul actually instructed his staff to obscure Klein's company name and address from promotional copies of "Let It Be" by sticking small pieces of black tape over them. To make matters worse, Brian Epstein's brother, Clive, who now controlled his family's interest in the Beatles — Nemperor Holdings, which held their management contracts and collected royalties on their behalf — was somehow convinced to sell, on February 17, 1969, 70 percent of its shares to the powerful Triumph Investment Trust. Even more upsetting to the Beatles' precarious Apple cart was the sale of the portion of Northern Songs owned by their music publisher, Dick James, to Sir Lew Grade's Associated Television Corporation for a princely sum. This, as they say, was the last straw. For now it seemed the Boys would be singing only for a boardroom of tired business suits whose only concern was to figure out just what to do with the millions of pounds generated by the Beatles' own peculiar brand of rock 'n' roll.

Musically, too, the Boys had some very real troubles. George and Ringo were intent on busting out on their own and no longer felt the need to restrict their musical presence to the sometimes stifling boundaries of the Beatles' framework. The Fabs were also becoming aware that their prolific output could no longer be easily contained on one or even two conventional LPs. "The last four years, every time we've made a record, it's been a tough

THE BEATLES "Let it be"

APPLE
An **abkco** managed company
presents

TECHNICOLOR® **United Artists**
Ⓖ Entertainment from Transamerica Corporation

Ringo and long-time Beatle aid, Mal Evans, with Paul, Linda, and her daughter, Heather, following the McCartneys' wedding on March 12, 1969, in London.

The McCartneys marry in Marylebone, 1969. Accompanied by his new wife and young stepdaughter, Paul strikes out on his own.

decision whether to carry it on from there," says John. "In the old days Paul and I would knock off an LP together, but nowadays there's three of us writing equally good songs and needing that much more space. The problem is, do you make a double album every time, which takes six months of your life, or do you make only one? We spend a good three or four months making an album, you know, and maybe we get only two or three tracks on each LP. *That's* the main problem."

Paul, ever the wide-eyed entertainer, found it increasingly difficult to identify with John and Yoko's avant-garde musical offerings and nearly hit the roof when on November 29, 1968, they shed all remaining bonds of conformity by appearing nude on the cover of their "Two Virgins" LP. Following John's lead, Paul released his first solo album, "McCartney," on the Apple label on May 2, 1970. (In November 1966 Paul had scored the soundtrack for the British film *The Family Way*, starring Hayley Mills, later released as an album under his name. The music, however, was actually recorded by "George Martin and his Orchestra" at the EMI studios. Today it is one of the most highly sought-after Beatle-related records.) Not surprisingly, "McCartney" immediately entered the British *Melody Maker* charts at number ten. Six days later the Beatles' long-awaited "Let It Be" was released and skyrocketed straight to number three, thereby pitting the two works directly against each other.

Paul had been lying low with his new wife, Linda, and stepdaughter, Heather, at their rambling, rustic farm in Argyleshire, Scotland, trying to avoid the controversy of his forthcoming LP and struggling to come to terms with life without the Beatles. Both the media and Paul's more fervent fans, however, were clamoring for some answers on the ultimate fate of the group. By now the rumors and rumblings circulating on Savile Row had grown much too public for even the Beatles' well-paid "Apple bonkers" to sweep under the lush green carpet of Sgt. D. W. Taylor's press office. At the eleventh hour Paul decided to include a self-penned "interview" with himself in the promotional copies of his new album to try and ward off the more ruthless members of the British press corps, but the plan backfired when his caustic "anti–Beatle/Lennon" remarks added yet more fuel to the fire. Paul's personal Declaration of Independence caused quite a furor among London's gossip mongers but made little impression on John Lennon, who only regretted not being the first Beatle to bail out of the flagging supergroup!

QUESTION   Why did you decide to make a solo album?

PAUL McCARTNEY   Because I got a Studer four-track recording machine at home, practiced on it, liked the results, and decided to make it into an album.

QUESTION   Were you influenced by John's adventures with the Plastic Ono Band?

PAUL   Sort of, but not really.

QUESTION   Are all the songs by Paul McCartney alone?

PAUL   Yes, sir.

QUESTION   Will they be so credited?

PAUL   It's a bit daft for them to be Lennon/McCartney–credited, so "McCartney" it is.

QUESTION   Did you enjoy working as a solo artist?

PAUL   Very much. As I only had *me* to ask for a decision, and I generally agreed with myself! Remember, Linda's on it too, so it's really a double act.

QUESTION   What is Linda's contribution?

PAUL   Strictly speaking, she harmonizes, but of course it's more than that, because she's a shoulder to lean on, a second opinion, and a photographer of renown. More than all this, she believes in me, constantly.

QUESTION   The album was not known about until it was nearly completed. Was this deliberate?

PAUL   Yes, because normally an album is old before it even comes out. Witness "Let It Be."

QUESTION   Why?

PAUL   I've always wanted to buy a Beatles album like "people" do and be as surprised as they must be. So this was the next best thing. Linda and I are the only two who will be sick of it by the release date. But we love it really.

QUESTION   Assuming all the songs are new to the public, how new are they to you?

PAUL   One was from 1959 — "Hot As Sun" — two from India — "Junk," "Teddy Boy" — and the rest are all pretty recent.

QUESTION   Why did you play all the instruments yourself?

PAUL   I think I'm pretty good.

QUESTION   Will Paul and Linda become a John and Yoko?

PAUL   No, they will become a Paul and Linda.

QUESTION   What has recording alone taught you?

PAUL   That to make your own decisions about what you do is easy, and playing with yourself is very difficult but satisfying.

QUESTION   Is it true that neither Allen Klein nor ABKCO have been nor will be in any way involved with the production, manufacturing, or promotion of this new album?

PAUL   Not if I can help it!

QUESTION   Did you miss the other Beatles and George Martin? Was there a moment when you thought, "I wish Ringo were here for this break?"

PAUL   No!

QUESTION   Assuming this is a very big hit album, will you do another?

PAUL   Even if it isn't, I will continue to do what I want, when I want.

Paul's first official promotional shot as a solo performer.

Paul McCartney in the late sixties.

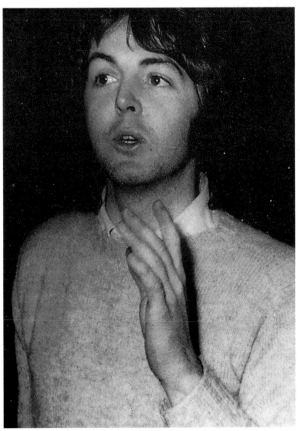

QUESTION   Are you planning a new album or single with the Beatles?

PAUL   No.

QUESTION   Is this album a rest away from the Beatles or the start of a solo career?

PAUL   Time will tell. Being a solo means it's "the start of a solo career . . ." and not being done with the Beatles means it's just a rest. So it's both really.

QUESTION   Is your break with the Beatles temporary or permanent, due to personal differences or musical ones?

PAUL   Personal differences, business differences, musical differences, but most of all because I have a better time with my family. Temporary or permanent? I don't really know.

QUESTION   Do you foresee a time when Lennon/McCartney becomes an active songwriting partnership again?

PAUL   No.

QUESTION   What do you feel about John's peace efforts? The Plastic Ono Band? Giving back his MBE? Yoko's influence?

PAUL   I love John and respect what he does, but it doesn't really give me any pleasure.

QUESTION   Were any of the songs on the album originally written with the Beatles in mind?

PAUL   The older ones were. "Junk" was intended for "Abbey Road," but something happened. "Teddy Boy" was for "Let It Be," but something happened again.

QUESTION   Were you pleased with "Abbey Road?" Was it musically restricting?

PAUL   It was a good album (number one for a long time).

QUESTION   What is your relationship with Klein?

PAUL   It isn't. I am not in contact with him, and he does not represent me in *any* way.

QUESTION   What is your relationship with Apple?

PAUL   It is the office of a company which I partly own with the other three Beatles. I don't go there because I don't like offices *or* business, especially when I am on holiday.

QUESTION   Have you any plans to set up an independent production company?

PAUL   Yes, McCartney Productions.

QUESTION   What are your plans now? A holiday? A musical? A movie? Retirement?

PAUL   My only plan is to grow up!

Arriving at Abbey Road for work on the "white" album.

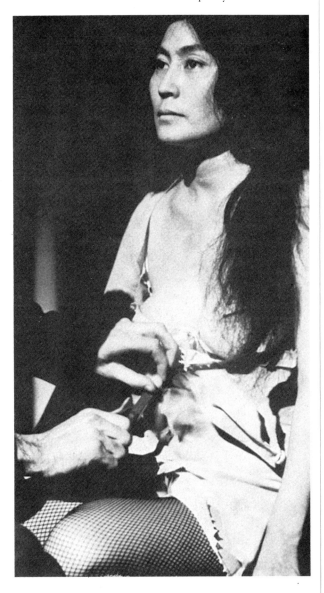

In her famous "Cut Piece" at the "Destruction of Art" symposium in London, 1966, Yoko allowed the audience to snip away pieces of her clothing until she was left completely naked.

The final, formal end of the Beatles came about almost as casually as their getting together in the first place. In June 1970 Lee Eastman wrote to Allen Klein, politely requesting that the Beatles' partnership be dissolved immediately. Hoping that the Beatles could somehow settle their differences amicably and carry on making music — and millions — Klein tried to sidestep the inevitable confrontation with Eastman by simply ignoring the request. Paul, however, was not so content to let it be and late that August dashed off a terse note to John suggesting that the Beatles break up once and for all. Four months later, on December 31, 1970, tired of the insufferable rows and anxious to put the group behind him, McCartney filed suit against the Beatles and Company. For John, Paul, George, and Ringo the dream was over, but an astronomically expensive legal nightmare had just begun that would take well over a decade to resolve.

One individual who was very closely associated with John and Yoko toward the end of the sixties is rock commentator Ritchie Yorke. During 1969 and 1970, while they were still intensely committed to their campaign for global peace, Ritchie spent more time with them than probably even the other Beatles. He was a highly visible member of their entourage as they shuffled around the world spreading the good word in Denmark, London, and Ritchie's adopted homeland of Canada. When not traveling with the couple, the young Australian-born writer could usually be found acting as their private press liaison or peace envoy in such countries as Japan, Thailand, Italy, France, Australia, Holland, America, and even the People's Republic of China. In addition, Ritchie collaborated with John and Yoko on the creation of many of their famous programs, including their infamous peace festival, the International Peace Vote, the Year One A.P. (After Peace) campaign, their "Live Peace In Toronto" concert, and the "War Is Over If You Want It" poster project. He also organized numerous press conferences, business meetings, and social events for the outrageous, peace-loving husband-and-wife team. In the hectic aftermath of the Beatles' breakup in 1970, Ritchie went back home to Canada, where he resumed his career as author and journalist. He was interviewed in Toronto late in 1984.

GEOFFREY   How did you first become associated with John?

RITCHIE YORKE   Well, in 1968 he was starting to move away from the Beatles and doing things by himself, like the Plastic Ono Band. I was working for the *Globe and Mail* in Toronto in those days, so I wanted to interview John and find out about his various activities.

GEOFFREY   Let me ask you about Apple. What kind of place was it?

RITCHIE   It was chaos. It was a great *idea* — very groovy, you know — but in a practical sense it was absurd. A lot of the employees were just milking it dry. It was a giant game. Swinging London was at its height, and the ultimate thing to do was to work at Apple.

Ritchie Yorke and Ronnie Hawkins offer a unique "message to Mao" at the Chinese border. 1969.

GEOFFREY   You were around the Beatles when they were beginning to realize that Apple was never going to work, is that right?

RITCHIE   Yeah, it was starting to go a bit sour. There were some very unpleasant meetings with everyone shouting and screaming at each other. John was trying to get Allen Klein in as their manager, and Paul wanted his father-in-law, Lee Eastman, running things. It was a very dodgy scene.

GEOFFREY   How did John relate to you his feelings about the Beatles?

RITCHIE   The Beatles were over as far as John was concerned. Phil Spector was remixing "Let It Be," and none of them even showed up at any of the sessions because no one really liked the album. John just didn't want to be a part of it anymore. And of course they couldn't be bothered doing the sort of things he wanted to do. They were always off on holiday somewhere, it seemed. I mean, the drive of the group had almost completely gone by late 1968. "Abbey Road" was basically done with each of the guys in the studio separately. It wasn't a group effort anymore. As a matter of fact Paul put together that whole medley on side two almost entirely on his own.

GEOFFREY   How were John and Paul interacting at this point?

RITCHIE   It was bitter, very bitter. John wouldn't go near Paul. John always sent Ringo to do any dirty work with Paul.

GEOFFREY   Surely Yoko was a catalyst in the breakup, wasn't she?

RITCHIE   Not really. That's not to say, however, that John didn't impose her presence on them — he certainly did. During the filming of *Let It Be*, for instance, John would never have been there if Yoko wasn't included, and that, of course, helped to build up the Beatles' resentment against her. It wasn't Yoko's idea to try and snuggle up to the Beatles or anyone else, for that matter. John wanted to demonstrate his independence from the Beatles in a very practical way. He was basically saying, "Hey, I do what I like, boys, and you do what you like." That was his attitude.

GEOFFREY   How did you go from interviewing a guy to becoming one of his closest associates, Ritchie?

RITCHIE   We just happened to hit it off, I guess. Actually, I realized that John wanted to make some serious statements with his music in the face of everything that was happening in the late sixties, and I just wanted to lend a hand if I could.

GEOFFREY   So give me a typical day in the life of John Lennon during the final days of the Apple kingdom.

RITCHIE   Well, they'd drive in from Tittenhurst Park and arrive at the office at around eleven o'clock in the morning. Then they'd usually just stay in the office for the afternoon and see people, generally people they felt were important to the youth movement. For example, Tom Donahue, the guy who started underground radio, came by a few times, as did Ken Kesey and the poet Richard Brautigan. I mean, everyone would be trying to hit on them in those days. Remember, John and Yoko were the world's most famous couple. They also had a few friends from the media who dropped in occasionally, like Ray Connolly from the *Evening Standard*. Believe me, it was a real zoo. Very often some kid with an idea would get John's ear (if he happened to be there when the phones had stopped ringing), and John would invariably give him his shot.

GEOFFREY   John and Yoko traveled to Denmark in 1970. Did you accompany them on that trip?

RITCHIE   Yeah, and quite a "trip" it was, too. They went to Denmark to meet with Yoko's ex-husband, Anthony Cox, and see Yoko's little daughter, Kyoko. We all stayed at his farmhouse in the middle of this great snowy expanse in the Jutland region of Denmark. Cox made the two of them go through a kind of purification process before he'd allow them to see Kyoko. So they fasted for a few days, meditated, and some guy named Dr. Don Hamrik, who fancied himself a warlock, tried to hypnotize them into giving up smoking. John and I had to sneak outside whenever we wanted a smoke! And last but not least, Cox somehow managed to talk them into getting their hair chopped off in celebration of the new decade. So I arranged for this lady barber called Aase Hankrogh to come out from the hotel in Aalborg and do the job. The next morning every paper in the world carried the story in banner headlines!

GEOFFREY   What were John's spiritual beliefs at that time?

RITCHIE   He was into peace and human beings. A very intense humanist.

GEOFFREY   Tell me about the bed-in in Montreal. What did they hope to accomplish with that?

RITCHIE   Publicity for peace. Remember, they couldn't get into the States, but they wanted to get their peace message across to the nerve centers of the world. In England they were considered a bad joke by the media, so they couldn't very well do it there. They did a bed-in in Amsterdam originally, but the idea was always to get the attention of America. They flew down to the Bahamas, but it was too hot there to stay in bed for a week and still a bit too far removed from the American press corps, so they settled for Montreal. It was about as close as they could get.

GEOFFREY   You traveled on your own quite a bit for John during the campaign, right?

RITCHIE   Ronnie Hawkins and I both went around the world spreading John's peace message. The idea was to try and set up John and Yoko centers everywhere so that we could produce their events internationally. We planned on using Telstar at one point in order to syndicate things like the peace festival. Anyway, in Hong Kong someone at a press conference said, "Okay, it's fine telling us all this, we think peace is great, but why don't you go and tell the Red Chinese!" So we said "Sure" and had one of the locals paint up a couple of "WAR IS OVER" signs for us. So we climbed into an old beat-up Volkswagen with a local reporter named Sybil Wong and a couple of photographers and drove down to the first border checkpoint at

With the press in Toronto's King Edward Hotel.

In Toronto. 1969.

133

The Beatles' much bootlegged Christmas album. This original can fetch up to $200 at auctions.

WAR IS OVER!

IF YOU WANT IT

Happy Christmas from John & Yoko

Lokmachau. Somehow or other we managed to convince the guards to let us pass, and we just drove right up to the top of this hill, which was the Chinese no-man's-land. Anyway, we held up the signs facing China, and of course immediately all the guards rushed out and were going to arrest us. Well, we talked our way out of that one, but the strange thing was, the next day the CIA confiscated all of our films, as they somehow thought that this little peace protest might escalate into an international incident! Incidentally, a week later someone was shot simply for standing in the same area!

GEOFFREY   Were you aware of that possibility before you went in?

RITCHIE   Oh yes. I didn't care, but Ronnie Hawkins was a little worried about it. Remember, this was long before anyone from the West had gone into China, not even the ping pong players!

GEOFFREY   How did John react?

RITCHIE   He thought it was the greatest thing that happened on the entire trip!

GEOFFREY   Tell me about the infamous Mosport Park John and Yoko Peace Festival.

RITCHIE   Well, the original idea was to hold the biggest music festival of all time.

GEOFFREY   Of course all the Beatles were going to be there.

RITCHIE   Yes, George was agreed, Ringo certainly would have done it, and Paul was yet to be confirmed, but John was very hopeful about it. The intention was to get every major rock star in the world there. Even Elvis was going to do it!

GEOFFREY   Was it to be a free festival, or were people expecting to get paid?

RITCHIE   Well, John wanted everyone to get some money. He figured that no one should be working for nothing, but they were certainly free to donate some of it back into a big peace fund if they wanted to. The main problem with the festival was the total lack of any real organization. It was such a mammoth undertaking that eventually it got buried under the strain of its own weight.

GEOFFREY   Whose idea was it to hold the festival?

RITCHIE   Mainly mine, but the whole thing was being handled by the Brower and Walker agency out of Toronto. I went for the idea because after the incredible success of Woodstock a beautiful sequel devoted to world peace was absolutely the right thing to be doing. Eventually I took off with Ronnie on this global peace tour, and by the time we got back, John and Yoko were becoming pretty disenchanted with the whole thing.

GEOFFREY   Tell me about John and Yoko's meeting with Canadian Prime Minister Pierre Trudeau. Did you arrange it all?

RITCHIE   Yes, we talked to Ottawa from the Bag office quite a few times in order to sound them out.

GEOFFREY   Could John get through to anyone in the world he wanted to?

RITCHIE   Yes, but up until that time no political leader had ever met with him. In England John and Yoko were generally regarded as a big joke. Somehow they managed to antagonize the old establishment something terrible. He had to get through to a prominent politician to lend credibility to his peace movement, and of course we were hoping to try and wrangle an endorsement. Trudeau was willing to meet them as long as there was no advance publicity, so we did it and then announced it afterward.

GEOFFREY   Beyond the publicity, what was the meeting all about?

RITCHIE   Just to talk about peace and music.

GEOFFREY   How was Trudeau disposed toward John and Yoko?

RITCHIE   Very, very friendly. He thought the whole thing was great and even offered the use of the Canadian army for security! John was extremely nervous, having never actually met a world leader on a one-to-one basis before. But afterwards he felt fantastic.

GEOFFREY   What do you think John would have to say about the nature of his own death?

RITCHIE   I think he expected it in a way. There was always the chance it would happen. John was a very misunderstood guy and a sincere, dedicated man as well as a great humanitarian. He believed that things didn't really have to be the way they are. Things could be different if people set their minds to it. And all any of us can do now is to try and keep John's spirit alive.

The Beatles very near the end of their rope together.

7

I'll Be On My Way

The Solo Years

"To get a good relationship between two people is the start. If we two can make it, then possibly we can make it with you. Maybe then you can make it with you and yours. It's only that you know there's no 'big answer'." JOHN LENNON

"The spirit of the Beatles, brash and earnest, was ironic and idealistic all at once. In the 1960s John Lennon and the Beatles captured the imagination of the entire world. In the songs he composed he leaves behind an extraordinary and permanent legacy. His work as an artist was far from done." JIMMY CARTER

"Here lies John Lennon, in life sang many songs
He had his joy and sorrow, was ofttimes sad at heart
May his sleep here be peaceful beneath God's clear blue skies
While passing drop a flower where John Lennon lies." TINY TIM

John at his white piano.

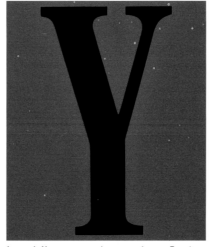

oko Ono was born into a wealthy, aristocratic banking family in Tokyo, Japan, on February 18, 1933, and grew up quietly in an environment of over-protective nannies and servants both at home and abroad in America. But her idiosyncratic mother, Isoko, made sure that Yoko developed a firm sense of independence from the stringent dictates of Japanese patriarchal society. Yoko was educated at the best girls' schools on both sides of the Pacific, ending up at the exclusive Sarah Lawrence in the mid-fifties. Linda Eastman attended the same school, as did noted writer Betty Rollin, who remembers Yoko as rather pushy and overtly ambitious "in much the same way twenty-year-old actresses often are." By this time the intellectually adventurous Yoko had become tired of the tame conventionality of her well-bred classmates and abruptly ended her college career by marrying Japanese avant-garde composer-musician Toshi Ichiyanagi in 1957. Her parents were not happy with their daughter's decision and summarily cut off the newlyweds without so much as a dollar of Yoko's intended dowry.

Life was hard for the rebellious, artistically ambitious young couple, but at least the Village provided them with a safe haven in which to expand their creative talents. Yoko especially enjoyed the offbeat mix of artistic people she met there and quickly became a fixture at all the hippiest

John's guitar rests against his hand-drawn poster promoting love and peace.

underground galleries, comfortably rubbing shoulders with the likes of as yet largely undiscovered artists such as Andy Warhol, Robert Rauschenberg, Claes Oldenburg, composer John Cage, and choreographer Merce Cunningham. Yoko's marriage ended in divorce after only five years. Despondent over the breakup and depressed that her highly conceptual artworks were not being more readily received in America, Yoko decided in 1961 to return to Japan in the hope of receiving a more favorable response to her minimalist, Buddhist-inspired compositions among the intellectual Japanese. However, once again the critics missed the point of her fanciful creations, and in despair she attempted to take her own life. Badly shaken, her family sent her to a mental hospital where she was visited by an old friend from New York, American filmmaker Tony Cox. Shortly thereafter Yoko and Cox were married, and in 1962 their only child, daughter Kyoko, was born.

Returning to New York, the Ono-Coxes settled into their new life together. Then in 1966 Yoko accepted an invitation to participate in something called "The Destruction of Art" symposium in London, England. Excited by the possibility of finally sharing her work with an appropriately intellectual audience, Yoko went on ahead of Tony and Kyoko and set up house in a tiny cold-water flat. Low on cash and on her own, Yoko was nevertheless optimistic about her chances for success in London. The psychedelic season was in full swing, and fortunately for her, many of the illicit chemical compounds making the rounds seemed to open up people's minds to the humor and irony in her highly esoteric art. When Tony arrived, the couple went straight to work producing an outrageous film commentary on people's inhibitions entitled *Bottoms*. Consisting solely of 365 of underground London's most celebrated naked rear ends, the unusual project succeeded in drawing attention to Yoko and Tony and was even favorably reviewed by several of London's most respected art critics, one of whom jokingly called it "totally asinine."

Yoko Ono first met John Lennon on November 9, 1966, at a special VIP preview of her exhibition called "Unfinished Paintings and Objects" at John Dunbar's Indica Gallery. One of her pieces, "Hammer a Nail In," invited the viewer to add to the work by pounding a nail into an all-white plywood box for the princely sum of five shillings. John was, as usual, flat broke, so when he approached the artist to pound in his nail, he wryly suggested he pay with an imaginary coin. Yoko was amused and impressed by John's wit and intelligence, and soon the two became not only close friends but also partners in several artistic ventures together, including another exhibition of Yoko's works entitled "Yoko Plus Me" at the Lisson Gallery and a joint showing in May 1968 at the London Arts Lab. With Yoko's encouragement John even staged his own exhibit, "You Are Here," at the Robert Fraser Gallery in Mayfair in July of that year.

John was thrilled at the prospect of finding someone with whom he could share his innermost thoughts and feelings, but not everyone in the close-knit Beatles circle felt the same. George, for one, never really liked Yoko

The Lennons with Yoko's daughter, Kyoko, in Toronto. 1969.

RICHARD LESTER's
"HOW I WON THE WAR"

MICHAEL CRAWFORD   JOHN LENNON

COLOR   UNITED ARTISTS

A valuable lobby card from the film.

John at the artillery while co-star Michael Crawford looks on in Dick Lester's antiwar classic, *How I Won the War*.

The "Wedding Album," John and Yoko's extravagant gift to their fans. The lavish boxed set included a press book, a replica of their marriage license, a photographic piece of the wedding cake, and the record. Like their previous albums, it didn't fare well with either critics or the public.

John and Yoko during their stay with Ronnie Hawkins in Mississauga, Ontario. December 1969.

and made it clear from the very beginning that he considered her presence in the studio to be an intrusion. He even went so far as to ask Bob Dylan's opinion of her, and Bob none too generously reported back that she was often accused of giving off bad vibes and was maybe even a little crazy. Paul and Linda, too, were cool toward John's new woman and made a point of avoiding any prolonged conversation with her and John if they met them at the office or even out on the town.

It was really only good-natured Ringo and his unassuming wife, Maureen, who genuinely embraced the couple and, when they needed a place to set up house, graciously offered the use of one of their flats in fashionable Montague Square. It was here that many of John and Yoko's most outrageous artistic projects first saw the light of day. "We took the infamous nude "Two Virgins" photo at Ringo's place and even planned several of our first avant-garde happenings there," remembers Yoko. "It was basically very tiny and cluttered but definitely gave us a place to be alone and seriously consider the course we wanted our relationship to take." Other people too, it seemed, had ideas about the happy twosome's unconventional lifestyle. As a result their apartment was unceremoniously raided on October 18, 1968, and they were arrested on drug and obstruction-of-justice charges. To make matters worse, Cynthia Lennon initiated divorce proceedings against John soon afterward, and three weeks later Yoko suffered a dangerous miscarriage.

Despite the many difficulties, however, John and Yoko bounced back and were quietly married on March 20, 1969, in a simple ceremony in Gibraltar. Realizing that their celebrity status would never allow them the luxury of a truly private honeymoon, they jetted off to Amsterdam, where they announced plans to hold a four-day "bed-in for peace" at the Amsterdam Hilton. "What we're really doing is sending out a message to the youth of the world or anybody, really, who's interested in protesting for peace," explained John at the time. "We say that peace can only be achieved through peaceful methods, and to fight the establishment with their own weapons is no good, because they've been winning for thousands of years. But anyone can go to bed for peace or give up a week of their holiday for peace. There are many ways of protesting, and this is simply one of them." Fuelled by an absolute blitz of international media attention for their peaceful passion, the couple soon staged similar happenings in the Bahamas and Montreal later that year.

Some months after the Montreal bed-in, John and Yoko held their first formal press conference at the Ontario Science Centre in Toronto to announce plans for the John and Yoko Peace Festival to be held at Mosport Park in the summer. Ambling fearlessly into the lion's den dressed all in black, John and Yoko took their place center stage among the reporters and dived right into the session. Questioned on everything from what they thought about reincarnation to which kind of toothpaste they preferred, the couple remained good-natured under the cross-examination and fielded many difficult inquiries with the aplomb of seasoned politicians.

Arriving at the Toronto "Peace Conference."

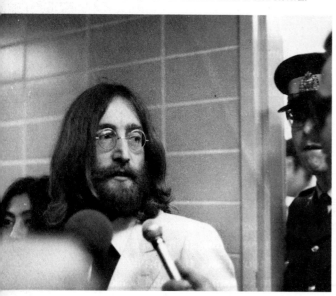

John backstage at Varsity Stadium waiting to perform at the Toronto Rock 'n' Roll Revival.

QUESTION   There are a lot of experts around the world trying to promote global peace. Why do you feel you can succeed where they have failed?

JOHN LENNON   It's like saying, "Why bother keeping Christianity alive because Jesus was killed." You see, we don't think people have really tried advertising before. I mean, when somebody brings out a new product — let's pretend peace is new, as we've never had it — they start advertising. Now whatever gimmickry is happening during the advert, it's the drink or the car that people go out and buy in the end.

QUESTION   How do you answer accusations that the kind of thing you are doing is bordering on naiveté?

JOHN   If anybody thinks our campaign is naive, then that's okay, let them do something else, and if we like the idea maybe we'll join in! But otherwise we'll carry on. We're artists — not politicians, not newspapermen, and not anything. We do things the way that suits us best. Publicity is our game, and because of the Beatles that's the trade I've learned.

QUESTION   I remember you saying you thought we'd have peace by the year 2000. Do you still believe that?

JOHN   I'd sooner say 1970. You see, I believe in positive thinking. I think we'll get it as soon as people realize that they have the power, and it doesn't solely belong to Mr. Trudeau, Mr. Wilson, or Mr. Nixon. The people are the power, and they can have whatever they want. And if it's a case of people not knowing what to do, then let's advertise and let them know they have a real option.

QUESTION   But what can they do?

JOHN   They've got the vote, haven't they? I mean, the youth will be the establishment soon, so there's no point in breaking it down, because we'll just have to build it up again. That's all we're saying.

QUESTION   Are there any circumstances in which you personally could support a war?

JOHN   No. I don't believe in killing, whatever the reason.

QUESTION   What is the possibility that your manner of clothing and hairstyle will tend to alienate more people than it would ever convince to come over to your side?

JOHN   Yes, I understand that. Many people say to me, "Why don't you get a butch haircut and a nice suit." (*Laughter*) But that's what the politicians do! I just try and be as natural as I can under the circumstances. We both do.

QUESTION   John, you are now endowed with more influence over the young people in the world than all the bishops, rabbis, and priests put together. Do you ever feel any sense of fright at the power you have?

JOHN   It's a very abstract power though. Say we wanted to plug a certain product that wasn't peace, and I contacted the press people I know and

Giving peace a chance.

At the Queen Elizabeth Hotel in Montreal, June 1, 1969, during their bed-in for peace.

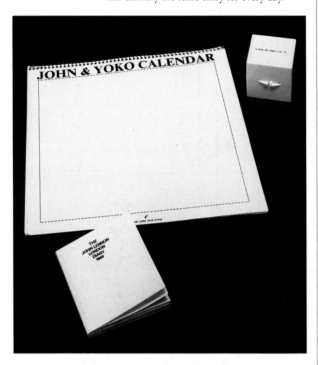

Three conceptual art pieces by John and Yoko. *Left to right* Their thirteen-month calendar, Yoko's "Box of Smile," and John's "London Diary," which had basically the same entry for every day.

tried to get it over, there's a very good chance it wouldn't work. So I haven't really got a power I can get hold of.

QUESTION   Do you believe in God?

JOHN   Yes. I believe He's like a vast powerhouse, but He's neither good nor bad nor left, right, black, or white. And that we can tap into that supreme source of power and make of it what we will. With electricity, you can kill people in an electric chair or you can light the room. I just think God *is*.

YOKO ONO   Also, we talk a lot about having a great belief in youth, but you know, youth includes everybody that is mentally or spiritually youthful.

QUESTION   It's been said that Jesus made the mistake of trying to save the whole world as one man. Is this why you don't believe in leadership?

JOHN   I just believe that father figures are the big mistake of all the generations before us, and we can't rely solely on Nixon or Jesus or whoever we tend to rely on. It's just a lack of responsibility on our part to expect somebody to do it for us. The Beatles were never leaders, you know, but people imagined we were, and now they're finding out the truth.

QUESTION   Could you give us your personal definition of peace?

JOHN   Peace? Just no violence, and everybody grooving, if you don't mind me using the word. Of course we all have violence within us, but we must learn to channel it. We have a hard time making people think we mean what we say in Britain. It's like telling your parents, "Look, I want my hair long." We consider this like our Cavern period now. We haven't really gotten out of Liverpool with this campaign yet, and we've got to break London and America. It's like that. I don't care how long it takes or what obstacles there are. We won't ever stop, you know.

QUESTION   Is there any one particular incident that got you started on this peace campaign?

JOHN   It just built up over a number of years actually, but the thing that really struck it off was a letter we got from a guy called Peter Watkins who made a film called *The War Game*. It was a very long letter stating just what's happening — how the media is really controlled, how it's all run, and everything else that people really know deep down. He said, "People in your position have a responsibility to use the media for world peace." And we sat on the letter for about three weeks thinking, "Well, we're doing our best. All you need is love, man." That letter just sort of sparked it all off. It was like getting your induction papers for peace!

QUESTION   Are you still as involved in Eastern philosophy as you once were, John?

JOHN   If I'm involved in anything, it's Yoko's version of Zen Buddhism. All the philosophies have a good basis, and all the religions are right. But I just haven't the time or the capability of reading through two million years of philosophy. Because to me the only answer is "yes" and "now."

Dressed in full balaclava headgear, John and Yoko hover over the tiny market square of Lavenham, Suffolk, during the shooting of one of their experimental, avant-garde shorts for Bag Productions. December 6, 1970.

QUESTION   How about meditation?

JOHN   Occasionally I use it. I'm not really very good at getting up in the morning and doing my exercises, you know. Meditation is a mental exercise. It works all right, it definitely does all they say.

YOKO   And our mantra is "Peace," thankfully.

QUESTION   Do you think the peace movement could be a solution for the problems that a lot of young people are having today with drugs?

JOHN   Everybody seems to need something, the way society is, because of the pressures. I know the only time we ever took drugs was when we were without hope. And the only way we got out of it was through hope. If we can sustain that, then we won't need drugs, liquor, or anything.

QUESTION   But could you have ever achieved that hope without the success of the Beatles behind you?

JOHN   The Beatles made it four years ago, stopped touring, had all the money and fame they wanted, and found out they had nothing. And then we started on our various LSD trips, the Maharishi, and all the other mad things we did. It's the old line about money, power, and fame not being the answer. We didn't lack hope just because we were famous though. I mean, Marilyn Monroe and all those other people had all the things the Beatles had but were still very unhappy. John and Yoko have the same problems, fears, hopes, and aspirations that any other couple on earth has, regardless of the position we're in or the money we have. We have exactly the same paranoias as everybody else, the same petty thoughts — everything goes just the same for us. We have no super answers that came through the Beatles or their power. The Beatles in that respect are irrelevant to what I'm talking about.

QUESTION   As a result of the Beatles, though, you are in a better position to go around the world and see these things that other people cannot.

JOHN   Ah yes. But Yoko wasn't a Beatle, but she had hope and was doing things for peace without being in a bloody pop group! Yoko and I were in different bags originally, but we both had a very positive side. I was singing "All You Need Is Love," and she was protesting in Trafalgar Square in a black bag. When we met we only had one thing in common: we were in love. But love is just a gift, and it doesn't answer everything. It's like a precious plant that you have to nurture and look after. What goes with love, we thought, was peace. We were planning on getting married, then not getting married, thinking what we're going to do and how we're going to do it. So we finally said, "All right, all right, what can we do together?" Yoko can't really come play with the Beatles and sing about peace, and I'm certainly not going to stand around Trafalgar Square in a bag, because I'm too frightened. Anyway, we went through every possible way of doing something for peace until we came up with the bed event. You see, we knew we were going to get press, so we had two choices — hiding from the press and having them all around as we were having our honeymoon or just

Mr. and Mrs. Lennon meet Canada's charismatic former prime minister, Pierre Trudeau. Ottawa 1970.

Sending out a strong message.

saying, "Okay, we give in. Ask any questions you want, for seven days and all the time we'll just keep plugging peace," and that's how it all got started.

YOKO   I think we were really meant to meet, you know. I didn't realize it at first because I was such a thoroughly conceited artist. I thought I was doing brilliantly as far as my protests were concerned. But then we met and started to fill each other in with our ideas. I've always thought that it's better to work on your own, but it's not.

JOHN   Two heads are definitely better than one!

Ronnie Hawkins, Canada's number-one rockabilly singer known affectionately to his fans as "the Hawk," prefers these days to be referred to as "a legend in his *spare* time." During the Lennons' 1969 international peace blitz, the couple touched down briefly at Ronnie's Mississauga, Ontario, farm and immediately proceeded to turn the rocker's life into a whirl of more congenial craziness than anyone around those parts had seen before or since. Erotic lithographs were signed, garages set on fire, joints smoked, ceilings washed away, and two of the Lennons' peace doves eaten by a crafty weasel. Still, Ronnie treasures it all and, despite the $16,000 phone bill John accidentally left behind, feels it was worth every penny. We talked about all this and more in Toronto in January 1985 during a break in a photo session for the cover of Ronnie's latest album.

GEOFFREY   So tell me, Ronnie, how did John and Yoko come to live with you?

RONNIE HAWKINS   Well, I got a phone call from England one day from John's right-hand man, Anthony Fawcett, who asked me if they could stay at my house, as they'd just been through the bed-in and wanted some privacy.

GEOFFREY   You never knew John before he rang you up?

RONNIE   I'd met him when the Beatles played Maple Leaf Gardens in Toronto. I didn't really know him though — just enough to say hello. When I met the Beatles at the Gardens, they were familiar with some of my old tunes I had out in the fifties, because I'd been to England long before they'd even gotten into music. I'd done a couple of TV shows over there, and if you watched TV at all you had to see me, because the BBC has only one or two channels and that's it.

GEOFFREY   So what did you say to Fawcett?

RONNIE   I said it would be fine because I lived out in Mississauga on a farm, so it wasn't very crowded. They wanted to be out in the country, but someplace where they could still get into town for business. Anthony said it would mean a lot of good publicity for us, and there was also their peace festival, which I'd heard quite a lot about, so there was a lot happening. Then there was that damn phone bill affair. It wasn't really John's fault that

I got stuck with it, you know. It ended up being about sixteen thousand dollars and change, I think!

GEOFFREY   What happened?

RONNIE   Well, the peace festival just went bankrupt, so I was stuck with all the bills. I learned a good lesson from that one, all right!

GEOFFREY   There's a story about John and Yoko taking a bath at your house.

RONNIE   Yeah, they went upstairs to run the water, went to sleep, and simply forgot all about the tub. I finally said, "Anthony, look, the ceiling is coming in," so he went up and knocked on the door, but nobody ever wanted to disturb them. Anthony was the one in between them and everybody else, because they certainly couldn't talk to everybody. It was very embarrassing for them at times, I think. John had an awful lot of fun though. I had some skidoos out back, and evidently he'd never done any of that, because I was told later that he ordered three or four of them and had them sent over to his home in England. I saw that John was being bugged quite enough by everybody else, so all I did was show him where the bedroom was and then stayed completely clear. If they said hello in the morning I'd say hello, and that was about it.

GEOFFREY   How did you get involved with the "War Is Over" poster campaign? You were at your house in Mississauga one minute, and the next thing we know you're in Red China protesting for John!

RONNIE   They just took a liking to me, I guess, especially John. At that time we were talking about the "Land of Bag." I don't know whether you've heard about that or not. The Land of Bag was a conceptual country that Yoko tried to have become a member of the United Nations! It's imaginary of course, but it was to be a place with all the right laws and rules. No guns at all, and everybody would always be happy and helping one another out.

GEOFFREY   And you were an ambassador?

RONNIE   No, John wanted me to be the first knight — "Sir Ronald the Good Knight," he called me. So I got down on my knees and went through the whole thing just like it was really ancient England.

GEOFFREY   So you got caught up in his vision, then?

RONNIE   Oh yeah. He said to me, "It's just a dream, you know, but it could be reality. All people would have to do is stop being so greedy. Just stop the fighting, and the world would be an unbelievable place. There's no reason for anyone to ever steal or hurt anyone in Bag Land because people would already have everything they ever wanted."

GEOFFREY   So tell me, Sir Ronald, about when John sent you on your first international mission to preach the gospel of Bag.

RONNIE   Well, at that time Ritchie Yorke was one of the top writers for *Rolling Stone* magazine, and they were behind it all, so we went right around the globe together. I was promoting my new album, and Ritchie

John rides an Amphicat snow vehicle at Ronnie Hawkins's Mississauga, Ontario, farm. December 1969.

Relaxing in Montreal during a lull in the madness of the bed-in.

was organizing the peace conference to help spread John and Yoko's philosophy. John asked me to do all this stuff for them, and they called a few people in Japan for us, so it was just unreal. The connections Yoko had all over the world were absolutely unbelievable. I don't think anybody since World War Two had been treated as well as I was in Japan! Yoko put out the front grease for me, right? I saw things that very few people have ever seen, I'm sure. The underground movement in Japan was very highly organized. I mean, they were five hundred thousand strong and could be mobilized and out on the streets in about an hour!

GEOFFREY After you did the Chinese border protest, Ritchie said you phoned John at home and told him about it.

RONNIE Well, actually, it hit the front page of every paper in Hong Kong. I was a little nervous because I knew my room had been searched many times by several different international agencies. The only thing that separates Hong Kong from mainland China is just a barrier in the road, you know.

GEOFFREY How do you remember John?

RONNIE I remember John as being exactly the opposite of what I had expected.

GEOFFREY Cynical, mean, and egotistical?

RONNIE Yeah, that's what you'd expect from somebody who was such a superhero, and I was really very surprised he handled things the way he did — after I saw everything he had to go through just to keep from making people mad at him. No wonder they hid out in their room every night. I wouldn't want to see anybody I didn't have to either.

GEOFFREY What about Yoko?

RONNIE Well, Yoko was very different. She was so educated she was very much above and beyond me. She could speak, read, and write about eight different languages.

GEOFFREY Could you understand the attraction between John and Yoko?

RONNIE I couldn't really, no, because when I look at John, the leader of the Beatles, I know he could have had fifteen or twenty of the most glamorous movie stars in the world swarming all over him.

GEOFFREY He got tired of it though, Ronnie, I'm sure.

RONNIE Yeah, he probably did. He probably wanted someone as intelligent as Yoko who had some highly creative ideas of her own.

GEOFFREY Anything else you'd like to say about John?

RONNIE Just that to me he was so damn sensible. Really more like a humble English country boy than a big rock star. Yoko was more business-minded, it seemed to me. She talked straight-ahead business, whereas John worried about people's feelings much more than Yoko did. If Yoko didn't like somebody she would just say, "We don't want anything to do with you," because she could see right through people. John could see

John and Yoko rap with reporters about world peace at the Ontario Science Centre. Toronto 1969.

An unpublished shot of John during sessions for his "Imagine" album at his own Ascot Studios at Tittenhurst Park.

through people too, I think, but he didn't ever want to hurt anybody's feelings.

Despite their well-known sociopolitical escapades John and Yoko were amazingly productive during the final hectic days of the late sixties. From mid-1968 to December 1969 they recorded four albums together: the highly experimental "Unfinished Music No. 1 — Two Virgins," "Unfinished Music No. 2 — Life With The Lions," the lavishly packaged multimedia souvenir of their wedding entitled "Wedding Album," and the hard-rocking soundtrack of John's first public foray sans the Beatles, "Live Peace In Toronto." They also produced a number of semiautobiographical, avant-garde films that showed their keen eye for cinematic introspection and surreal juxtaposition of time and space.

Yoko herself published a clever collection of instructional poetry entitled *Grapefruit* and recorded four solo albums for Apple over a three-year period: "The Plastic Ono Band — Yoko Ono," "Fly," "Approximately Infinite Universe," and "Feeling The Space." In addition, John produced six top-selling albums during the seventies: "The Plastic Ono Band — John Lennon," "Imagine," "Mind Games," "Walls And Bridges," "Rock 'N' Roll," and "Shaved Fish."

By late 1971, though, the Lennons had tired of the laid-back lifestyle they were living in England and returned to New York for good. In June 1972 their fifth and perhaps most uninspired joint album was released. Aptly entitled "Sometime In New York City," it was supposed to be a sort of *Threepenny Opera* gone rock but ended up sounding somewhat haphazard and almost trivial. Nevertheless, it represented two important milestones in the couple's whirlwind life together. First, its blatantly left-wing lyrics aroused the suspicions of the conservative Nixon government, leading to John's difficulties with the immigration department. Second, it was the last time John and Yoko seriously recorded together until "Double Fantasy" was released in 1980. Hard times temporarily subsided, however, when on October 7, 1975, the U.S. District Court of Appeals overturned a previous deportation order against John and ended his three-year battle to live and work in America. Two days later, on John's thirty-fifth birthday, Sean Ono Taro Lennon was born. "I feel as high as the Empire State Building!" declared John to a crowd of reporters. "God bless America!" For the next five years John devoted himself exclusively to looking after Sean. "It seems as if I've been under contract to produce a hit record, artsy book, or some daft film since I was about fifteen, and now I'm tired. I've made my contribution, and it's time to just cool out and be with my family," John said at the time. "I quit. Let someone else carry it on from here." Thus the self-described "male chauvinist piglet" became the world's most celebrated househusband, steadfastly shunning all offers to either perform or record.

What followed then for the Lennon clan were five years of relative peace and contentment punctuated only by periods of world travel to such places

In the studio with the sixties' whiz kid of pop, Phil Spector.

At the opening of Yoko's one-woman show at the Everson Museum of Art, Syracuse.

as India, Egypt, the Bahamas, and Yoko's native Japan. Then in August 1980 John and Yoko began to record what was to become possibly their best-known work together, "Double Fantasy." An ambitious world tour was planned to promote the album starting in Japan and working its way westward to New York via Europe. But it was not to be. For on December 8, 1980, at 10:49 P.M., John Ono Lennon was gunned down in front of his apartment building while Yoko looked on in horror. The assassin was subsequently arrested and sentenced to twenty years in prison; but simply knowing that justice has been done cannot possibly begin to mitigate the tremendous loss to the world of John Lennon's masterful wit, generous intelligence, and beautiful, insightful music. Above all, one fact becomes painfully clear: we have lost a genuine pioneer of the human spirit whose like we will probably not see again in our lifetimes.

After the Beatles' bubble finally burst, Ringo Starr was left the most uncertain as to what direction his career should take. Ironically, his initial solo recording was actually released in 1970, while the Beatles were still working together. Entitled "Sentimental Journey," the album featured twelve easy-listening standards including "Bye Bye Blackbird" and "Night And Day." "I wanted to do something me mum and her friends would enjoy," said Ringo. Always a devoted fan of good old American hillbilly music, Ringo's next LP, released later that year, was a salute to his favorite country tunes recorded in Nashville with the aid of veteran producer and musician "Sneaky" Pete Drake. Both the album and the single were called "Beaucoups Of Blues," and while neither did exceptionally well in the charts, they did show that Ringo was every bit as versatile as his fans had always suspected. Next came the well-known "Ringo" album in 1973, with all four former Fabs pitching in to make it a success by contributing several catchy tunes — "I'm The Greatest" (John), "Six O'Clock" (Paul and Linda), and "Sunshine Life For Me (Sail Away Raymond)," "You And Me (Babe)," and "Photograph" (George and company). Produced by Los Angeles bigwig Richard Perry, the slick, good-natured disc surprised no one by sending two tunes, "You're Sixteen" and "Photograph," straight to number one in the U.S. in just a few short weeks. So positive was the response that John Lennon even sent Ringo a telegram wistfully entreating him to "write *me* a number-one tune!"

Inspired by this acclaim, Ringo threw himself enthusiastically into his next recording project, "Goodnight Vienna." John composed the catchy title track and assisted in its production, and the album also featured a tune called "Snookeroo," written by Elton John. Released in late 1974, several cuts did a fine job of showcasing Ringo's talent for doing schmaltzy pop rock. But it was the campy, sci-fi jacket art, depicting Starr as an alien landing his souped-up flying saucer on earth, that stole the show. Unfortunately the record-buying natives weren't very friendly, and the album failed

John's personal reference card from Barclays Bank of New York.

Part of the promotion for John's "Walls And Bridges."

JOHN LENNON

051-84350-1

117 ~~3254~~

BARCLAYS BANK OF NEW YORK is hereby authorized to recognize any of the signatures below in the payment of funds or the transaction of any business for this account. It is agreed that all transactions between the Bank and the undersigned shall be subject to the Account Agreement, the rules and regulations of the Bank, and the Uniform Commercial Code and other laws of the State of New York.

☑ Individual   ☐ Partnership   ☐ Trade Style   ☐ ....

Signatures: Required - 1 (For Mr. Lennon) "or" 2 Attorneys. All checks in excess of $2500.00 are to be signed only by Mr. Lennon

H. Comart   Helen Z. Bikman   David Miller   Gertrude Levine

Date Opened ....   Initial Deposit $ ....   Account Accepted by ....

Tax ID # 127-52-1582

REGULAR CHECKING ACCOUNT

SIG 1-(9-68)

John and Yoko stroll through Central Park in the summer of 1980. John decided to cut his hair just days after this photo was taken because he believed his long, flowing locks made him too easily recognizable to his many New York fans.

to fly. Ringo was busy meanwhile forming his own label, Ring O'Records, to help develop new talent and oversee his personal business interests, but the ill-fated venture soon bottomed out after only one album and three singles.

"Blast From Your Past," Ringo's fifth release on Apple, was also the last Apple album ever. Issued in the U.S. in November 1975, this compilation of his greatest hits sold well and delivered exactly what it promised — the very best of Ringo's recorded works from the previous five years. Included were "It Don't Come Easy," "Back Off Boogaloo," "Early 1970," and "Photograph," among others. By March 1976 Ringo had parted company with EMI and was now signed to Polydor. In September they released his first album under the new contract, called "Ringo's Rotogravure." Produced by the legendary Arif Mardin, it featured three tunes from his old partners including John's "Cookin' In The Kitchen Of Love," George's "I'll Still Love You," and Paul's "Pure Gold." The next year Ringo released "Ringo The Fourth" for the Atlantic label. Once again a lineup of the most impressive Los Angeles session musicians was assembled, but sales were disastrously low, and his contract was summarily canceled. Ringo then moved on to the CBS-owned Portrait label, where he produced "Bad Boy" with his old pal Vini Poncia. This time public response was even more negative, and consequently Ringo's recording career hit an all-time low.

Plagued by a series of stubborn health problems, Ringo lay low during most of 1979 but resurfaced early in 1980 to begin filming the prehistoric comedy *Caveman*. Co-starring was the lovely American actress Barbara Bach (whose film credits included *The Spy Who Loved Me* and *Force Ten from Navarone*). Ringo was soon very much in love. Fortunately Barbara reciprocated, and by the end of filming the happy couple were already hinting at marriage. For the first time in many years Ringo was a truly happy man. He and friend Harry Nilsson planned to holiday in the Bahamas and then travel on to New York with Barbara and friends to work with John Lennon on "Life Begins At Forty," his contribution to Ringo's forthcoming LP, "Can't Fight Lightning." All that changed forever when Ringo received word of John's death. Several months later the LP was released, but without John's tune and with a new, more appropriate title, "Stop And Smell The Roses."

On his own, George Harrison was finally free to pursue his solo interests without the many constraints of being a Beatle. His first project was to ready for release the ambitious three-album set he'd been working on since the latter days of the Fabs, "All Things Must Pass." Culled from an extensive backlog of material, the package boasted several hits. Foremost was "My Sweet Lord" followed by "What Is Life," the Bob Dylan composition "If Not For You," and the ethereal "Isn't It A Pity." The 1970 set reached number one in both Britain and America — an auspicious start to George's career.

The Lennons arrive for the final mixdown of their
last album together, "Double Fantasy."

In Manhattan only weeks before his death.

A year later Apple released George's next project, the celebrated
"Concert For Bangla Desh" featuring old friends Bob Dylan, Eric Clapton,
Ravi Shankar, Ringo Starr, Leon Russell, Billy Preston, Badfinger, and a
host of pop's most celebrated sidemen and backup vocalists. The star-
studded benefit was held on August 1, 1971, at Madison Square Garden
and raised upwards of $12 million. George's next release, in 1973, was the
hauntingly beautiful "Living In The Material World." Although many found
its soulful, Krsna-consciousness meanderings something less than inspira-
tional, it sold reasonably well and was a milestone in George's long and
winding road to success as a first-rate craftsman of finely tuned, intelligent
music. It also yielded one smash hit with "Give Me Love."

George soon began to feel restless, however, so in the fall of 1974 he
embarked on an ambitious solo tour of North America under the banner
"George Harrison and Friends." As it turned out, the list of friends was long
and impressive and included Ravi Shankar (complete with a superb sixteen-
piece Indian orchestra), George's old pal Billy Preston, ace horn player and
arranger Tom Scott, powerhouse bassist Willie Weeks, super session guitarist Robben Ford, and the well-known percussionist Andy Newmark.

Organized and promoted by the legendary rock 'n' roll impresario Bill
Graham, the tour kicked off with much publicity in Vancouver but soon
turned into a veritable media circus. Right off the bat many reviewers
objected to the inclusion of Shankar's "Indo-pop infusions" into the show
and scoffed at George's persistent tirades to "chant the name of the Lord."
Even his upbeat, eclectic music came under fire for being pretentious and
overly preachy. His basically untrained voice became weak and raspy,
slowing the natural momentum of the shows, and the last gig, at New
York's Madison Square Garden, had more stars in the audience than onstage.
All in all not a very good experience, as evidenced by George's refusal to
commit himself to ever touring again. He held a press conference in Los
Angeles just before the ill-fated tour began.

QUESTION   Why did you decide to return to America?

GEORGE HARRISON   Oh, I've been back here many times, but this is the
first time I've had an H-1 working visa since '71. I had the same problem as
John — I was busted for marijuana way back in '67.

QUESTION   Why are you doing this tour?

GEORGE   This is really a test. I either finish this tour ecstatically happy
and want to go on tour everywhere, or I'll end up just going back to my
cave again for another five years.

QUESTION   Looking back, what do you consider the crowning glory of
your career as a musician?

GEORGE   As a musician, I don't think I've achieved that yet, but as an
individual, just being able to sit here today and be relatively sane. That's
probably my biggest accomplishment to date.

QUESTION George, are you involved in any serious negotiations to get the Beatles back together for just one night?

GEORGE No. The point is, it's all just a fantasy. If we ever do play again, the only reason will be because everybody's broke! And even then, to play with the Beatles I'd rather have Willy Weeks on bass than Paul McCartney, and that's the truth with all due respect to Paul. The Beatles were like being in a box, and it's taken years to get comfortable playing with other musicians again, because we were so isolated together. It became very difficult playing the same old tunes day in, day out. When I made "All Things Must Pass," it was so nice for me just to be able to work with other artists. I really don't think the Beatles were all that good, you know. I mean, they were fine . . . fine. Ringo's got the best backbeat I've ever heard, and he can play great twenty-four hours a day. Paul is a fine bass player, but a little overpowering at times, and John has gone through his scene, but it feels to me like he's coming around now. To tell you the truth, I'd join a band with John Lennon any day, but not with Paul, and that's nothing personal. It's only from a musical point of view.

QUESTION What's your relationship with John and Paul these days?

GEORGE It's very good actually.

QUESTION Are you ever amazed by how much the Beatles still mean to people today?

GEORGE Not really. I realize the Beatles did fill a big space in the sixties, but all the people they really meant something to are all grown up. It's like anything that people grow up with — they get attached to it. I can understand that the Beatles, in many ways, did some nice things, and it's very much appreciated that people still like them. But the problem comes when they want to live in the past.

QUESTION What are your hopes for Dark Horse records?

GEORGE I want it to remain reasonably small. Actually, I've been here just over a week now, and if I signed all the people who gave me tapes I'd be bigger than RCA!

QUESTION Do you still meditate?

GEORGE It's a difficult question to answer really. You see, there's a state of consciousness which is the goal of every living entity, but I haven't sat down and really meditated for some time now. At the same time, however, I constantly try and think of the Lord in one fashion or another, just remember Him, which is another kind of meditation.

QUESTION Can you foresee a time when you'll give up your musical career?

GEORGE I'll give up this sort of touring madness certainly, but music — everything is based upon music. No, I'll never stop my music.

QUESTION There's a paradox there between lifestyles, though, I think.

GEORGE It is difficult, yeah, but the point is, it's also good practice in a

A sensitive portrait of Ringo.

Ringo extends a greeting to the inhabitants of planet earth on the cover of this 45 record jacket.

Ringo looking terribly top-drawer during filming for *The Magic Christian*, an antiestablishment film also starring Peter Sellers, Richard Attenborough, Christopher Lee, Spike Milligan, Wilfred Hyde-White, and Raquel Welch.

DOORS OPEN 12:30
For "MAGIC CHRISTIAN"

832-3511   FREE PARKING
BRITTON   75¢   UNTIL 1:30
BRITTON PLAZA SO. DALE MABRY   EVERYDAY EXCEPT
SUNDAY & HOLIDAYS

HOLD OVER!
2ND WEEK!

Who knows
what evil lurks
in the
heart of man?

The
Magic
Christian
do.

Peter Sellers & Ringo Starr
in "The Magic Christian"

RAQUEL WELCH   COLOR

Recommended For Adults
(GP)   1:30-3:40-5:45
8:00 & 10 p.m.

MATINEES ONLY!

An autographed shot of Ringo.

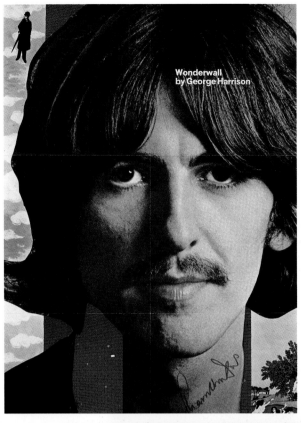

Wonderwall
by George Harrison

apple presents
ERIC CLAPTON
BOB DYLAN
GEORGE HARRISON
BILLY PRESTON
LEON RUSSELL
RAVI SHANKAR
RINGO STARR
KLAUS VOORMAN
as well as BADFINGER
JESSE DAVIS
JIM HORN
JIM KELTNER
CLAUDIA LINNEAR
and CARL RADLE

THE CONCERT FOR BANGLA DESH

Now you can experience it, hear it, live it as never before.

THE CONCERT FOR BANGLA DESH

Directed by Soul Swimmer · Produced by George Harrison and Allen Klein · Music Recording Produced by George Harrison and Phil Spector
Technicolor® apple/20th century-fox release   Original Sound Track Available On Apple Records   G

A promotional poster for *Wonderwall* autographed by sitarist Shambu Das.

George's humanitarian effort for the war-torn refugees of the India-Pakistan war.

A program from George's "Concert For Bangla Desh" autographed by Billy Preston, Ravi Shankar, Eric Clapton, Alla Rakha, and Leon Russell.

George in Los Angeles.

A rare 1975 poster promotes the entire George Harrison catalogue.

In concert 1974.

Overleaf
Beatle-related music books from the sixties and seventies.

way. As they say, "To be *in* the world but not *of* the world." You can go to the Himalayas and miss its secrets completely, or you can be stuck in the middle of New York and become very, very spiritual. Most people think when the world finally gets itself together we'll all be okay, but I don't see that happening. I think, one by one, we'll all free ourselves from the prisons we're chained to. But I don't think that suddenly something magical will happen and liberate everyone in one big go!

QUESTION   You said you had an experience which made you believe in the Lord. Was this a specific experience?

GEORGE   No, it was just certain things that happened in my life which left me thinking, "What's it all about, Alfie?" I remembered that Jesus said, "Knock and the door shall be opened," and so I said (*knock, knock*), "Hellooo!" From the Hindu point of view each soul is potentially divine, and the goal of life is simply to manifest that divinity. The word *yoga* means union — the union between the mind, body, and spirit. Yoga isn't lying on a bed of nails or standing on your head. There are various forms of yoga, which are all branches on one big tree, and the Lord has a million names. A guru once said he found no separation between man and God except man's "spiritual unadventurousness," and that's the catch. Our consciousness has been so polluted with the material energy that it's hard to try and pull it away towards anything spiritual. Everyone has within them a drop of that ocean, and we have the same qualities as God, just as a drop of the ocean has the same qualities as the entire sea. Everybody's looking for something outside, but it's all right there within ourselves.

By late 1974 George's yogic devotion was in full bloom and supplied momentum for his next effort, "Dark Horse." Released in America to coincide with his tour, it spawned only one minor hit with its semiautobiographical title track and is probably best remembered for George's raspy, uneven vocals, because he all but lost his voice during the tour. His next LP, "Extra Texture," was his final release on the rapidly fading Apple label. To give his critics something else to write about besides his recent weak albums and rather shaky tour, a photograph of a deliberately sardonic-looking composer appeared on the inner sleeve with the cryptic caption, "OHNOTHIMAGEN." However, the album only confirmed what was already becoming apparent — George wasn't having much fun playing rock 'n' roll anymore, and what was worse, his audience wasn't really enjoying listening either.

Over the next few years George's sputtering recording career produced several well-written, well-produced, well-played, but often commercially unsuccessful albums — "33⅓," "George Harrison," and his first after John's death, "Somewhere In England." His singles often did better than his LPs, and from 1976 to 1980 he had several popular 45s — "Crackerbox Palace," "This Song," "Blow Away," and the chart-topping tribute to John, "All Those Years Ago," which also featured the talents of Paul and Linda, Ringo, Denny Laine, and George Martin.

During the Beatles' last days together it was Paul McCartney who fought the hardest for their reconciliation, but once it was certain that the end was near, he also pushed the most vehemently for the group's dissolution. Wanting to perform live again, he formed his band, Wings. The original lineup included Paul on bass and lead vocals, Linda on keyboards and backups, Denny Seiwell on drums, and Denny Laine on lead guitar. Paul's first solo release had been the appealing one-man show "McCartney," followed by the eccentric "Ram." His first Wings LP, "Wild Life," was largely underrated. Early in 1972 Irish guitarist Henry McCullough was added to the group, and that February the newly expanded Wings took flight and embarked on a college tour of Britain. "The whole idea was just to turn up somewhere unannounced and play," remembers Paul. Later the band headed for Europe, where they reconsidered this rather haphazard touring style and began booking themselves properly through local agents.

Over the years Wings underwent many personnel changes but continued to tour and record. It released several commercially successful albums and singles, all aimed at showing what Paul McCartney without the Beatles could really do. Their releases included "Red Rose Speedway," "Band On The Run," "Venus And Mars," "Wings At The Speed of Sound," "Wings Over America," "London Town," "Wings' Greatest," and "Back To The Egg." Paul also turned out a number of highly polished rock videos to coincide with these releases. Eventually, though, Paul disbanded Wings and once again struck out on his own.

A collection of stationery from George's many companies.

Wings' Denny Laine and Paul McCartney.

Paul trades licks with Pete Townshend during the Concert for Kampuchea in London. December 1979.

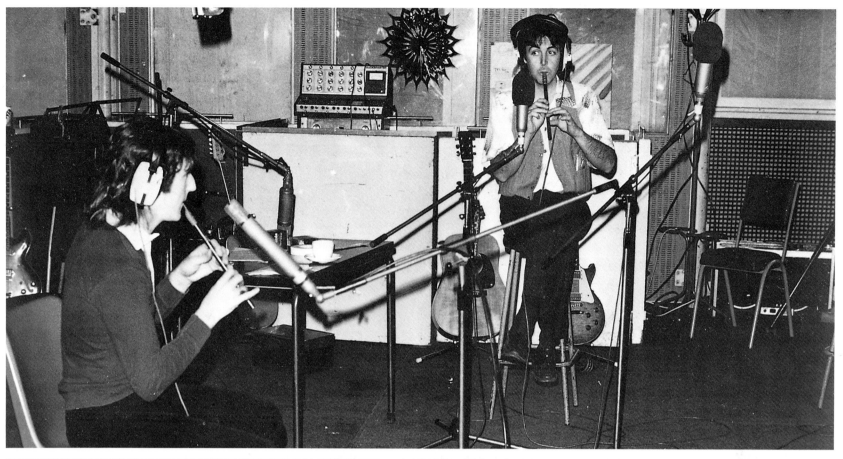

8

Pink Litmus Paper Shirt | *The Beatles as Artists*

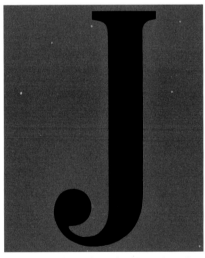

"I should have been a painter."
JOHN LENNON

"I've always done a bit of drawing, you know. It relaxes me."
RINGO STARR

"We're not necessarily learning to be painters or writers. We're learning to be, that's all."
PAUL McCARTNEY

"We'll go round and round in circles, doing films, trying out new things. Then after films we'll try something else. But as for this life, we haven't done anything yet." GEORGE HARRISON

A detail from the only known art piece created by all four Beatles.

ohn Lennon, founder and leader of the Beatles, was also chiefly responsible for turning on the other three to the serious pursuit of "high art." Even as a child John had a richly imaginative inner life. At the ripe old age of twelve he established a witty, hand-printed, schoolboy journal called "The Highly Esteemed Daily Howl." Illustrated throughout with caustic (often downright insulting) cartoons, the "Daily Howl" poked fun mercilessly at John's fellow students and teachers at Quarry Bank Grammar School — even its dour, humorless headmaster. While no known copies of the journal exist, several of John's drawings from this period were reproduced on the sleeve of his solo album "Walls And Bridges." What we have left to remind us of his fearless wit and devilish prose are his two funny, satirical books, *In His Own Write* and *A Spaniard in the Works*, published at the height of Beatlemania in 1964 and 1965.

Early in 1969 John was asked by a friend to begin work on a series of elegant, limited-edition lithographs to be published by the prestigious Cinnamon Press of New York. In response John produced fourteen highly erotic, personal studies relating to his recent marriage and honeymoon. Dubbed by John "Bag One," the stylish portfolio sold for only a thousand dollars, but today complete sets in good condition have been known to

163

fetch up to $70,000. A follow-up series based on the *I Ching* was planned (and even proofed), but owing to the Lennons' somewhat unpredictable lifestyle this project was never completed. Influenced by Yoko's "con art" (her name for the often pretentious conceptual art so prevalent in the mid-sixties), John discovered a whole new area of exploration for his powerful sense of the absurd. Over the years John and Yoko collaborated on countless artistic projects together, including showings at the Robert Fraser Gallery in London in 1968 and upstate New York's Everson Museum of Art in 1971. But much of John's best work was achieved on his own, and there must still be hundreds of as yet unpublished drawings, paintings, literary works, and recordings all safely stored away in the fortress-like Dakota.

"As a kid our Paul was always doodling around on one thing or another," remembers Mike McCartney. "Mind you, now that I think about it, so was I. I guess we were a very artistic family!" Paul likes to draw and paint. But like everything else he does, he does it in a very big way. In the early 1980s he published a selection of his engaging, humorous line drawings in a lavish, oversize paperback entitled *Paul McCartney: Composer/Artist*. "Macca [pet name for Paul] absolutely loves to draw," reports one longtime MPL employee. "Just take a good look at the walls of our office — Paul's pictures are everywhere!" But it is in his home that Paul feels most comfortable working. While Linda works on her photography Paul writes, composes, and creates his colorful, swirling abstracts and caricatures on large, prestretched canvases brought down from London. He designed the Beatles' first logo, sketched out first drafts for many of their most famous album covers (including "Sgt. Pepper" and "Abbey Road"), and designed picture sleeves, promotional posters, and press kits for many 45s. Like the other Beatles Paul dabbles in 35-mm photography, and why not? He just happens to be roommates with one of the world's most celebrated rock photographers! He also has his own fan magazine, *Club Sandwich*, in which to showcase his and Linda's best work.

George Harrison's mother, Louise, always thought her son was artistically inclined. "As a boy he was constantly drawing and sketching clever little racing cars and things in the margins of his school notebooks," she says. "As far as I'm concerned, he could have been anything he ever wanted." Few of those original boyhood drawings exist today, but there are still many fine examples of George's artwork around. His distinctive, far-out album cover artwork for Zapple's "Electronic Sound" is perhaps his best-known venture into graphic illustration. In 1967 George and his pal Klaus Voorman also cooked up some very heady designs for one of Harrison's many motorcars and a spacey, tantric-inspired mural for the white stucco exterior of his fashionable Esher bungalow, "Kinfauns." All the Beatles adorned their personal letters and postcards with imaginative caricatures

John's humorous vision of the Beatles signaling "thumbs up" to their fans in this obscure 1969 line drawing.

A 1964 Christmas card designed by John and sold in aid of Action for the Crippled Child, a nonprofit organization researching a cure for childhood polio.

Many editions of John's two best-selling books and of Yoko's *Grapefruit*.

The stylish, white Italian leather portfolio designed by John and Yoko to hold the lithographs.

John patiently signs his name to a never-ending pile of lithographs at Ronnie Hawkins's Mississauga, Ontario, home. 1969.

FILMS BY YOKO ONO-JOHN LENNON

Everson Museum of Art
401 Harrison Street
Syracuse, New York
Tel: 474-6064

	7:30	9:30
Friday, October 15	A	B
		Advance ticket sales
Saturday, October 16	C	D
Sunday, October 17	A	E

	12:00	2:00
Tuesday, October 19	B	C
Wednesday, October 20	D	A — Tickets sold at the door first come basis.
Thursday, October 21	E	C
Friday, October 22	B	D

A   TWO VIRGINS, ERECTION, FLY, GIVE PEACE A CHANCE (short), 90 minutes

B   APOTHEOSIS, RAPE, FREEDOM FILM No. 1 JOHN, FREEDOM FILM No. 2 YOKO, 110 minutes

C   GIVE PEACE A CHANCE (feature), INSTANT KARMA, BALLAD OF JOHN AND YOKO, 85 minutes

D   FLY, ERECTION, UP YOUR LEGS FOREVER, 117 minutes

E   FLY, ERECTION, SMILE, COLD TURKEY, 98 minutes

Advance ticket sales for the Friday, Saturday and Sunday evening performances will be available at the Book Center on Marshall Street and the Sales Gallery at the Everson Museum. Admission is $1.00 for each performance, free to members.

and doodles, and George's squiggly, offbeat creatures and intricate patterns rivaled even John's and Paul's for their creativity and free expression. Several of his works can be seen in his limited-edition musical autobiography, *I Me Mine*, as well as in Derek Taylor's outrageously funny Apple log, *Fifty Years Adrift*. As a Beatle George had his say in the design of their many album covers and was instrumental in choosing the "personalities" pictured as the backdrop on the "Sgt. Pepper" cover. He has also been an avid amateur photographer for many years now.

As director of photography on the Beatles' innovative fantasy film *Magical Mystery Tour*, Richard Starkey, MBE, had the opportunity to flex his artistic muscles in a way he never had before. Almost solely responsible for the project's complicated photography, Ringo tackled the job successfully and had a major hand in the final editing of the made-for-TV movie. Of all the Beatles Ringo was the most involved in exploring the boundaries of photography and became the group's unofficial photographer in charge of documenting many events in their personal and professional lives. As a painter he was inspired by his first wife, Maureen, who was perhaps the finest all-round artist within the Beatles' close-knit group. Often working together at their comfortable Weybridge home, the couple explored many artistic forms, including photo collage, oil painting, drawing, and even a little rudimentary modeling in clay. Ringo has contributed ideas and designs for many of the Beatle album covers, his ten solo LPs, and his own label, Ring O'Records. In addition, Ringo and John were commissioned to illustrate the tunes "Snookeroo" and "Bennie And The Jets" for the book *The One Who Writes the Lyrics for Elton John*. Perhaps his most noteworthy artistic achievement, however — apart from his music — was designing and manufacturing a line of very avant-garde, futuristic steel and glass furniture with his partner and friend, London artist Robin Cruikshank. Together they formed a company in the early seventies called Ringo Or Robin Limited to market the strangely appealing sculptural creations.

A rare flyer advertising Joko Films to accompany Yoko's "This Is Not Here" multimedia conceptual art exhibit at the Everson Museum of Art in Syracuse, New York.

A poster from Yoko's "This Is Not Here" exhibition showing many of her and John's enigmatic constructions.

John's response to a request to jot down his thoughts about a new magazine, *Harmony*, devoted to macrobiotic cooking.

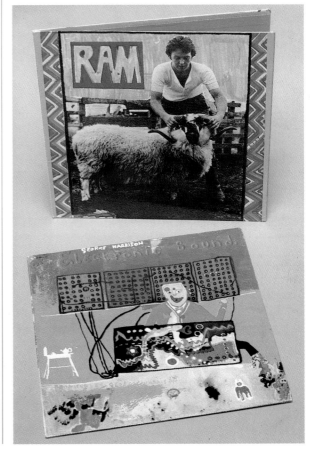

Top The front cover of Paul and Linda's 1971 "Ram" LP. The distinctive jacket art is by Paul. *Bottom* George Harrison's inventive painting for his almost completely unknown "Electronic Sound" LP released on Zapple Records May 23, 1969.

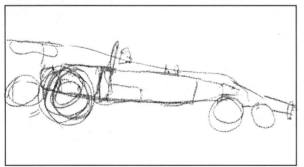

Shambu Das and George on Juhu Beach, Bombay.

George's love of motor racing is shown in this casual drawing of a formula-one racer.

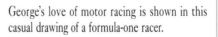

A caricature of John drawn by Ringo.

Pattie Harrison in Kashmir. 1966.

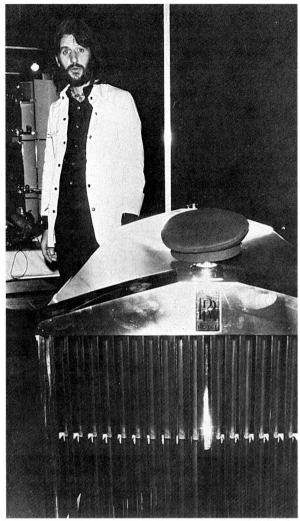

Ringo at Liberty's in London promoting his "Rolls Royce" coffee table made from two front grills.

Ringo's free-style snapshot used to illustrate the Beatles Fan Club 1969 Christmas record.

One of Stuart Sutcliffe's abstracts from his post-Beatles period.

From Ascot in Berkshire, from Weybridge in Surrey, from St. John's Wood in the Borough of Marylebone and from Apple in the West End, John Ringo Paul and George send you these tapes of love and greetings soldered into a collective disc by the iron wrist of Maurice Cole. The Beatles wish all of you a happy Christmas and may the Seventies Give Peace a Chance.

Cover design by Richard Starkey and Zak Starkey

The Official
Beatles **FAN CLUB** of Great Britain

presents

THE BEATLES SEVENTH CHRISTMAS RECORD

HAPPY CHRISTMAS
1969

© 1969. The Official Beatles Fan Club

THIS SPECIAL RECORD MAY BE FREELY BROADCAST BUT IS NOT FOR PRIVATE OR PUBLIC SALE. IT IS DISTRIBUTED FREE OF CHARGE TO MEMBERS OF THE OFFICIAL BEATLES FAN CLUB IN THE UNITED KINGDOM. PLAY AT 33⅓ R.P.M. USING A NORMAL L.P. STYLUS. UNAUTHORISED COPYING OF THIS RECORD PROHIBITED. ALL RIGHTS RESERVED.

THE OFFICIAL BEATLES FAN CLUB
National Secretary: Freda Kelly
P.O. BOX 12, LIVERPOOL 1

33⅓
R.P.M.

Printed in England by West Brothers · Printers · Limited, London, S.W.19

9

Not Unknown

Friends and Family

*"We are the best thing we can
ever give each other."* JOHN LENNON

*"All I want to do is be with my
family."* PAUL McCARTNEY

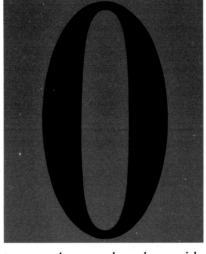

Over the years John, Paul, George, and Ringo have met tens of thousands of people, all eager to make an impression on them. The following special people have each shared a unique relationship with at least one of the Beatles and have generously agreed to share with us the individuals they found behind the myth.

"I was always mates with Julian. He's a very nice kid." PAUL McCARTNEY

John Charles Julian Lennon, the only child of John and Cynthia, was born on April 8, 1963, at Sefton General Hospital in Liverpool. When Cynthia discovered she was pregnant, John decided they should get married immediately. While Julian (named in memory of John's mother) was growing up, his dad was seldom at home. When he did manage a few days off from the rigorous Beatle tours, he was generally so exhausted he slept for days at a time. By the fall of 1966, however, the Beatles had decided to discontinue touring, giving them more time to spend with their growing families, and John devoted almost all of his leisure hours to playing with his young son. Some of that play turned out to be very productive for the Beatles; for example, a drawing Julian did at school became the inspiration for John's "Lucy In The Sky With Diamonds," and another was used to illustrate the

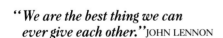

At Tittenhurst Park. 1969.

171

Father and son. London 1968.

sleeve of the Beatles Fan Club 1968 Christmas single. Soon, however, John met Yoko Ono, and his affections were directed elsewhere. The highly publicized estrangement and sensationalized divorce proceedings that followed drove a painfully deep wedge between John and his first family, and until the mid-seventies Julian only rarely visited his father. Cynthia married again, this time architect John Twist, and moved to Ruthin, North Wales, where she opened a bistro. Julian went to school, learned to play the guitar, and caught up on a lot of the great old music he'd missed when he was younger, including the music of the Beatles. On the evening of December 8, 1980, three thousand miles away in Manhattan, a nameless assassin stepped out of the night and tore the life out of John Lennon with a .38-caliber Charter Arms revolver, dashing any hopes Julian might have had of ever growing closer to his father. Within two days he was on a plane to New York City to try and console Yoko and his half-brother, Sean.

Julian Lennon ultimately decided on a career in music. For eighteen months he contemplated the route his career should take and the reaction he could expect if it wasn't launched properly. "I would like to keep the family tradition going, but in *my* way. No one can ever top what my dad did, especially me, but I still want to try and keep the Lennon name singing, writing, and performing." In 1983 his manager, Dean Gordon, sent a demo tape of Julian's tunes to the British-based Charisma Records, which reviewed the engaging, energetic material and promptly signed Julian to an extended recording and publishing contract. In North America he was signed to the Atlantic label, and his first album, "Valotte," was released on October 25, 1985, to a flood of critical acclaim. His second LP, "The Secret Value Of Day Dreaming," was issued in April 1986. When asked what he thinks his father might have said about his decision to become a musician, Julian comments, "I think he'd say, 'Go ahead and do it, but just don't blame me if it doesn't work out.'" But as we all know, it certainly has, and John must be very proud. This interview was conducted in Toronto in 1985, shortly after the release of "Valotte."

GEOFFREY   Julian, did you many years ago bring home a drawing of a little girl named Lucy?

JULIAN LENNON   Yes, well, I was waddling along up to the house with this big picture in my hand which was all watery and blurry. I mean, how well can you paint at five? It was just a school friend called Lucy that I'd drawn in this picture. It had green grass at the bottom, a dark blue sky at the top, and some very rough-looking stars. I also painted in these long, golden, curly locks of hair on my girlfriend, Lucy. Dad just said, "Well, what's that?" I said, "That's Lucy in the sky — you know, with diamonds." So the song just got worked up from that.

GEOFFREY   Does the drawing exist anywhere, or is it long gone?

JULIAN   I'm sure it's long gone by now.

Julian Lennon. 1984.

Julian in concert. Toronto 1985.

GEOFFREY   Ringo's son Zak is about your age now, and he's a drummer. Have you ever considered working with him?

JULIAN   He's a fantastic drummer — I mean, just incredible, but . . .

GEOFFREY   "Son of Beatles" might be a bit too much?

JULIAN   Yes, but also our attitudes aren't quite the same either.

GEOFFREY   How are you going to find your own identity as an artist and a person?

JULIAN   Well, I don't know. I hope everything will fall into place. I think it's just a question of working at it, but who knows when?

GEOFFREY   Do you like Beatle music, Julian?

JULIAN   Oh yes, pretty much so. There are a couple of tracks on "Valotte" that reflect the Beatles' style, I think.

GEOFFREY   Your bio suggests you're interested in acting.

JULIAN   No, that was years ago — well, a couple of years ago anyway. I don't like the idea of mixing medias too much. I want to continue with one career, and if I'm going to do music, I'll stick to that. Being silly once in a while on video is okay, but I think one career is enough for me.

GEOFFREY   Sam Peckenpah directed the two videos for "Valotte," and everyone expected something to blow up or machine guns to go off because of his reputation! But surprisingly, it was a very laid-back, nontheatrical video, not at all like the ones you see with all these sexy girls dancing around everywhere.

JULIAN   Originally we weren't even going to do a video. We had no intention of doing a video, but it does help to get the music across, I suppose.

GEOFFREY   There was a story in the press a while back that you had one of John's demo tapes and were going to be recording some of his last tunes. What's the story on that?

JULIAN   Fred Seaman, who used to work for my dad and Yoko in New York, apparently stole some stuff, and he gave me this tape of Dad's, you see, which was great. There were some really wonderful songs on there. He was just playing an acoustic guitar placed in front of a microphone at home, you know? Anyway, he sent along a guitar of Dad's with it as well. So I thanked Yoko, and she said, "Thanks for what?" And I said, "The guitar and the tape," and she said, "What are you talking about?" Anyway, she found out about the whole plot, and so off they went, back to America.

GEOFFREY   So no plans to record any of John's unreleased material?

JULIAN   Oh, no chance, no.

GEOFFREY   How did you feel about recording with ex-Wings drummer Steve Holly?

JULIAN   He's great. He's my number-one favorite drummer at the moment.

GEOFFREY   Do you remember seeing this? It's the Beatles Fan Club 1968 promo 45 RPM given only to club members, and you are credited on back as contributing to the sleeve design! Did you know it existed?

The Beatles Fan Club 1968 Christmas single. A free-form collage by John probably done at his Weybridge home, "Kenwood," sometime in 1967 or early 1968.

A painting by Julian on the back.

Harry Nilsson (r) with Ritchie Havens at a fund-raising event for the gun control lobby. New York 1984.

JULIAN   No, I didn't.

GEOFFREY   Is this the first time you've seen it?

JULIAN   Yes.

GEOFFREY   But you did it as a child, look at your name there.

JULIAN   Yes, incredible!

GEOFFREY   It's very rare these days, you know. Your dad did the front cover collage, and you did another of your famous drawings on the back.

"When I first heard Harry in 1968 and then later met him, it was strong — heterosexual, if you don't mind — love at first sight, and I knew that he should be introduced to John. Our heroes eventually met in Surrey. Both were quite tentative with each other, like very little children at a birthday party handing gifts to each other and blushing. Later, of course, he became friendly with the fab other three, and with Ringo, too, he has formed a magical team."   DEREK TAYLOR

Born in New York on June 15, 1941, Harry Nilsson moved with his parents to the West Coast at the age of eleven. After completing his education, he found himself a job at the Security First National Bank in the San Fernando Valley as a computer programmer but soon left to pursue a career as a singer. His first album for RCA, "Pandemonium Shadow Show," caught the attention of Derek Taylor, who was so impressed he sent along several copies to the Beatles. They especially liked Harry's interpretation of the Lennon/McCartney number, "You Can't Do That," and when John and Paul were asked in a 1968 interview who their favorite group was, they offhandedly replied, "Harry Nilsson."

It was, as they say, the start of a beautiful friendship. One of Harry's biggest hits, "Without You," was written by Apple's talented house band, Badfinger. George and Ringo performed on several tracks of his "Son Of Schmilsson" LP. Derek Taylor produced his "A Touch Of Schmilsson In The Night" album, while John Lennon did the same for "Pussy Cats" in 1974. Later that year Harry tried his hand at acting, in the title role of Apple Films' obscure monster-movie parody, *Son of Dracula*, and in the short, autobiographical *Harry and Ringo's Night Out*. Harry's musical contributions to various Beatle-related solo recordings include "Goodnight Vienna," "Ringo's Rotogravure," and "Ringo" for Ringo, "Walls And Bridges" with John, and "Every Man Has A Woman Who Loves Him" for Yoko. After John's murder Harry became a powerful advocate for the gun control lobby and today dedicates much of his time to traveling around the globe speaking to people on this issue. He was interviewed in New York in 1984.

GEOFFREY   Harry, I understand you're very good friends with Yoko and that you're working on the Birthday Album [working title for "Every Man Has A Woman Who Loves Him"] with her. How is she feeling about the handgun laws today?

John and Harry's "Pussy Cats" LP and Rapple Records' "Son of Dracula" soundtrack. Both autographed by Harry.

The Beatles and company have been headline news now for over twenty years. A few of their more outstanding cover stories.

Harry and the author doing their bit to aid the National Coalition to Ban Handguns at a charity benefit in New York following John's death.

HARRY NILSSON   Well, she's against all forms of violence. I'll tell you something about Yoko: I know why John fell in love with her. She is one of the most ingratiating people in the world — one of the kindest, nicest, most honest, and most pursued people on the planet. I don't want to turn this into some kind of epitaph, you know, but look — she's wonderful. We clash a little bit about how to deal with handguns, but it's fine. She'd rather not know about violence, and I don't blame her.

GEOFFREY   How did your relationsip with John get started?

HARRY   He called me up and said, "Harry, you're fucking great, man," and I said the same to him. Later we became friends, and over the years we just hung out together.

GEOFFREY   How do you remember John?

HARRY   It's not how I remember him, it's how I miss his great wit. John was one of the world's wittiest men, you know. He'd always beat you to the punch.

GEOFFREY   How did the album you recorded with John, "Pussy Cats," come about?

HARRY   We were bored . . .

GEOFFREY   And the lost weekend in L.A.?

HARRY   Oh, the lost weekend is history. We were getting very bored at a Joni Mitchell session one night peeing in ashtrays and that sort of thing when John just jumped up and said, "I'm gonna produce Harry Nilsson!" I didn't know whether he was drunk or what, so a couple of days later he says to me, "What do you think?" I said, "If you're serious about it, man, you bet."

GEOFFREY   What was it like living in a house with Keith Moon, Ringo, and John? Did you party twenty-four hours a day?

HARRY   Of course not, you can't do that. We just lived a normal, reasonable life. We'd wake up in the morning — well, about one o'clock actually — and eat breakfast prepared by this couple we had serving us. Klaus Voorman went out for a swim in the ocean quite a lot. My wife, Una, used to take long walks on the beach. John and May would sleep late, I'd sleep later, and then at six o'clock the limos would show up, and we'd drive over to Warner Brothers to record, finishing about two o'clock in the morning. Then we'd come home, open up the brandy bottles, and listen to the tapes very loudly, get drunk, and tell each other how wonderful we were.

GEOFFREY   What about any unreleased material — do you have anything still in the can that you did with John?

HARRY   Yes, there are a couple of tunes we started writing. Years ago we wrote a song together called "You Are Here." It's something we started to write but never really finished. I never heard the final product, but we used to send tapes back and forth to each other — and postcards. He would sign them "You Are Here." Oh shit, I miss him very much. I'd like to say I was

An original poster for Ringo and Harry's *Son of Dracula* for Apple Films.

very close friends with the man, but I wasn't. No one was a very close friend to John other than the Beatles.

GEOFFREY   Did he miss the Beatles?

HARRY   Well, someone recently told me that they once saw John walking on the street wearing a button that said, "I LOVE PAUL." And the girl who told me about it said she asked him, "Why are you wearing a button that says, 'I LOVE PAUL'?" And he said, "Because I love Paul."

GEOFFREY   How's your relationship with the rest of the Beatles these days?

HARRY   Ringo and I speak a couple of times a week. He was the best man at our wedding, he's the godfather to our children. He's one of the dearest friends you can have in life, and I hope he considers me one of his best friends. George and I are very good friends, and Paul is just Paul. I don't really know Paul. I've spent time with him over the years, but I don't actually *know* him like Ringo or George. Paul is an amazing guy. He just smokes his joints and whistles his way through life, and God bless him for it too!

GEOFFREY   He shouldn't take them to the airport though.

HARRY   How about when Yoko went over to England, and they searched her cold cream! First of all she's not a drug taker. She's the most beautiful fifty-one-year-old woman in the world! I read in a magazine the other day that she was taught not to smile in public because only shopkeepers smile in public in order to ingratiate themselves. That's a very heavy thing to think about. Yoko's one of the most fascinating women I've ever met in my entire life.

GEOFFREY   What about Sean?

HARRY   Sean is one of the brightest children I've ever known as well. I have two or three bright children, but Sean is so loose, open, and bright. He's very fragile too and aware, but he says things that are very accurate. He's honest and admirable — a wonderful, wonderful little boy.

Mike McCartney has lived too many years in the giant shadow of his famous brother. Although the two have remained close, it must have been difficult for Mike to forge a career in show business without the inevitable Beatle comparisons. In the early sixties he teamed up with the well-known Liverpool poet Roger McGough and humorist John Gorman to form the highly successful musical comedy trio, the Scaffold. In 1964 their irreverent, high-spirited assaults on the English language won them a regular spot on the British television show "Gazette" and several other TV specials and programs of their own over the years. George Martin produced their first single, "2 Day's Monday" backed by "3 Black Jellyfish." But it wasn't until they recorded the upbeat novelty tunes "Thank U Very Much," "Lilly The Pink," and "Liverpool Lou" that they scored big with the British record-buying public.

Mike McCartney.

Two fine albums from Mike "McGear" McCartney,
"The Scaffold" and "McGear."

In 1968 Paul offered to produce the group, and together they turned out the popular "McGough and McGear" LP, which featured a surprise guest appearance by the late Jimi Hendrix. Six years later the brothers met in the studio again to record Mike's now classic solo album, "McGear," which included several first-rate rocking numbers written by the ambitious McCartneys. For a brief period in the mid-seventies Mike was a member of the Bonzo Dog Doo Dah Band satellite group, Grimms, which also included Vivian Stanshall, Neil Innes, John Gorman, Roger McGough, Zoot Money, and others. Together this tribe of unpredictable musical fools performed live throughout England and recorded two albums for Island Records — "Grimms" and "Rockin' Duck."

Mike is also a talented writer and has published several children's books as well as a tongue-in-cheek biography of the McCartney clan, *Mike McCartney's Family Album*. He has been married twice. He and his first wife, Angela, were wedded in Wales on June 8, 1968, and together they had three daughters. They separated, and some years later Mike tied the knot with a lovely Liverpool woman by the name of Rowenia (who joins us for this 1983 interview in Liverpool). Mike is one of the City of Liverpool's foremost roving ambassadors and enthusiastically donates his time, talent, and money to support local drug rehabilitation centers and other community-oriented programs. He is a frequent guest lecturer at Beatle conventions in England and North America and never tires of relaying his witty remembrances of the golden days of Beatlemania. He is one of the few from the Beatles' circle who still lives in Liverpool, and today he makes his home in Heswall, just across the river Mersey.

GEOFFREY   What was your name again, McGear or McCartney?

MIKE McCARTNEY   *McGertney*. Establish where we are — go on.

GEOFFREY   We're in a delightful restaurant in a wonderful old baronial home in Liverpool.

MIKE   It was our first home, you know, but they kicked us out because we couldn't afford the bloody rates! (*Laughter*)

GEOFFREY   I went by your old homes today actually.

MIKE   You know, they once offered me twenty thousand pounds to do an exclusive Beatle tour of Liverpool for all the executive Japanese, Americans, and Torontonians.

GEOFFREY   How intimidating was it to get into show business with your group, the Scaffold, with Paul McCartney being your brother?

MIKE   Paul McCartney! Darling, darling! He's going to say "Be Ba Bea, Beat . . .

GEOFFREY   I'm going to say "Beatles" next, that's right.

(*Laughter*)

MIKE   Actually, it was no problem at all. The only way to survive was to choose a theatrical comedy concept. If I had chosen pop music I'd be dead by now.

GEOFFREY   Would you have liked to go into straight pop music but thought you couldn't because of Paul?

MIKE   Look, Brian Epstein once said to me at the height of the Beatles' success, "Michael, would you like to be a pop singer? Please, come and join our organization." This was when they were just getting Gerry and Cilla organized. I said, "Brian, you must be jokin'. We've got one up there already who is doin' rather well, thank you." To try and emulate that, to try and put myself up there and draw on Paul as a comparison would be a pretty dumb thing to do. I'm as good as he is. He's a natural singer and a natural player of instruments, but I'm a natural singer too, though I've never been relaxed enough to really let anybody hear it.

GEOFFREY   I spoke to George Martin recently about the song "Her Majesty." I said, "Yeah, what about when you and the Beatles clipped off that last note on "Her Majesty?" And he said, "Oh, did we?" I said, "What do you mean, 'did we?' There's a million guys in America right now who were high on LSD during the sixties reading the meaning of life into your leaving that note off, and you didn't even know you did it?"

MIKE   That's right. That's exactly what the whole Beatle thing was, doing it in complete *innocence*. You are just a being, you do what you do because it's your job, and you can't go into it any more than that. Sometimes I suppose they used to tease the listeners a bit. Particularly John, I think, would love to fool around with people's heads.

GEOFFREY   Did the Scaffold ever play on the same bill with the Beatles?

MIKE   No. We played the Cavern, though, but we didn't go down too well because they were used to pop groups, and we'd come on spoutin' poetry and bloody comedy.

GEOFFREY   Well, the Beatles were always edging towards comedy.

MIKE   John was a great comedian all right, a natural.

GEOFFREY   Paul was no slouch either.

MIKE   No, no, but John was the heavy one, and Paul was a very good feed. Two good comedians. But then again, Ringo's a very funny guy as well.

GEOFFREY   George came out with a few zingers too, you know.

MIKE   Oh yeah. Well, you've been to Liverpool now, and all the people reading your book will understand that when they come to Liverpool, they might actually see why the Beatles are so big. Liverpool life is the best apprenticeship in the world, because our families are virtually gold mines of upbringing. Without that grounding I doubt very much whether the Beatles would have stayed at the top for so long or kept their sanity when all about them so many died. Of course an enormous contribution to that longevity was their sense of humor. They always say in Liverpool you've got to have a sense of humor to survive.

The *Beatle Fun Kit*, inspired madness from the editors of *Dig* magazine. 1964.

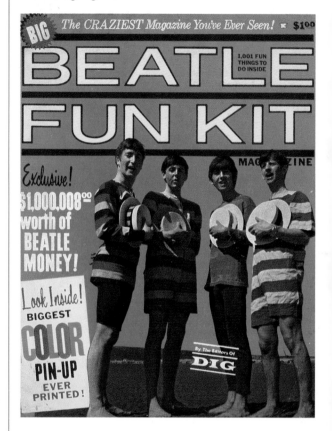

The SCAFFOLD

JOHN GORMAN

Born in Birkenhead on 4th January 1937. He has fair hair and blue eyes and is 5'11" tall. He was educated at St. Anselm's College, Liverpool and later served his National Service in The Royal Air Force.

MIKE McGEAR.

Born in Walton on 7th January 1944. He has blue eyes and brown hair and is 6 feet tall. He was educated at the Liverpool Institute. His earlier career has included employment as a Bible representative, tailoring and hairdressing.

ROGER McGOUGH

Born in Liverpool on 9th November 1937. He has brown hair and blue eyes and is 5'11" tall. He was educated at St. Mary' College and at Hull University where he obtained a Bachelo of Arts degree in French and Geography. He has successfull combined a teaching career with writing much of the materia used by the group.

A postcard from Mike McCartney to the author.

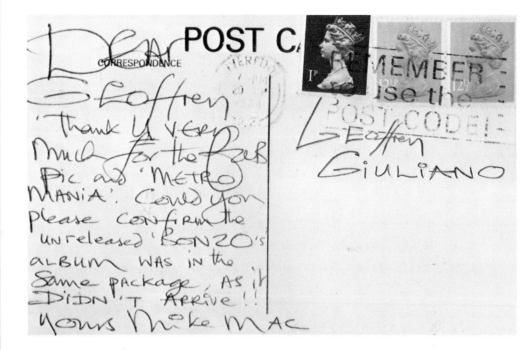

George's hat from *Magical Mystery Tour* surrounded by an assortment of buttons.

Paul as a solo performer.

GEOFFREY   I went around to their boyhood homes today, and I can see where you'd have to keep a sense of humor, because it all seemed so harsh.

MIKE   Hold on. There's two ways of looking at it. Ringo's neighborhood was heavy. Now I don't particularly know what George's was really like, as he was in Speke, and I only vaguely remember going up to his house. Paul would have known George in Speke when we lived in Harwood Grove. George lived about three streets parallel to us. I remember walking up the back alleyway with some fireworks under my arm going to George's one night. I can't remember George as a kid particularly. He lived very close to us, and from there we moved to Forthlen Row.

GEOFFREY   Which is very near John's.

MIKE   Oh, very near — just down the road. So the point you were making was about all this poverty we were brought up in. The reality was quite different! We were actually lower, working middle class. My dad was a cotton salesman, which was a good job, very well respected. He was earning good money. And my mother was a midwife — again, a highly respected position. Look at John's place on Menlove Avenue. It's bloody posh.

GEOFFREY   I've met Paul and Linda, and they're the nicest people you would ever want to meet. How can you take a guy, give him everything that most people just get a taste of, and have him end up so cool?

ROWENIA McCARTNEY   The Beatles weren't particularly star-struck though, you know what I mean? A lot of the groups today seem to be.

MIKE   The Beatles were immediate stars too.

ROWENIA   Yes, but it didn't go to their heads. The Beatles still got around — I mean, they went on every chat show. They did most everything they were asked to do instead of saying, "No, we're far too big for that." They realized that being amiable was much better. I can imagine your father taking the piss out of Paul if he ever got too big for his boots.

MIKE   Yes, that's right. But again that can only come from your upbringing. And that's why you don't get thrown when you're at the top, when the pressure's really on. Paul was always in contact with his relatives. Families tend to cut one down to size, so suddenly it isn't that big a deal being rich and famous as in Paul's case. I know family life is more important to him. And when you get too big for the family — ah, then that's very uncool.

GEOFFREY   Was it the same for the rest of the Beatles? Did they have strong family roots as well?

MIKE   Yes. You just said to me in the car what a magical, amazing place Liverpool is.

GEOFFREY   So what you're telling me is that one of the most significant factors in the Beatles' success was simply being from Liverpool?

MIKE   Yeah.

GEOFFREY   Okay, what about the Maharishi?

The McCartneys arrive at Tokyo airport shortly before the infamous pot bust.

Paul obliges a happy fan with an autograph outside his St. John's Wood home in the early seventies.

MIKE I did his meditation for two years. But I suddenly realized it was costing me a fortune and taking two hours of my life every day! So I stopped, because that's the trick. That is what Maharishi is telling you: "Okay, gang, what are you coming here for? Go get the answers for yourself! Self-realization is the whole thing, and I am just a tool of my Guru Dev." You know, these TM people, God love them, are very nice, but they think of him as a god. There's also an idea that Jesus is a god as well. But as soon as you think of any human being as a god, then you've lost the answer.

GEOFFREY When I met Paul I certainly felt a bit of a flutter in my throat. Same thing with George.

MIKE It's called "the reason that John got killed," and it's a worrying feeling. It's in everybody who is enamored with anybody else. As soon as you are overly impressed, then you're finished. What you don't realize is that the people you're talking about go through the very same thing. I know a few occasions in my life when I've been in the presence of people that I admired, and I've done exactly the same. I lost my bottle, and suddenly you're not yourself. Let's face it, it's the hardest thing in the world being yourself all the time. In a star situation — when you're with somebody famous — you naturally change, like a chameleon, according to your environment, fear, embarrassment, degree of adulation.

GEOFFREY You know, when I met Paul, I could feel him trying to compensate for other people's nervousness.

MIKE That's right. He was trying to help them understand themselves. Listen, the Beatles themselves have been flipping out for years listening to Elvis, Chuck Berry, Ben E. King, and Ray Charles. In the old days Paul and I used to like the Everly Brothers, listening to every word, every nuance, every bit of feeling to get it exactly right. Paul imitated Little Richard and was one of the few white people that Richard had ever acknowledged as being a good interpreter of him! Therefore we were influenced by our peers as well. Now the most important thing to remember when an idol comes around is that he's just a guy who picks his nose and performs all the other bodily functions every other little god on this earth does. Don't forget that the person is still a human being.

GEOFFREY Mike, did you say you had a tape of the Beatles that no one has ever heard?

MIKE I have.

GEOFFREY And no one ever will?

MIKE Someday. But I have to think of it in another light now. I've got four children, and it's their heritage, right?

GEOFFREY Did you collect a lot of things over the years?

MIKE I have. I'm one of those terrible people that can't throw anything away. I'm a natural hoarder. Ringo, I think, is one as well, but unfortunately his house in Los Angeles burned down.

GEOFFREY   Do you ever see many people from the old days?

MIKE   I saw John's mate, Pete Shotton, in Liverpool when Queenie Epstein opened up Beatle City. I didn't meet him though, but I did meet Pete Best.

GEOFFREY   You did? What was that like?

MIKE   Very good. I thought he was very much like he always was — quiet, dignified, and shy.

GEOFFREY   They say he got canned from the Beatles because he was too good-looking and Paul didn't dig it, so he said, "Let's find the ugliest drummer we can who's got a cool drum kit."

MIKE   Nonsense. It was just fate that decreed he should go. It's like they said, "Something's got to happen. Somebody's got to go, and it's not us." It could have been any one of them that fate chose. George could have been the one, you know. None of them was that strong. But when they all got together, that's when the magic happened. The other three were very quick, but Pete was moody, magnificent, and good-looking. The girls screamed for him, and that was an *asset*. They wouldn't have sacked the sod for that! Think about it. That would have been much bigger, a good-looking drummer with Paul, John, and George fronting him. It was basically down to his drumming ability in the end. There were quite a few drummers around Liverpool, and I used to go home and tell Paul about Ringo. I often saw him play with Rory Storm. We didn't think about how ugly he might have been or even about the little white streak in his hair. It was just that this guy with Rory was a very inventive drummer. He goes around the drums like crazy. He doesn't just hit them — he invents sounds.

GEOFFREY   There's a nice story about you reopening Apple Studios in the mid-seventies. You guys went down and recorded something, and Paul couldn't believe he was actually back there.

MIKE   It was his decision to join me there.

GEOFFREY   What did you record?

MIKE   It was very good for him. It's called "Knocking Down Walls Of Ignorance."

GEOFFREY   Was that the name of the track?

MIKE   It is now! We were there in London but I couldn't find a drummer, so I was ringing around to different people. Linda was saying, "Get hold of John Bonham." So Paul came in on the conversation. "I'll drum for you down at Apple." So we went there and did it. The track that he drummed on I presented to EMI, and the young A & R man then in charge listened to the track and said, "Very good, but the drummer certainly leaves a lot to be desired." (*Laughter*) I didn't tell him it was the drummer who played on their best-selling "Band On The Run" album. I just didn't have the heart. So I walked out, got on the train, and went back home to Liverpool.

Steve Holly, Wings' sexiest drummer, joined the group in 1978 after his predecessor, Joe English, quit to return home to America. Holly's debut

This valuable 45-RPM picture cover is actually an obscure Wings recording composed by Paul's dad, Jim, and later released under this peculiar pseudonym for contractual reasons.

A singles jacket featuring Steve Holly and Wings in the basement rehearsal hall of Paul's London office building.

Wings near the end of its career: Laurence Juber, Denny Laine, Linda, Paul, and Steve Holly at the drums.

with Wings was in the promotional film for "With A Little Luck" off their popular "London Town" LP. Although Steve stayed with the band for only a little under two years, he fit in so well with its carefree, bopping image that by the time it was all over in 1980, at least as far as many of the fans were concerned, Wings never had another drummer. He worked on three album projects with Wings — "Back To The Egg," the live LP "Concerts For The People Of Kampuchea," and some early demos for "Tug Of War." Steve also figured rather prominently on Wings' delightful disco tune "Goodnight Tonight" and just about stole the show on the Roaring Twenties–inspired video. Since leaving Wings, Steve has done session work in both England and America with artists such as Denny Laine and Julian Lennon. Recently married to a promising New York actress, Steve makes his home in the Big Apple, where he was interviewed in 1984.

GEOFFREY   How did you come to join Wings?

STEVE HOLLY   Well, I was living in a village in England where I'd lived since I was about eight years old. Denny Laine moved into the same village, and we became drinking buddies at the local pub. We had a few parties, and he didn't even know I played the drums until one evening, when there was nobody around that could play, I just sat in. He looked at me and said, "My God, I've known you all this time and didn't know you played." So then I did some solo work with him, but more importantly, I did an album with Kiki Dee that Elton John produced. Later Elton asked me to play on the "Single Man" album, and when I had done that, I think Denny realized that I could hold down a professional gig, so he asked me to audition for Paul McCartney and Wings.

GEOFFREY   Were your aspirations professional from the start?

STEVE   Yes. There's never been anything else in my life. When I was going to school, I used to get these little savings certificates for about twenty-five cents and save them up. I was saving for a drum kit of my own when I was only eight years old.

GEOFFREY   Tell me about the audition. Did you feel apprehensive about it?

STEVE   I was fine when I first got there. It was held in the basement of Paul's offices in Soho Square, and I was feeling great when I arrived with Denny. Laurence Juber and I were auditioning together, but I was a nervous wreck by the time he finally arrived, because I'd had hours of twitching in the cellar of his building just waiting for him. But after we got playing it was very comfortable, and he made me feel at ease, so we had a good time.

GEOFFREY   What did you do, old rock numbers?

STEVE   The usual kind of twelve-bar boogies and generally just bashed around a bit. We played some reggae tunes and a few little contrasting things just to give an overall picture of what I could do, I guess.

GEOFFREY   Did you feel you were there to be the new Wings drummer or that you were just having a bash?

STEVE   I knew that if I was good enough I would probably get the gig, because they didn't want to go through a big, long-drawn-out audition, and Paul wanted to get things moving fairly quickly. I felt that as long as I was at least adequate, I would have a good shot.

GEOFFREY   The particular lineup of Wings you were in probably had the most appeal of them all. How did you find out you got the job?

STEVE   It was at the end of that afternoon. We played for about two or three hours, and Paul suddenly said, "Fine. That's a good group, sounds great, let's go for it." He made his decision then and there, which is the fastest I've personally been through any audition! Denny and I went out afterwards, had a few drinks together, and celebrated. Denny was kind of welcoming me aboard, and then we flew out to America to meet with Lee Eastman and discuss the terms of our contracts and salaries.

GEOFFREY   Was life with the McCartneys social, or was it mostly work?

STEVE   There wasn't a tremendous amount of social activity. It was more of a working situation. I think Paul's opinion of it from the word go was at odds with mine. I felt as if I was in a group I wanted to be part of for a long time, and I was very upset when it fell apart. Of course I was more specifically upset about Paul's pot bust in Japan and that tour not coming off, because I felt that somehow, if that tour had gone on, then we would have become a very strong group. But looking at the twenty-two shows we played in the U.K., there were obviously problems that we had to iron out before we could take on the world, as it were.

GEOFFREY   What about Linda's musical contributions to Wings?

STEVE   Well, her thing is that she's so close to Paul that he just wants her around.

GEOFFREY   Does she actually play though?

STEVE   She can play single-note lines, and she plays pack chord stuff, but it's all pretty much programmed. She's the first person to admit she's no virtuoso keyboard player. I mean, she can't whiz around the board with lightning fingers or solo with the guys when they're just jamming, but she is certainly capable of learning parts and playing them.

GEOFFREY   Were you still with Wings when John was assassinated?

STEVE   No. But it was close on the heels of the Japanese tour. It was a period in Paul's life when it was just one upset after another.

GEOFFREY   Did Paul ever talk to you about it?

STEVE   No. I mean, I felt I couldn't really speak to him. It was much too personal, and I wasn't the person to ring him up and say, "Hey, I'm very sorry about John." There were plenty of other people doing their best to console him and plenty of press guys on his trail to get his comments, and I felt my calling him would just complicate matters, so I stayed completely out of the picture. In fact for four or five months afterwards I didn't even

Wings in their final configuration.

Paul McCartney

Linda McCartney

Steve Holly

Denny Laine

Laurence Juber

Vivian Stanshall — portrait of the artist as rock star.

see him. Then of course, when we did see each other again, it was after they'd decided that the band was to be no more, so it was a fairly strained period of time.

GEOFFREY   What is life around the McCartney farmyard like? Is it like Paul's song "Heart Of The Country," with kids running around barefoot, Shetland ponies, and dogs chasing about everywhere?

STEVE   You've just put it into a nutshell — that's exactly what it is! Of course there's the corporate side to the man, but predominantly he keeps that down-home flavor as firmly entrenched in his life as he can. I'm a great admirer of his lifestyle and the way he runs his life. The kids are very unspoiled. They go to regular schools, and they've all got great attitudes.

GEOFFREY   How does Paul handle the fans?

STEVE   He's a perfect gentleman. He goes out of his way. It doesn't matter who it is — he'll take time, he'll speak to people. He's amazing. I think he was always the one that kept the Beatles' image so clean. He always went out of his way to shake people's hands, to do this, to do that. John, I'm afraid, was far more critical of that situation altogether.

GEOFFREY   Let me ask you about the infamous pot bust in Japan. Where were you when you first realized what was happening?

STEVE   We were all there at the same time, and we were told at the airport that there was a minor complication, so we should go on to the hotel and that we'd be meeting later. I remember I was very tired, as it was an eighteen-hour flight, so I checked into my room and went to sleep. Later I was woken up by Linda at seven-thirty in the evening. She was kind of laughing very nervously and said, "Hey, Paul's been busted." And because she was laughing, I thought she was kidding around, so I just said, "Yeah, yeah. Great, Linda, I'll see you downstairs for dinner." I left it at that and just got up, had a shower, got dressed, went down to the bar, and there were a lot of MP staff sitting around with very forlorn faces and a lot of plainclothes police everywhere. The fans were going crazy, and I suddenly realized that she must be telling the truth. I hung out for a couple of days, hoping that they would find some way around it and the tour would pick up, but after three or four shows had been missed, I realized there was no way they were going to save the tour — or the band, for that matter.

As headmaster of the celebrated Bonzo Dog Doo Dah Band and later as a solo artist, Vivian Stanshall produced more affable madness than any composer/performer in recent memory. Born in Shillingford, Oxfordshire, he moved with his family to Leigh-on-Sea near Southend-on-Sea when still a boy. As a youth he joined the Merchant Navy and sailed the bounding main for almost a year. Near the end of his tour of duty Vivian shaved his head and enrolled in London's Central School of Art. "I wanted to be a painter and sculptor, full stop," he remembers. "It never occurred to me to be anything else. I met Larry ["Legs" Larry Smith] at art school when I first moved to London. Later I roomed with Rodney Slater, who was a practicing

"Legs" Larry Smith and Vivian Stanshall.

fascist and a part-time musician of some renown. Together we eventually formed the Bonzos." Seven years later the group broke up, and Viv worked briefly with two other bands, Freaks and then Grimms. Since that time he has collaborated with other prominent artists such as Stevie Winwood, Mike Oldfield, and the late Keith Moon. In 1980 Eel Pie Publishing (one of Pete Townshend's pet projects) printed Vivian's brilliant screenplay, *Sir Henry at Rawlinson's End*. The film itself, a biting satire of the English leisure classes starring Trevor Howard as the irascible old Sir Henry, was lauded by critics, loved by audiences, and chosen best film of the year at the prestigious Oxford Film Festival. Over the years Vivian has released a number of successful solo albums in Britain. These days he acts as host at his own floating riverside restaurant in Bristol, appropriately named The Old Profanity Showboat. This interview was conducted just outside London in 1983.

GEOFFREY   How did the Bonzos' appearance as the house band in the *Magical Mystery Tour* come about?

VIVIAN STANSHALL   Brian Epstein used to own a place called the Saville Theatre, and Paul and John used to sneak in occasionally to see us, because we supported the Cream a couple of times and the Bee Gees. Yes, I think the *Mystery Tour* was just dropped on us. Paul suddenly phoned up and said, "Do you fancy it?"

"LEGS" LARRY SMITH   We were doing a week's cabaret in somewhere wonderful like Darlington, which is up in the north of England, and our roadie came rushing back from the telephone and said, "You're not going to believe this." It was an almost definite confirmation that we'd gotten the *Mystery Tour*. The Beatles had personally invited us to perform.

VIVIAN   Someone nicked all our instruments, though, didn't they, from outside of that alley — don't you remember? All the saxes went, your kit went — we had to hire everything to do the film.

LARRY   It was pretty rushed because as I said, we were doing a week in Darlington. And believe it or not, the manager we had at the time was wondering whether we could get out of doing the gig, if I recall. And we had to rush around to find a substitute to play. We got Gene Pitney, as he was flying over.

GEOFFREY   You must have been personal favorites of the Beatles, or you wouldn't have been asked.

LARRY   Surely, yeah. That's very nice to know.

GEOFFREY   Were you around on the bus with them and all that?

VIVIAN   Oh no, we just did that one bit, and it was finito. Then they had that ruddy great party wherever the hell it was, where they all —

LARRY   At the Lancaster Hotel.

VIVIAN   Oh, we had a great jam that night, didn't we? God, I wish I had that on tape.

A rare Bonzo Dog promotional poster from the sixties.

GEOFFREY   Who was involved?

VIVIAN   Well, I was up onstage with Lennon doing vocals on "Lawdie Miss Clawdy," "Long Tall Sally" — you know, all the oldies. We screamed our heads off. Who was on the kit? Must have been Ringo, I should think, and Klaus Voorman played bass.

LARRY   George got up and blew some saxophone.

VIVIAN   That's right. By god, it was a great row!

LARRY   I remember going out into the lobby and overhearing Lulu speaking on the phone: "Hello, Mother? I'm in London having a great time. I just *can't* come home yet. I'm with the Beatles!" For me the most wonderful costume event of the evening was George Martin and his wife storming the cocktail area as Prince Philip and the Queen. For a moment everyone thought, "Can it really be them?" (*Laughter*) I mean, they just looked so right.

GEOFFREY   Tell me how Paul got involved in producing the band.

VIVIAN   Well, they wouldn't let him back into Poland. (*Laughter*) Actually I was more chummy with John myself, riding around in that absurd psychedelic Rolls of his. I think I just phoned Paul up and said, "Look, I think we could do with a hit record." So he said, "What have you got?" And so we sent him over some stuff, and when he heard "Urban Spaceman" he said, "That's the one. I'll come and do it, you fix up the studio," and he came down and we did it. Just to put us at our ease, he sat down and said, "I've just knocked this song off, what do you think of it?" and he played us "Hey Jude." So I said it was all right, apart from the verse! (*Laughter*)

LARRY   And I told him religion will *never* be a hit. You can't write about that! Anyway, we worked really efficiently, it was quite nice. We did the whole thing in about five hours. I don't know why he wanted to be called Apollo C. Vermouth on the record though.

VIVIAN   That was my idea. I didn't want the thing to sell on his name alone. It was nothing to do with anything contractual on his side, he was quite happy to have it out there with his name on it, but I just didn't think that would be a fair measure.

GEOFFREY   Do you know he put out a few tunes under the name of Bernard Webb? He also penned a few songs for other artists that Epstein had under assumed names, just to see if they would sell on their own or if everything was just selling because he was Paul McCartney. And he had a big number-one hit. Tell me about this relationship with Lennon.

VIVIAN   There's not a lot to tell really. Just the absurd anomalies of the time. We'd wind up at the Speakeasy or some other god-awful club, get sloshed, and he'd say, "Want a ride home, wack?" I'd say, "Okay, John," so he'd drop me off in my crabby basement in Islington that I was rat-hunchbacked in, and he'd be in his Rolls full of birds and things and just drive off!

LARRY   And I'd have been up two hours worrying where he'd been all night. (*Laughter*)

Neil Innes.

"What should have happened is that the Bonzos and the Beatles should have turned into one great Rutle band with all the Pythons and had a good laugh."

GEORGE HARRISON

"When I was about seven, my parents thought my brother and I ought to take some music lessons," recalls Neil Innes, "and I quite enjoyed the exercises until the day came when I had to do something different with both hands! By the time I was fourteen, though, the only reward for perfecting a piece was to be immediately given another, harder one. Well, I soon realized that this was nothing but a mug's game and called it quits." After finishing his basic education, Neil applied to three London art schools and to his surprise was accepted by all of them. He settled on Goldsmith's, where he concentrated on painting and design. It was during this period, while rooming with a friend in Blackheath, that Neil first met Vivian Stanshall and Rodney Slater in a New Cross pub. Just a few weeks later the nucleus formed of what was to become Bonzo Dog, and they performed their first gig at a South London pub called the Bird in the Hand. Years later Neil summed up their musical contribution: "Bonzo has probably stood the test of time because the music we made was 'human-sized'. That is, it was very easy for everyone to relate to, as just about everybody enjoys a good laugh."

Like the other members of the band Neil went on to a successful solo career, performing in several top-notch groups — Freaks, Grimms, the World, McGuinness Flint — and later with Monty Python. He appeared with the Beatles in *Magical Mystery Tour*, played "Baby," George's female nanny in his "Crackerbox Palace" video, and shared the screen with Mr. Harrison in the wonderfully absurd Beatle parody, *The Rutles*. He also worked on several of George's Handmade Film productions — *Monty Python Live at the Hollywood Bowl* and *The Life of Brian* — and Michael Palin's titillating one-off, *The Missionary*. Neil has also masterminded a handful of solo recordings — "The Rutle Soundtrack LP," "How Sweet To Be An Idiot," "Off The Record," and his popular 1984 hit single, a "techno-pop" remake of the Bonzos' classic "Humanoid Boogie." He was interviewed at his comfortable country home near Ipswich, Suffolk, in June 1983.

GEOFFREY   I understand that you met the Beatles while you were recording your first Bonzo single, "My Brother Makes The Noises For The Talkies," at Abbey Road.

NEIL INNES   Not to talk to. It was during those days when they looked like the Blues Brothers. They all had dark glasses on, black suits, and were all coming through the hall grinning.

GEOFFREY   That must have impressed you.

NEIL   We didn't care a toss, quite frankly, about anything that was going on.

GEOFFREY   Many of the big pop stars were quite enamored of the Bonzo Dog Band, weren't they?

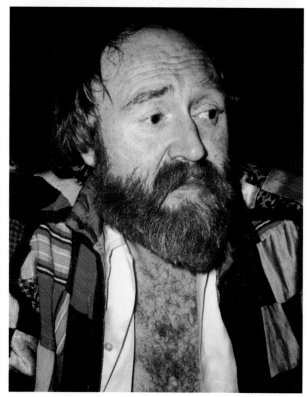

Vivian.

Two rare, autographed Bonzo albums, "Tadpoles" and "Gorilla."

NEIL   At the *Magical Mystery Tour* party, when Larry came out with his false tits on to do a tap dance, John was dressed as a rocker and yelled out, "Come on, Larry, show us your tits, we've all seen them!" (*Laughter*) I think people like Eric Clapton and Jimi Hendrix secretly admired us a great deal.

GEOFFREY   *Magical Mystery Tour* stands as one of the few appearances of the Bonzos on film.

NEIL   I know, that's the irony of it. The Bonzos were always such a visual act, and there's very little movie evidence of that left, and a whole new generation has grown up listening to the records, never having seen them!

GEOFFREY   Tell me how the Rutles project came about, and specifically how you did the soundtrack music for it.

NEIL   By the time we'd formulated the idea of doing *The Rutles*, I'd made a couple of inroads into song-writing. We needed about fourteen Beatle-style songs which ran the whole gamut, from "I Want To Hold Your Hand" to the psychedelic stuff. It was a curse in a way, because I've been labeled as a parodist ever since. But it was a real labor of love, because I just thought, "Ah, I remember that kind of song," and I just started writing them up. Anyway, the Rutles got together, and I thought, "This is one of the few astute things I've done in my career, to insist that we rehearse together for a fortnight as a group in a grotty little place, in Hendon . . ." So we more or less went through the experience, the "rags to riches" thing. By the time we left the place, we felt like a real group, and it was really good, because we had none of the inhibitions about having to make it. We knew we were going to make it (*Laughter*), because we were going to be doing a film in a few weeks' time! So everybody was very up. We made the record in about two weeks. In fact the only part of the project that came in under budget was the album!

GEOFFREY   Your Lennon spoof, "Cheese And Onions," surfaced in a very peculiar way.

NEIL   Yes, Eric Idle and I went to America to do another "Saturday Night Live," and I did the "Cheese And Onions" thing with the white piano and the long hair as a takeoff of John. Just before the Rutles came over here, the *New Music Express* rang me up and said, "We've got a rather interesting question to ask you. We've heard one of the Rutles' songs on a Beatle bootleg album — what have you got to say about it?" "I don't know. Could you tell me a bit more about this song? Play it to me." So they did, and I just fell about laughing. "That's me, you fool, what's it doing on a Beatle bootleg album?" I suddenly figured it must have been taken from "Saturday Night Live." The poor journalist thought he'd got a scoop, almost caught me with my fingers in the till, as it were.

GEOFFREY   Tell me about the filming of *The Rutles*.

NEIL   Oh, that was great fun. The wonderful thing was that Eric and Mick Jagger are very good pals, and Eric just said, "These are the names of the characters. You just tell us the story." So Mick sat back in his hotel room and made up a load of crap about this imaginary band called the Rutles. The same with Paul Simon. George had cleared it with the other three for us to use real footage of the Beatles. Because when we looked at the Shea Stadium footage from the stage, it could have been anywhere. You don't actually see the crowd, so you could cut in, and this is where Gary Weis, the director, was so clever, because he insisted that the labs come out with exactly the right sort of print that would match that one perfectly. A lot of care was taken on that sort of thing. So we hired a big C stage at Shepperton, put black curtains behind it, got a couple of rent-a-cops to stand in front, and cut it in with the old footage, and it was fine.

GEOFFREY   The film was pretty heavy on Yoko, making her a Nazi.

NEIL   Well, you see, it wasn't actually Yoko, this was the Rutles.

GEOFFREY   Let's put it this way — it was a fond look back at the Beatles. It wasn't too heavy on any of the Beatles, except Yoko got put into a Nazi uniform. It certainly looked like a swipe at her all right.

NEIL   You'd have to ask Eric about that, that was his vision of it. I kept myself to a very large extent to the music.

GEOFFREY   George's being involved in the production validated it somewhat, didn't it?

NEIL   In many ways the story needed to be told. There's lots of things that are too heavy about the real story to make it entertaining at the end of the day. So for example, "All You Need Is Cash" was a pretty good way of saying from their side what it was like, but without making it too heavy. It must have been quite grueling that just because you've made some popular records, folks will bring people in wheelchairs up to you so that you can touch them and make them better. On the whole it doesn't make for a very healthy ego, all of that stuff, but I think the Beatles survived the madness of it quite well. You can't do it with any other group. The Beatles hold a very special place in history, and we all respect them a great deal.

Season's greetings from the Rutles.

Neil and George. London 1979.

"Legs" Larry Smith and Neil Innes.

The Rutles in a rare photo.

10

A Candle Burns

The Fab Three

> *"The Beatles saved the world from boredom."* GEORGE HARRISON

> *"Give peace a chance. Remember love. The only hope for any of us is peace. Violence begets violence. You're all geniuses and you're all beautiful. You don't need anybody to tell you who you are or what you are. You are what you are. Go out there and get peace. Think peace. Live peace and breathe peace. You'll get it as soon as you like."* JOHN LENNON

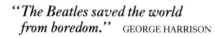

The formidable gates to Friar Park.

Just behind the striking wrought-iron gates of George Harrison's palatial Oxfordshire estate, Friar Park, is a small green and gold sign advising all uninvited guests to "get your ass outta here" in fourteen different languages. But for the favored few who sail past the star-struck masses, it is a vastly different story. Close friends like Jon and Vicky Lord, sixties crooner Joe Brown, Eric and Tanya Idle, Elton John, "Legs" Larry Smith, Ringo and Barbara, ace guitarist Alvin Lee, David and Ginger Gilmore, Derek Taylor, Eric and Pattie Clapton, Neil and Yvonne Innes, and Ray Cooper are greeted by one of Sir Frank Crisp's crafty legends carved in stone above the main entranceway: "Walk in and welcome, honest friend repose. Thief get thee hence, to thee I'll not unclose."

George's home is definitely his castle. Friar Park is without a doubt his most prized possession and an inspiration for his work as an artist. Built in 1889 by Sir Frank Crisp on the remains of an ancient friary, its polished red-brick and yellow low-stone exterior boasts a number of intricately carved friars and gargoyles, each illustrating in a humorous, tongue-in-cheek manner a parable from the quasi-religious philosophy of its eccentric founder. As for the grounds, it took a team of landscape artists over twenty years to lay out the elaborate system of split-level lakes, topiary gardens,

George at home in his twenty-four-track studio.

mazes, artificial caverns, and the miniature replica of the famous Matterhorn. After Sir Frank died in 1919, Friar Park was sold to Sir Percival, a decorated English aristocrat who shortly afterward turned the property over to an order of Salesian nuns, who converted it into an exclusive private girls' school. By the mid-sixties Friar Park School was deeply in debt, and the aging sisters were unable to care for the property. In 1970 it was put on the market and eventually sold to George and Pattie Harrison for an estimated $336,000. An enthusiastic sun worshipper, George also has houses in Hana Maui, Hawaii, and on Hamilton Island thirty miles off the coast of Australia, but he reserves most of his time for the quiet, pastoral life he so much enjoys in Henley-on-Thames.

George has many professional interests these days. Most important is his role of executive producer and chief idea man for Handmade Film Productions of Cadogan Square in London. In order to produce his first Handmade project, *The Life of Brian*, filmed in 1978 with his old Python pals, he had to put up Friar Park as collateral to secure a large enough loan. Other Handmade properties include *Monty Python Live at the Hollywood Bowl*, *The Long Good Friday*, *Time Bandits*, *Privates on Parade*, *Scum*, *Bullshot*, *The Missionary*, *Private Function*, *Water*, and *Shanghai*.

Since John's death George has released only two major albums, "Somewhere In England" (which includes the much publicized Beatle reunion number, "All Those Years Ago") and "Gone Troppo." The only other official releases from George have been an old Bob Dylan composition entitled "I Don't Want To Do It" showcased on the soundtrack of the movie *Porky's Revenge* and a spot as backup vocalist and producer on the title track from *Bullshot*, sung by "Legs" Larry Smith. A note should be added here concerning Warner Brothers' radical readjustment of George's "Somewhere In England" LP shortly before its American release. It seems that when George finally delivered the master tapes to the A & R department in Los Angeles, four songs — "Flying Hour," "Lay His Head," "Sat Singing," and "Tears Of The World" — were judged to be "musically below par" and deleted from the album. A few advance copies had already been distributed within the industry, however, and eventually the tunes made their way onto numerous Beatle and George Harrison bootlegs around the world. Ironically, among hard-core Harrison collectors and connoisseurs these four "inferior" tracks are some of the most popular of his *unofficial* releases.

Today George Harrison looks back on the Beatle years with very mixed emotions. On one hand he is intensely proud of what the band accomplished, but he also believes the persistent manic adulation they attracted may be in some way responsible for John's death. "The whole Beatle thing is like a nightmare to me. I don't even like to talk about it," he told me coldly when we first met in Henley two years ago. "It was all absolute madness." The following conversation took place at keyboardist Jon Lord's sprawling country estate, Yewden Lodge, in the company of Olivia Harrison just before Christmas 1984 and is reconstructed from detailed notes

Friar Park shortly after the Harrisons moved in.

A rare picture postcard of Friar Park as it was in
the early 1900s.

FRIAR PARK, HENLEY-ON-THAMES.

London gallery owner Mary Tambini, George, Olivia, and "Legs" Larry Smith at Friar Park.

George and Olivia in Henley during the shooting of Handmade Films' drawing room feature *Bullshot*.

The unreleased cover of George's "Somewhere In England" LP. Although counterfeit copies have been found, this one is original.

Ringo in the early eighties.

made immediately following the Harrisons' departure on that rainy, windswept night in rural Oxfordshire.

GEOFFREY How do you remember Srila Prabhupada?

GEORGE HARRISON Prabhupada always used to say that he was "the servant of the servant of the servant of Krsna." He was very humble. The thing about Prabhupada, he was more like a dear friend than anything else. We used to sit in his room in my house and talk for hours.

GEOFFREY I understand that on his deathbed he called you his "archangel," took a ring from his finger, and instructed his disciples to make sure you got it. Did you?

GEORGE Yes, I got it. I have it.

GEOFFREY Were you his disciple?

GEORGE As far as being a full-fledged devotee, no. I liked him and his philosophy though. I never followed all the rules and regulations that strictly, however.

GEOFFREY What is your attitude towards spiritual life these days?

GEORGE Well, I was at the airport in Honolulu recently, and I met a guy dressed in these old saffron corduroys. He approached me with a book and said, "My guru wants you to have this." I didn't make out if he recognized me or not. I said, "What do you mean your guru wants me to have this book? Does he know I'm here?" The book said, "Something Something Guru, The World's Spiritual Leader." Now I read the book, and this guy doesn't like *anybody*. He ran down Sai Baba, Yogananda, Guru Maharaji, and everybody. It seemed very dogmatic. I'm just not into that. It's the organization of religion that turns me off a bit. I just try to go into myself. Like Donovan said, "You've got to go into your own temple once a day." It's a very personal thing, spiritual life.

GEOFFREY How do you feel about the Beatles myth today?

GEORGE All this stuff about the Beatles being able to save the world was rubbish. It was just people trying to put the responsibility on our shoulders. The thing about the Beatles is that they saved the world from boredom. I mean, even when we got to America the first time, everybody was running around in Bermuda shorts, brush cuts, and braces on their teeth. But we didn't really create any great change, we just heralded that change of consciousness that happened in the sixties. We went along with it, that's all.

"Ringo is just Ringo, that's all there is to it. And he's every bloody bit as warm, unassuming, funny, and kind as he seems. He was an only child, you know, so we three were always like brothers to him. He was quite simply the heart of the Beatles."   JOHN LENNON

On Monday, April 27, 1981, at London's Marylebone Register office, Ringo Starr married American actress Barbara Bach in a quiet civil ceremony attended by a few close friends, his immediate family, and of course George Harrison and Paul McCartney. Although the weather was less than perfect, the whole affair went off without a hitch. That is, except that Ringo's lifelong friend and mentor, John Lennon, wasn't there to share his joy. "John always had the biggest heart of us all," said Ringo shortly after his murder. "It's impossible to imagine that he's really gone." So deep in fact was Ringo's regard for John that he even purchased his former home in Surrey, Tittenhurst Park.

Today Ringo's low-key lifestyle at home with Barbara reflects his realization that nothing lasts forever and that every moment of life with someone you love is precious. As he has been plagued most of his life with several recurring health problems, Ringo's cavalier bachelor life has taken its toll, and he has been forced to party just a little less heartily than he used to. Now a typical day in the life of Ringo Starr might begin with an impromptu drum lesson for his stepson or a stroll through the grounds to watch Barbara ride one of her beloved prize throroughbreds. Afternoons might be spent conferring with his longtime secretary, Joan Woodgate, on pressing business matters or discussing upcoming recording ventures with chief aid, Mike O'Donnell. Evenings are generally reserved for family functions such as dinner in town with Ringo's children from his previous marriage or a drive into Henley to visit George, Olivia, and Dhani Harrison.

Ever since Ringo met Barbara on the set of *Caveman*, the two have been virtually inseparable, both personally and professionally. Together they co-starred in the CBS miniseries "Princess Daisy" and worked with Paul and Linda McCartney on the MPL-produced cinematic short *The Cooler* and on *Give My Regards to Broad Street*. The Starrs have become familiar figures on the international variety show circuit, guesting on "The Tonight Show" and "Saturday Night Live." Current projects include Ringo's role as an uppity turtle in Irwin Allan's television adaptation of *Alice in Wonderland* and some session work for the soundtrack of George's recent film *Water*. In the summer of 1983 Ringo embarked on an ambitious twenty-five-hour program for the ABC radio network based on his remembrances of the Beatle years, entitled "Ringo's Yellow Submarine" (written by ace Canadian producer Doug Thompson). In 1984 he took on the task of narrating a twenty-six-episode children's series for British television entitled "Thomas the Tank Engine and Friends."

Of course music continues to be Ringo's first love, and throughout the eighties he has performed live and on record with such artists as the Beach Boys, George Harrison, Paul McCartney, and the legendary Carl Perkins. He has also released two solo albums. The first, "Stop And Smell The Roses," was a joint venture using the talents of five producers. Ringo explains, "I figured using so many different producers would make things more interesting. George looked after the single, "Wrack My Brain," which he wrote, sang backup vocals on, and played guitar. Paul produced three of the tracks — "Private Property," "Sure To Fall," and "Attention." He also

Royal Dalton Toby mugs modeled on the "Sgt. Pepper" cover. 1985.

A few of the many Beatle fan magazines published over the years.

Paul and Linda's elegant, Georgian-style town-house in London's fashionable St. John's Wood, just around the corner from Abbey Road. 1983.

PHOTO: LINDA McCARTNEY

© 1982 MPL COMMUNICATIONS LTD   PRINTED IN ENGLAND

POST CARD

mpl

A postcard personally autographed by Paul, Linda, Ringo, Barbara, and George Martin at the taping of the McCartneys' "Take It Away" video in London.

A photo by the author of Paul in Covent Garden.

sang backup and played bass and piano. But it wasn't really like old times because I was on the move when I recorded the album. We worked in London, New York, Nice, and the Caribbean. Besides, the three of us didn't ever work together at one time." Other tunes were produced by Rolling Stone Ron Wood, Harry Nilsson, and Stephen Stills. Ringo's next record, "Old Wave," released in 1983, had all the elements of a smash hit. Produced by ex-Eagle Joe Walsh, it featured stirring performances from Eric Clapton, Ray Cooper, Chris Stainton, John Entwistle, and Walsh himself. However, the album falls short of its goal of being a free-and-easy celebration of good-time rock 'n' roll, but happily, the irrepressible, good-natured Ringo still rambles on.

"Songwriting is still my great love, but I took turning forty as a cue to develop in different directions, to do some of the millions of things that have interested me in my life but which I've never had time to explore. I know it's a cliché, but what's important to me is nothing that I've achieved, none of the fame or even the money. It's only the family, my kids, their health, and safety. And Linda's really the warmth of the family. When I was eighteen, I deliberately said stuff that was clichéd and which, as it happens, was wrong. So what should I do now? Still try to sound clever or just keep trying to get it right?" PAUL McCARTNEY

Although Paul McCartney wasn't exactly pleased with many of John's remarks concerning their tempestuous twenty-four-year relationship, he was nevertheless stunned by the news of his senseless murder. "I have hidden myself in my work today," he told a handful of reporters stationed outside his Sussex home on December 9, 1980. "I feel shattered, angry, and very, very sad. He was pretty rude about me sometimes, but I secretly admired him for it. There was no question that we were friends; I really loved the guy. In years to come I think people will realize that John was an international statesman. He often looked a loony and even made a few enemies, but he was really fantastic. His record 'Give Peace A Chance' helped to stop the Vietnam War. He made a lot of sense."

Severely unnerved by John's death, Paul took on several additional bodyguards and tightened security around his primary residence, "Waterfalls." The persistent invasions into his privacy by the press and the discovery of an alleged plot to murder him became too much for the McCartneys, so they flew to the Caribbean island of Montserrat to finish up work on Paul's latest album, "Tug Of War." It was around this time that Wings' loyal and talented co-conspirator Denny Laine decided he'd had enough of Paul's negative attitude toward touring and graciously bowed out of the group. "There is no row," said Laine's manager Brian Adams. "But Denny likes to tour, and Paul has decided that Wings will not be making any plans for performing in the near future." When it was finally released in April 1982, "Tug Of War" was well worth the wait for McCartney fans and was shipped out certified gold to record stores around the globe. Smoothly produced and orchestrated by George Martin and Paul, the album con-

Before writing this book, the author played Ronald McDonald, the clown, for McDonald's television ads in Canada. Paul sent this unsolicited greeting to the clown.

tained twelve new tunes and fostered over half a dozen hits — "Tug Of War," "Take It Away," the touching Lennon tribute, "Here Today," "Ballroom Dancing," "Wanderlust," "Dress Me Up As A Robber," and "Ebony And Ivory," McCartney's catchy plea for interracial unity co-written and -performed with Stevie Wonder.

A confirmed workaholic, Paul also readied two fine videos for release with the album, one for the title track, an outrageously campy tug-of-war between man and beast pilfered from the far-out thirties flick *Mighty Joe Young*, and one for *Take It Away*, an imaginative romp around the rock biz starring actor John Hurt, the Macs, Ringo and Barbara, George Martin, and almost the entire British chapter of the Wings' Fun Club!

Meanwhile, on the home front Paul and Linda have been busy looking after their children and doing their best to ensure a proper working-class upbringing for the unspoiled McCartney brood. Their eldest child, Heather, is Linda's daughter from her first marriage to American college professor John See, and Paul formally adopted her in the early seventies. Strikingly pretty but often painfully shy, like her mother she adores horses and has won several top awards in England for her original photography. She appeared in the film *Let It Be* and was the inspiration behind Paul's unreleased tune "Heather," recorded with Donovan. Mary McCartney (born August 28, 1969) has likewise figured in her father's illustrious career. As a baby she was pictured on the cover of his first solo work, "McCartney," peering cautiously out of Paul's jacket, and shared top billing with her parents in the November 7, 1969, issue of *Life* magazine. Stella (born September 13, 1971) wasn't even around when the Beatles were extending the boundaries of popular music and has only vague memories of her parents' years on the road with Wings. The beloved baby of the family, James Louis McCartney, rushed into the world on September 12, 1977, and like his sister Mary also appears on one of his dad's albums — "McCartney II," where he is seen on the inner sleeve tugging aggressively on Paul's shirttails. The McCartney children have all attended local Sussex schools and like other country kids do their fair share of farmyard chores.

Paul, of course, is a very shrewd business operator whose privately owned umbrella company, MPL (McCartney Productions Limited), manages the family's international holdings in everything from fine art to music publishing. MPL owns the publishing rights to a very eclectic catalogue of material including "Autumn Leaves," "The Christmas Song," "Stormy Weather," the Broadway musicals "Grease" and "Annie," and almost the entire portfolio of Paul's childhood idol Buddy Holly. Strangely enough, while Paul controls so many works by other artists, neither he nor George nor Ringo holds the rights to *any* of the Beatles' own compositions. In the early eighties Paul and Yoko placed a bid with copyright holder Sir Lew Grade for almost $40 million in an effort to buy back the Beatle catalogue. Ironically, it was Paul's old songwriting partner, superstar Michael Jackson, who finally scored the highly prized compositions for the whopping sum of $47.5 million.

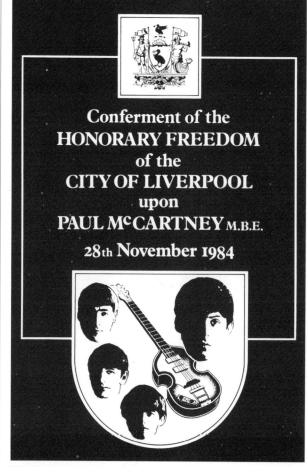

The brochure from the ceremony bestowing on Paul Liverpool's highest honor.

An unsolicited but highly prized memento from
Paul and Linda.

The author with the McCartneys. London 1983.

Paul's personal test pressing of the twelve-inch version of "I'll Give You A Ring".

The front entrance of MPL in Soho Square, London.

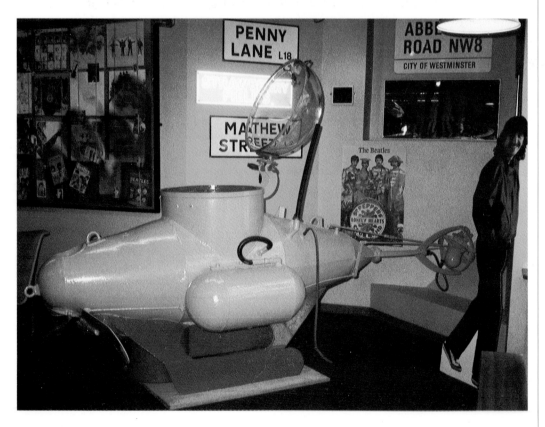

The interior of the Cavern Mecca (Beatle Information Centre) on Mathew Street in Liverpool, which unfortunately closed only months after it opened. This Yellow Submarine was used at the London premiere of the film in 1968.

One of the highlights of 1982 for Paul was the overwhelming success of his sultry R & B–inspired duet with Michael Jackson entitled "The Girl Is Mine," which appeared on Jackson's triple-platinum chart buster LP, "Thriller." Paul's next recording project, the stylish and easygoing "Pipes Of Peace," proved once again what a formidable production team McCartney and Martin were. Two of its tunes, "Say Say Say" and "The Man," were co-written with Michael Jackson and another, "Hey Hey," with famed jazz bassist Stanley Clarke. *Give My Regards to Broad Street*, Paul's imaginative "day in the mind of a pop star," took the ambitious, aspiring writer/actor over fourteen months of laborious preproduction work to pull together and many more months to finance, film, and distribute to movie theaters around the world. "I wanted to make the sort of movie that I like to see," says Paul. "It's an old-fashioned musical, a good night out — nothing heavy. Like most people, I go to the cinema to be entertained, not to see my problems up on the screen." Although the film was not very well received by the critics (especially in the United States), audiences generally seemed to enjoy following Paul's imaginative escapades through the surreal work-a-day world of a rock 'n' roll superstar. The project fostered only one bona fide hit in "No More Lonely Nights" but did manage to rack up a real winner for MPL in the clever animated featurette, "Rupert's Adventure," which the industrious McCartney clan had been working on sporadically for fifteen years!

On July 13, 1985, Paul joined the *crème de la crème* of pop and over a billion enthusiastic fans the world over to lend a helping hand to the hunger-stricken continent of Africa by performing at the celebrated Live Aid Concert. Closing the star-studded Wembley show, Paul led the audience in a sing-along version of "Let It Be" and then teamed up with the entire ensemble for a rousing chorus of "Do They Know It's Christmas."

The first thing one notices when meeting Yoko Ono is her tiny, geisha girl handshake. She is a peaceful, elegant woman whose well-known burden rests on her diminutive shoulders with grace and dignity. One instantly recognizes that John Lennon was right: Yoko is a remarkable woman and a competent, creative, and important artist. The press was wrong about her all along. By the time she met the Beatles, there was precious little left to break up.

Inside the Dakota in 1983 one wonders whether anyone could ever forget what happened there on that unusually mild December night when John and Yoko decided to forgo a late dinner and come right home to look in on Sean. One senses the presence of another age, far removed from New York's current state of deep decline. The elderly woman at the reception desk announces my partner, radio producer Allan Lysaght, and myself as the loudest buzzer in the city summons us into the cavernous hallways of this remarkable building and right up to a large wooden door marked "Studio One." Inside there are pictures of John and Yoko every-

The Dakota Apartments.

With Yoko and Sean in the Dakota. February 1983.

John in the recording studio. 1966.

where, while wall-to-wall filing cabinets house the Lennon's cultural legacy to a generation. On one wall the platinum albums for "Double Fantasy" face off against letters to John and Yoko from world leaders. A single, strategically placed bumper sticker declares "Peace Will Reign Over The Earth" from an office bulletin board that also holds several gun control pamphlets. "You know the way to the apartment, don't you?" asks George Speering, number-one troubleshooter for Lenono, the clever name of John and Yoko's music publishing company. Jenny Myers, our official record company escort, replies, "Yeah, sure. See you," as we head for New York's only water-pressure-operated elevator and, seven floors above, the incomparable Yoko Ono Lennon. Soon afterward we are ushered into a large, light, all-white room that beautifully enshrines John's pure white piano. Family and childhood pictures of John and Yoko sit elegantly on top of the piano, while a particularly sardonic-looking John smiles out of one tiny, hand-painted frame, proudly wearing a T-shirt that says, "The Greeting Committee."

GEOFFREY   You know, I met a man in London recently who said, "That Yoko Ono, she lived in the same building as me, and I had a little stepladder I used to get into my apartment with, and one day it was gone, but I found a note under the door saying, 'Please come and see your stepladder at the Indica Gallery,' so I went there, and it was painted white!" Did you do that? Did you steal someone's stepladder?

YOKO ONO   No, well, we didn't actually *steal* it. We borrowed the stepladder really. He was a very nice fellow, and he was very kind to lend it to us. After the exhibition opened, I couldn't find a proper ladder! So we just painted that one white, you know. Some of the gallery people said, "Well, we can pay you for this. After all, it's just a ladder, isn't it? Aren't you happy it's in an art exhibition?" But he was saying, "No, I would like it back, and I don't particularly like it white." We paid for it in the end, but it was rather strange. I think the gallery people thought he'd be very delighted that suddenly his ladder was an art piece!

ALLAN LYSAGHT   Was that the one you had when John climbed up the ladder and looked through a telescope at a small sign that said "Yes?"

YOKO   That's the one . . . These days I am resigned to the fact that all right, all right, so we were a couple for how many years? How many decades? When John was alive, I used to always try and keep my independence, because he was such a strong, powerful energy — with the whole world behind him as well, by the way. So if I didn't keep my independence, I would have just been swallowed up. Whenever somebody called me "Mrs. Lennon" I used to say, "Mrs. Lennon? Sorry, I'm Yoko Ono, thank you." Then after John died, somehow when people called me "Mrs. Lennon," I felt good about it. Also there was the feeling, "Yes, it's all right. I *am* Mrs. Lennon." People often write to me saying, "We grieved over John's death and just wanted to know how his widow was doing." That would have maybe made me feel a bit strange two years ago, but now I'm very grateful people are writing, because they love John and are concerned about his family.

GEOFFREY I've always felt that there was a great, though basically silent, following for Yoko Ono.

YOKO Look, you don't have to say that. Whenever I do something now, I feel that my first concern should be, "Do you think John would like this?" I don't want to do anything that would shame his name or embarrass him. When I'm doing something and I know John would have approved, I feel much better. Let's just say all this has mellowed me in a way. So that old independence thing is rapidly disappearing.

GEOFFREY You're talking to us about how you've grown through the whole thing.

YOKO Oh yes, it's really amazing. The first time my assistants downstairs showed me piles of letters and telegrams that had come in, I said, "Oh, it's too bad John's not here," meaning I automatically assumed that they were letters and telegrams sent to John. And they said, "No, Yoko, these are to you." So I was thinking, "Oh great, but why?" And from then on there was a nice dialogue going on with the fans. Of course it's very hard to send a reply to each letter, and so I sent out one to everyone. Some people were a little upset that it wasn't actually an individual reply.

ALLAN It's funny how your records are being accepted more today. I think you could rerelease some of your earlier work.

YOKO Probably one day. When I'm not making a new record, you know.

GEOFFREY How do you remember John?

YOKO He was a very direct person, but there was another side too, very shy and not open — a complex person. But that's what really woke me up in a way. I was just like most of the sixties crowd, getting more and more complex but becoming a little bit out of touch with my own body, shall we say. So along comes this man who was really very straight and honest. I was still into my old bag of being shy and not communicating, or if I did, communicating with a little symbolism, and here comes John and then later Sean saying, "Wake up! Come on, wake up!"

GEOFFREY You showed my wife and I that I can be yin sometimes and she can be yang. That's a very important thing that John and Yoko gave to a lot of people.

YOKO Well, the funny thing was, it has a lot to do with John too. I mean, if he didn't have the basic material, I couldn't have worked with him, you know? John was an Englishman, and you can just imagine being raised by an English couple — a strong-headed woman, independent but caring —

GEOFFREY Auntie Mimi, right?

Yoko's gift to the author following the interview.

A lithograph by John of Yoko in a pose reminiscent of the Mona Lisa.

210

A promotional poster for Yoko's "It's Alright" LP.

Sean Ono Lennon flashes a peace sign to *his* generation. The Dakota Apartments, February 1983.

John Ono Lennon
December 9, 1940–December 8, 1980
Forever in our hearts

IT'S ALRIGHT

yoko

YOKO ONO ON POLYDOR RECORDS + TAPES

All the Beatles' albums released by Capitol/EMI
— a hard-to-find 1981 promotional poster.

A scene from the London production of *Lennon*, starring Mia Soteriou, Jonathan Barlow, and Mark McGann. One of many stage productions about the slain Beatle.

YOKO   Yes. You know, I can just hear her saying, "It's time to get some milk for the cats, dear" and the men all tending the garden. That's how it was in a way, and that's all right. Making tea was very natural for him to do, it was very nice . . .

GEOFFREY   And baking bread.

YOKO   Yes. So there was nothing really new about that. John had a very vulnerable side, and I had the tough side, I suppose, as well as a vulnerable side. We can all exchange roles once in a while. You know, sometimes it's good to be alone, to have your own space. Loneliness of course is a very different thing. You can experience it in a crowd. Maybe because of how I dealt with the situation after John died, people think that I'm a very strong woman and therefore different, so when I say, "It's all right," they say, "Well, it's all right for you because you're especially strong!" No, it's nothing like that. I consider myself just normal. If somebody says something nasty about me, I get hurt and think about it for the whole day. And the way I coped with John's death was almost a miracle! Part of me was . . . well, part of me is *still* in shock . . . and the other side was a like a little baby — "Oh, why did this happen," and "I need a big teddy bear." So when I look back on what I did — all the videos, the album, and the public announcements — I think, "Wow, how did I do that?" So there are several people in me, and they somehow organized it. I was put into a situation, and I just coped with it.

GEOFFREY   You're getting on with your contribution to making the eighties the way John wanted, so that the man up in Washington doesn't have his way.

YOKO   I think that when you really look at the system, there is an automatic operation that stops anyone who's there, regardless of his personality, from going too far from what the people really want. Now it's our responsibility to give him a definite sign of what we want, a unified opinion. Even in a man-woman relationship, we know that when we're giving so many conflicting signals to each other, it makes it very difficult. We know that it's better to try to express our needs in a way our partner understands. We're getting wise on an individual level, so why don't we get smart about communication with the government? Now if we really present him with a unified opinion, he then has the responsibility to carry it out. The problem is that we don't have a unified opinion, or maybe we're just not expressing it. We should be very thankful that we have a system like we do. In a dictatorship they don't have to care about people's opinions, you know. This time around we have to really voice it. I'm suggesting a peace poll, all done on the congressional level. Every city, every town in all the states would do their own polling.

GEOFFREY   Work through the system?

YOKO   Yes, because the system is really very good actually, if it's used right.

GEOFFREY   Yoko, do you believe in God?

YOKO   God or Goddess? No, it's just a joke. Well, look, I do believe that there's some kind of big power that is beyond us . . .

GEOFFREY   And in us too?

YOKO   Right. But you can also explain it in a way that agnostics would understand. It's like a mass dream, a human race dream. For instance, we always wanted to fly, and finally, yes, we now have airplanes. Of course that's not quite the way we were thinking of flying! Also there was always a lot of talk in literature about the moon. So we eventually went to the moon. There's always a collective dream that we have as the human race. And this time around I think maybe the game is just to survive. There are three things we all want, you know: to love, to be happy, and to survive. There's nobody in the world who doesn't want those things. Even the people who are saying, "I want to commit suicide" — it's only a kind of reverse expression of wanting happiness. So that's what we're all interested in. And anybody who thinks they can somehow con us into thinking otherwise, they're the dreamers. We are the realists, and there are billions of us thinking the same thing. That is what I call the "great design" that is above us.

GEOFFREY   How do you think the world can find peace today?

YOKO   We'll do it. Step by step it will happen. The problem is in the way we think. It's too bad the economic situation is so poor, because there's a lot of people suffering, which is making the world very tense and violent. But that sort of thing can be solved rather easily through the political system that we have, I'm sure. And it's not true anymore to say that war is economically viable.

GEOFFREY   I heard that you and John were going to a protest march near that terrible time in 1980.

YOKO   The plan was, we were going to San Francisco that Thursday to join a march the next day for equal pay for Oriental people in the area. It was announced, we sent a statement there, and John was very happy about it, because John has a son who is half Oriental. So he was envisioning carrying Sean and saying, "Here's . . ."

GEOFFREY   Living proof of the harmony?

YOKO   Yes, but that was only one of the things we were going to do together. That probably indicated we were going to do a few things in that direction.

GEOFFREY   Do you believe in reincarnation?

YOKO   Well, I think we all have many lives probably.

GEOFFREY   John once sang, "I don't believe in Jesus, Krsna, Gita, etc." But when he went with you to Japan, he visited the temples of Buddha.

YOKO   Oh, sure. He believed in the "big power," and any expression of that he had a great respect for, as I do. I'd like to say that until I met John, I didn't really know what the Beatles were all about. I suppose I first heard

Strawberry Fields, the teardrop-shaped parcel of land in Central Park recently dedicated to John's memory by the City of New York.

214

John and Yoko preside over the opening of John's first one-man art exhibit, "You Are Here." He dedicated it "To Yoko from John, with Love." July 1968.

about them like most people in those days — not as fans, but rather as a social phenomenon. Elvis Presley was another social phenomenon that I wasn't involved with either but just sort of knew about. Since I've recently gotten more involved with Paul, I now know what he's done, and it's a very beautiful thing. After all, he's one of the Beatles, and that's what John did as well, and being Sean's mother, I'm part of it too. I feel a family pride in what they did. What the Beatles were all about was just simple love — "I want to hold your hand," that's the entire gist of it! It's a beautiful thing, and no wonder they were so popular! They changed the entire world. A working-class background was something to be ashamed of before that, especially in Britain. They changed everybody's consciousness. Before the Beatles maybe people wouldn't even listen to a young guy. It was a social revolution. And in that sense I really admire what they did.

GEOFFREY   Yoko, how do you remember the events immediately following the tragedy?

YOKO   Well, I was still shaking in bed, so to speak, in the old bedroom that John and I used to sleep in, which is on the 72nd Street side. All night long these people were chanting and playing John's records. So I continually heard John's voice, which at the time was really a bit too much. In a way I learned that I don't have all that much control over my destiny. That's just how it is, and I have to realize that. John and I thought we knew all about enlightenment, so there was that very arrogant side to us. And this was like a big silver hammer from nowhere saying, "Well, just remember you don't know it *all*. There's a lot more to learn!" Therefore I've said these last fifty-odd years are just a prelude to my life in the sense that I'm open to an unknown future.

ALLAN   Could you explain what you had in mind with the Central Park memorial to John, Strawberry Fields, with all the nations sending you stones, plants, and things?

YOKO   Oh, sure. It's getting to be very beautiful. The easiest part was to get the participation of all the countries. I didn't have very much trouble there at all. It seemed like they were all very agreeable. Also I didn't have any trouble with New York City in the sense that they're very happy about this international garden that will soon come to life and be so beautiful. Many people are sending money to me saying, "Will you please use this for Strawberry Fields?" So all the monies that are coming to me I put directly into the Spirit Foundation, which is a charity that John and I founded together. By the way, any money that's sent to us is directly used for whatever purpose we feel is important. In other words, the money is sent on to the people who really need it.

ALLAN   John once summed things up by saying, "I don't regret a thing, you know. Especially since meeting Yoko. That's made everything worthwhile." Does that sum it up for you as well?

YOKO   (*Weeping softly*) Well . . . that sums it up for me too, I suppose. I feel that now John is helping me through Sean.

A beautiful promotional poster for the Beatles'
Rock 'N' Roll compilation album.

Overleaf
The Beatles in the last official Beatles Fan Club
poster.

"I think the Beatles were great. If you listen to the radio in America, that's all you hear, isn't it? They play the Beatles twenty-four hours a day over here, right? I'm sure they will continue to be heard for a long, long time to come."

BOY GEORGE, 1984

"In our minds this 'British thing' is something of a phenomenon which somehow seems to be extraordinarily attractive to the younger generation at the moment. We certainly don't want to give the impression, however, that the 'Ed Sullivan Show' is simply a vehicle for popular rock 'n' roll acts like the Beatles. After all, it's only a fad and will almost certainly soon pass."

ROBERT PRECHT,
ED SULLIVAN'S SON-IN-LAW AND THE SHOW'S PRODUCER, 1964

"Umbrae umbrarum ritu soluimur"
Shadows we are and like shadows we depart

INSCRIBED UPON THE SUN DIAL, FRIAR PARK, HENLEY-ON-THAMES

"Et nunc progressi alibi observemus"
And now let us move along and observe elsewhere

Backword

"Like ice in a drink,
invisible ink,
or dreams in the cold light of day;
the children of rock 'n' roll
never grow old,
they just fade away . . ."

Four war babies grew up in an ugly duckling world that was just about to see its new reflection. They sang songs and made you smile to see them. They called themselves the Beatles.

And why not? Let's face it, show business isn't exactly new!

Yet in spite of the name, the haircuts, and the suits, they became immensely popular.

It could have gone on forever, but life got in the way.

Thank you, John, Paul, George, and Ringo. I choose to remember the Love, Hope, and Fun.

As you can Imagine.

NEIL INNES
Suffolk, England

ACKNOWLEDGMENTS

The author gratefully acknowledges the kind and invaluable assistance of the following persons and companies in the production of this work.

Paul A.
Don Adams—*Rogers Cable TV*
Ann and Pat—*McCreas Color Lab*
Clinton D. Baker
David Bandfield—*CBS Morning News*
Ingrid Berzins
Bill Bilby and Puppy
Sadie Mozelle Black
Raymond L. Black
Mark Bonokowski—*Toronto Sun*
The Bonzo Dog Fan Club (& Dean Cole)
Tony Bookbinder
Richard Boraks
Stefano Castino
Capital Records
CBS Records
Stephen Chesley
Vishvakarma Das—*ISKCON Toronto*
Sharon Kay Dear
Devi Deva Das
Dharma Prana Das
"Chef" Jerry DeFlippo
Sean Foley
Bob Gallo—*Emp-Hire Productions*
Sesa, Devin, and Lennon Giuliano
Peter Goddard—*Toronto Star*
Francis Goode—*TCT*
Gokula and Naradi—*ISKCON Atlanta*
Su Gold—*MPL Communications*
Goose Grey—*Camp Kenan*
Mark Griffiths—*The Ashford Hollow Foundation*
John Hamilton—*Penny Lane Records*
Henrik Hansen
Herb Hilderley
The Hit Factory (Dave and Franco)
Jim and Liz Hughes
Omid Irafas—*Irafas Images*
M. S. Irani—*Meher Baba Perpetual Trust*
Thom Jack

Bill King—*Beatlefan magazine*
Charles and Sharon Klotchbach
Tom, Mike, and Pat Klotchbach
Adam LaZarre—*Brockport State University*
Leif and Lia Leavesley
Pip Leavesley
Richard, Michael and Johnathan Lee
The John Lennon Memorial Club of Liverpool
Jeff Levy—*Bag Two Collectibles*
Tanya Long
Allan Lysaght—*Lysonic Productions*
David Lloyd MacIntyre
His Divine Grace Swami B. H. Mangalniloy Maharaj
Colleen Maynard—*Skyboot Productions*
Hillary Oxlade—*Merseyside Tourist Board*
Frank Poole
Eddy Porter
Vince Petti
David Pritchard—*Sonic Workshop*
Robbie—*Henley-on-Thames Travellers' Aid Society*
Onyo Rebon
Scott Rubin—*910 Promotions*
Brian Roylance—*Genesis Fine Art Publications*
Helen Simpson—*Beatle City of Liverpool*
Mr. Singh
"Big" Wendell and Joan Phyllis Smith
Tim and Brian Smith
Wendell Lee Smith—*Old Siam Wood Company*
Martin Soldat
John Sylvano
Derek Taylor—*West Kirby Enquirer*
Steve Thomson—*Backstage Productions International*
Dave Tollington—*WEA Music of Canada*
Ritchie Yorke
Ernie Williams—*New Sand Mountain Wildcats*
David, Vernon, and Kay Wolotko

Also a special thanks to Jill Kathleen Lee and all the people who graciously granted me interviews. Om tat sat.

CREDITS

PHOTOGRAPHS:

Astoria Theatre, London, page 213.

Atlantic Records, page 155 bottom right.

Bear Root Developments Ltd., pages 132, 146, 147, 166 top.

Beatle City of Liverpool (Helen Simpson), pages 75 bottom, 112 top.

Boardwalk Records, page 199.

Rodney Bowes, pages 10, 44, 48–49, 53, 54 top, 55, 57, 58 bottom left, 60 top, bottom left, 64 top, middle, 65, 66 top, 70 bottom, 78 bottom left, right, 80, 82 top left, 90, 95 bottom, 99 bottom right, 100 bottom, 106, 108 bottom, 110, 111, 112 bottom, 113 bottom left, right, 114, 126 bottom, 134 top, 140, 144, 151 middle, 156 top right, bottom right, 157 top, 158–159, 160, 165 top, 167 bottom right, 176, 178 top, 179, 180, 181 bottom right, 189, 191, 193 top, 198 bottom left, 200–201, 206 top left, 212.

The Cavern Mecca, pages 12, 22, 25, 28–29, 34–35, 39 top, 42 bottom.

CBS Records, page 161 top.

Devi Deva Das, page 100 top.

Everson Museum of Art, pages 166 bottom, 167 left.

Bob Gallo Productions, pages 39 bottom, 40, 66–67.

Geoffrey Giuliano, pages 15, 16 bottom, 17, 18, 19, 20, 26, 30–31, 33, 41, 56 top, middle, 70 top, 108 top, 117 top, 118 bottom, 122, 151 bottom right, 165 bottom, 169 bottom right, 175, 177, 178 bottom, 188, 190 bottom, 194, 202, 205 bottom right, 206 bottom left, right, 207, 210 bottom, 214.

The Giuliano Collection, pages 2, 28 top left, top right, 50 top left, 51, 52, 54 bottom, 56 bottom, 59, 60 right, 61, 64 bottom, 67 top, 74 bottom, 83 bottom, 86, 91 top, 98, 109, 113 top left, 118 top, 120 top, 127 top, 134 bottom, 139 middle, 154 bottom, 155 left, 156 top left, 169 top left, bottom left, 174, 181 left, top left, 184, 186, 197 bottom, 203 bottom, 204 top, 205 top, bottom left, 210 top, 217, 218–219.

John Hamilton, page 128.

The *Henley Standard*, page 198 top right.

Neil Innes, pages 190 top, 192, 193 bottom.

Irafas Images, pages 116 bottom, 143 bottom, 152, 153, 157 bottom, 203 top, 209, 211 left.

Jasmine and Peach Archives, pages 6, 8, 14, 16 top left, top right, 21, 22–23, 24, 27, 32, 36, 38, 43, 45, 47, 50 top right, bottom left, 58 top, bottom right, 62, 69, 74 top, bottom left, 75 top, 76, 77, 78 top left, top right, 79, 82 top right, bottom left, 83 top, 84, 85, 87, 91 bottom, 92, 93, 94, 95 top, 96 top, bottom left, 97, 101, 102, 103, 115, 116 top, 117 bottom, 119, 120 bottom, 123 bottom, 124, 126 top, 127 bottom, 129, 130,131, 133, 135, 136, 139 top, bottom, 141, 142, 145, 149, 150 top, 151 top, 154 top, 155 top right, 156 bottom left, 161 bottom, 162, 164, 167 top right, 168, 169 top right, 170, 172, 182, 183 bottom, 185, 187, 196, 197 top, 198 top left, 204 bottom, 211 top right, 215.

Tony Mansfield, pages 42 top, 46, 99 top, bottom left.

Karen Neilson, page 173 bottom.

Paul Petock, page 150 bottom.

Shiva Shakti Ltd., pages 68, 71, 72, 73, 81, 123 top, 208.

Ivor Sharp, pages 104, 105 left, 138, 143 top, 148.

Union Sun and Journal, page 183 top.

WEA Music of Canada, page 173 top, middle.

ILLUSTRATIONS:

Jahnavi Dasi, "The Divine Couple/Radha and Krsna," oil painting 1984, page 96.

Giuliano, "Under the Eyes of Dawn/The Beatles in Rishikesh," collage 1985, page 88; "Jai Raj Harisein," collage 1985, page 105 right; "Rainbow Beatles," silkscreen/collage 1973, page 211 bottom right.

Frank Poole, "William Evert Preston," charcoal drawing 1974, page 111 bottom.

Beatle memorabilia courtesy The Giuliano Collection.